A PRECARIAT CHARTER

FROM REVIEWS OF
THE PRECARIAT

'A very important book.'

NOAM CHOMSKY, *Massachusetts Institute of Technology, USA*

'Standing has produced a well-informed and important book investigating, for the first time in a comprehensive way, the direction in which global economic security is moving in the 21st century. The book is packed with statistics presented in a very readable form and drawing on extensive published research. It is a compelling account of economic insecurity...'

KEITH RANDLE, *Work Organisation, Labour and Globalisation*

'[T]here is much in The Precariat to recommend it to labor educators, labor studies scholars, and activists of all sorts...a book that provides a clear and detailed understanding of how the situation of precarious employment affects the lives of the "precariat" individually, collectively, day to day, and over the longer term. This is the book's greatest value. Standing does this with many international examples, even though his main intellectual base is in Britain. His analysis of the impact of precarity, along with the diversity of examples from around the world, makes this the primary book on the topic to date.'

JOE BERRY, *Labor Studies Journal*

'[T]he analysis and arguments are compelling, for *The Precariat* brings together and develops many current strands of thought within the (social science) literature, and builds on the materialist tradition which ultimately leads to a rejection of "neoliberalism". Standing captures some of the collectivist social policy tradition established by Richard Titmuss, but with more attention to all forms of work and notions of occupational citizenship...The social policy community needs to engage more with issues at stake here, making *The Precariat* essential reading.'

CHRIS DEEMING, *Journal of Social Policy*

'This is undoubtedly a significant book, highlighting the plight of an increasing number of people in the global economy. Importantly, it does away with the myth that precarious labour is mainly to be found in the Global South, in less developed countries. In reality, it is increasingly a common form of employment also in industrialised countries as what was once considered to be atypical labour becomes more and more the norm...This is a must-read book for both labour academics and activists.'

ANDREAS BIELER, *Capital & Class*

'This book should be read by everyone working in the humanities and the social sciences...This is an outstanding book [which] should transform how we think about justice, injustice, class, work and leisure.'

TARA BRABAZON, *Charles Sturt University, Australia*

'Guy Standing provides an incisive account of how precariousness is becoming the new normality in globalised labour markets, and offers important guidelines for all concerned to build a more just society.'

RICHARD HYMAN, *London School of Economics, UK*

'This important and original book brings out the political dangers, so clear in contemporary America, of failing to address the insecurities of the Precariat. It also suggests the way forward: a reconstruction of the concept of work.'

EILEEN APPLEBAUM, *Center for Economic and Policy Research, Washington, DC, USA*

'Over 90% of workers in India are informal, poorly paid, without any economic security. Guy Standing combines vision with practicality in outlining policies that are urgently needed to provide security to workers such as these around the world.'

RENANA JHABVALA, *Self-Employed Women's Association of India*

'Buy Guy Standing's book, *The Precariat*! Or nick/borrow it!'

JOHN HARRIS, *The Guardian*

A PRECARIAT CHARTER

From denizens to citizens

GUY STANDING

B L O O M S B U R Y

LONDON • NEW DELHI • NEW YORK • SYDNEY

Bloomsbury Academic

An imprint of Bloomsbury Publishing Plc

50 Bedford Square	1385 Broadway
London	New York
WC1B 3DP	NY 10018
UK	USA

www.bloomsbury.com

Bloomsbury is a registered trade mark of Bloomsbury Publishing Plc

First published 2014

© Guy Standing, 2014

British Library Cataloguing-in-Publication Data
A catalogue record for this book is available from the British Library.

ISBN: PB: 978-1-4725-1039-6
HB: 978-1-4725-0575-0
ePDF: 978-1-4725-0847-8
ePub: 978-1-4725-0798-3

Library of Congress Cataloging-in-Publication Data
A catalog record for this book is available from the Library of Congress.

Typeset by Fakenham Prepress Solutions, Fakenham, Norfolk NR21 8NN
Printed and bound in Great Britain

CONTENTS

PREFACE

There is an oft-repeated aphorism that has come to us from Heraclitus, 2,500 years ago: 'You never step into the same river twice.' This is how it felt in presenting *The Precariat*, the predecessor of this book, in numerous places around the world. Although the same book was being presented each time, the presentations evolved, as some aspects faded and some came into sharper focus. Often this was due to the reactions of the audiences and well-informed questions.

To write a book is an act of vanity. To think audiences would be interested in listening to its arguments is equally so. Therefore, it is a pleasure to use this preface to thank all those who have listened and responded, orally, in letters and, most of all, in emails. It has been an educational experience, often tempered by sadness or anger when hearing of people's personal stories of being in the precariat.

They are primarily responsible for the current book. It is the culmination of a long journey that began in the 1980s with papers and a series of national monographs on the growth of labour market flexibility, in the UK, Sweden, Finland, the Netherlands, Spain, Germany, Italy and Austria, some written with or by colleagues in the ILO or academia. The underlying thesis was that the neo-liberal model would generate more economic insecurity and fragmented societies.

Much of the 1990s was spent gathering data from factory and worker surveys on labour flexibility and insecurity. These yielded numerous papers and four books as well as a comprehensive ILO report entitled *Economic Security for a Better World*. In that period, I was fortunate to visit dozens of factories and firms, and interview managers, owners, workers and their families, in various countries, rich and poor. As an economist, I cannot describe these inter-views as 'scientific', unlike the large sample surveys we conducted. Nevertheless, I found myself agreeing with Alfred Marshall's dictate to aspiring economists: 'Get into the factory!' It is in seeing and listening to people in labour and work that one learns.

This book does not reproduce many statistics. That is not its purpose. It is intended to prompt others to focus on policies and institutional changes to reach out to the precariat. Political debate everywhere is in a state of disarray, with social democrats close to meltdown. They just do not appeal with their old messages. Worse, they do not seem to understand why.

Indeed, the energy needed to write this book stemmed from anger that mainstream policymakers and the media were so bereft of *empathy* with the precariat and the growing number of denizens in their midst. What has been happening is unnecessary and amoral. Anybody with a chance to speak should be shouting about the inequity and inequality that governments are fostering and oppositions are barely opposing.

In short, this book is an attempt to formulate an agenda for the precariat that could be the basis of a political movement, based not on a utilitarian appeal to a majority but on a vision of what consti-tutes a Good Society. It is also to some extent an attempt to respond to reactions to *The Precariat*.

One issue has preoccupied old-style Marxists. Is the precariat a class? An attempt is made in the book to respond to their assertions that it is not. However, there should be space for constructive debate. Precariousness (or 'precarity', as some prefer) is more than a 'social condition'. A social condition cannot act. Only a social group with common or compatible aims can do that. One way of expressing the claim underlying both books is that the precariat is a class-in-the-making that must become enough of a class-for-itself in order to seek ways of abolishing itself. This makes it transformative, unlike other existing classes, which want to reproduce themselves in a stronger way.

Another point that deserves emphasis is the distinction between 'work' and 'labour'. Numerous commentaries on *The Precariat* failed to come to grips with this point. So, the essential differences are reiterated here.

The opening chapters define the key concepts, before discussing the implications for the precariat of the economic crisis and why a Precariat Charter is needed to provide an alternative to utilitarian democracy. The second half of the book presents 29 Articles that might constitute a Charter. They are not comprehensive, and readers will have their own priorities they may wish to add. But it is hoped that the set presented here could provide a framework for action.

It remains to thank all those who have contributed to the ideas and writing. Once again, there are so many that it is best that I thank them personally. The essential point is to acknowledge that a book such as this is never the work of just the author.

These are momentous times, when we are in the midst of a Global Transformation, when a new progressive vision of the Good Society is struggling to take shape. The river is certainly flowing. Change is coming. Perhaps the piece of graffiti that lingers most in the mind was on a Madrid wall: 'The worst thing would be to return to the old normal.'

Guy Standing

September 2013

LIST OF ABBREVIATIONS

ACA	Affordable Care Act ('Obamacare')
APR	Annual percentage rate
CEO	Chief Executive Officer
CGIL	*Confederazione Generale Italiana del Lavoro*
CV	Curriculum vitae
DSA	Disability living allowance
DWP	Department for Work and Pensions
ESA	Employment and support allowance
EU	European Union
FDI	Foreign direct investment
GDP	Gross domestic product
ILO	International Labour Organization
IMF	International Monetary Fund
M5S	*MoVimento 5 Stelle* (Five Star Movement)
MWA	Mandatory work activity
NGO	Non-governmental organization
OECD	Organisation for Economic Co-operation and Development
OFT	Office of Fair Trading

PIP   Personal independence payment

SEWA   Self-Employed Women's Association of India

SNAP   Supplemental Nutrition Assistance Program

SWF   Sovereign wealth fund

UNCTAD   United Nations Conference on Trade and Development

UNESCO   United Nations Educational, Scientific and Cultural
              Organization

UNICEF   United Nations Children's Fund

WCA   Work capability assessment

1

Denizens and the precariat

Around the world, more people are being turned into denizens; they are having rights associated with citizenship whittled away, often without realizing it or realizing the full implications. Many are joining the precariat, an emerging class characterized by chronic insecurity, detached from old norms of labour and the working class. For the first time in history, governments are reducing the rights of many of their own people while further weakening the rights of more traditional denizens, migrants.

Mainstream politicians and political parties – on the right and left as conventionally defined – have become stridently utilitarian. While the past should not be romanticized, the class-based political parties that emerged in the late nineteenth and early twentieth centuries came closer to deliberative or participatory democracy. Groups debated and shaped class-oriented perspectives. By contrast, what has emerged in the globalization era could be called utilitarian democracy. Without class-based values or ideas of class struggle to guide them, politicians and old political parties have resorted to a commodified politics that focuses on finding a formula to appeal to a majority, often depicted as 'the middle class'.

It scarcely matters to these politicians that their policies deprive a minority of rights and push them into the precariat. They can win elections as long as they can sell themselves to a majority. But the minority is growing by the day. And it is becoming restless, as the millions demonstrating discontent in the squares and parks of great cities testify.

Citizens and rights

The idea of citizenship goes back to ancient Greece. It made a stride forward in 1789 with the French Declaration of the Rights of Man and the Citizen, that stirring emancipatory call stemming from the Renaissance and its message of escape from a slavish 'God's will'. Henceforth, a citizen was someone who had *rights*. This was what Tom Paine – the Englishman who helped forge the American Revolution and Constitution, and the French Revolution – intended in his epoch-shaping tracts, *Common Sense* and *The Rights of Man*.

It fell to T. H. Marshall (1950), writing after the Second World War, to define citizenship in its modern form as 'a status bestowed on those who are full members of a community'. To be a citizen meant having 'an absolute right to a certain standard of civilisation which is conditional only on the discharge of the general duties of citizenship'. While Marshall's later conception of the 'duties of citizenship' included a duty to labour, with which this book takes issue, he recognized the tension between rights and capitalism, noting that 'in the twentieth century, citizenship and the capitalist class system have been at war.' Citizenship imposed modifications on the capitalist class system, since social rights 'imply an invasion of contract by status, the subordination of market price to social justice, the replacement of the free bargain by the declaration of rights.'

That was roughly correct in the 're-embedded' phase of Karl Polanyi's *The Great Transformation* ([1944] 2001), the period of social-democrat supremacy between 1944 and the 1970s. In the subsequent 'disembedded' phase, contract has invaded status, and social justice has been subordinated to the market price.

There is also a tension between universal human rights, which should apply equally to everybody, and the idea of rights embodied in citizenship, confined to people with a certain status. Rights in the modern era have been depicted as 'melting' with citizenship (Bobbio 1990), with citizenship coming to be defined as *belonging* to an entity (usually a sovereign nation) and entitlement to rights seen as a function of that belonging.

In the early twentieth century, what Zolberg (2000) called 'the hypernationalist version of citizenship' predominated, leading to the 'nationalization of rights', which Hannah Arendt ([1951] 1986) identified as leading to totalitarianism. Countries also took advantage of international migration. Some operated discriminatory quota systems, as the USA did in the 1920s to restrict citizenship mostly to those from 'Protestant countries'. National citizenship became linked to obligations, notably to men's duty to perform military service.

The end of the Second World War led to an advance in the framework of rights, with the Universal Declaration of Human Rights of 1948 and a spate of international documents, including the 1951 United Nations Convention relating to the Status of Refugees and the 1966 International Covenants on Civil and Political Rights and on Economic, Social and Cultural Rights. However, while asserting universal rights, these reflected the conventional link between rights and national citizenship.

Thus the Universal Declaration (Article 13) interprets the right to freedom of movement as the right to emigrate – to *leave* a country – but not a right to immigrate – to *enter* a country. This is a recipe for leaving migrants without rights anywhere and without protection by national laws and institutions. As such, jurists have seen a contradiction between human rights and the territorial rights of national sovereignty embedded in the Universal Declaration. Similarly, the Refugee Convention asserts a principle of non-expulsion (*non-refoulement*) of refugees and asylum seekers, but does not grant them entitlement to the full rights of national citizens.

Rights are thus seen as a badge of citizenship, and only citizens have all the rights established in their own country. It is in this sense that most migrants are denizens – people with a more limited range of rights than citizens. But they are not the only group that fall into this category. As we shall argue, some migrants may have more rights than some 'nationals'. The reality is that in the globalization era more people are being converted into denizens, through losing rights.

A human *right* is universal, applying to everyone. If someone is to be denied a right, there must be legally established reasons and strict respect for due process in denying it. Entitlement to a right is not dependent on some behavioural or attitudinal conditionality, other than adherence to the law of the country and due process. It is crucial to emphasize these points, since a contention underpinning this book is that governments are abusing them with increasing ease and impunity.

A full citizen has access to five types of rights – civil, political, cultural, social and economic – as recognized by the 1966 Covenants and by regional equivalents stemming from the Universal Declaration. Marshall (1950) famously asserted that civil rights were the achievement of the seventeenth century, cultural rights of the eighteenth, political rights of the nineteenth and social rights of the twentieth century. If so, we might say that the challenge ahead is to ensure that economic rights will be the defining achievement of the twenty-first century.

However, as emphasized by Bobbio (1990) and others, the nation state is not the only form of association for generating rights. Most of us belong to associations that establish and enforce individual and group rights within specific communities. A right is what is granted to those who join and remain good members of a club. That perspective produces an image of layers of citizenship and layers of rights. So we can think, for example, of occupational citizenship, implying that some have a 'right to practise' a set of activities with designated titles, such as doctor, lawyer, carpenter or baker, along with a right to receive income, benefits, status and representation or agency – rights developed and legitimized within an occupation, often over generations, as in the legal and medical professions.

A fundamental aspect is the right to *belong* to a community or a self-identifying set of communities. This is why freedom must be interpreted as associational freedom, a perspective that stretches from Aristotle through Arendt, but which has been lost by modern social democrats as well as by libertarians and neo-liberals, who see freedom in individualistic terms.

THE MAIN TYPES OF RIGHTS

* Civil rights include the right to life and liberty, a fair trial, due process, equality before the law, legal representation, privacy and freedom of expression, and the right to be treated with equal dignity.

* Cultural rights are rights of individuals and communities to access and participate in their chosen culture, including language and artistic production, in conditions of equality, dignity and non-discrimination.

* Political rights include the right to vote, participate in political life, stand in elections, and participate in civil society.

* Social rights include the right to an adequate standard of living, social protection, occupational health and safety, housing, health care and education, and preservation of and access to the commons.

* Economic rights include the right to practise one's occupation, share in the economic resources of the commons, enjoy a fair share of economic growth, access all forms of income, and bargain individually and collectively.

Human rights are universal, indivisible and inalienable, meaning they cannot be taken away except in specific situations subject to due process. Thus a person convicted of a crime in a court of law may lose their right to liberty.

The term 'claim rights', or 'republican rights', is intended to mean rights that society should move *towards* realizing. As explained in Chapter 4, policies and institutional changes should be judged by whether they move towards realizing rights for the most vulnerable and disadvantaged in society.

Rights constantly evolve, at national and international levels. For example, a Charter of Emerging Human Rights, which highlighted distributional and ecological claims, was formulated as part of the Universal Forum of Cultures (Barcelona Social Forum 2004). It made little impact, but should be revisited.

Denizens and restricted rights

In the Middle Ages in England, a denizen was an outsider – an 'alien' – who was granted by the king, or an authority operating on his behalf, the right to settle and to work in a town in his proven occupation. He gained some of the rights of a citizen of the town, but rarely all of them and not necessarily forever.

As the idea of citizenship evolved, the notion of denizenship moved to national level. Writing his *Law Dictionary* in the early nineteenth century, Sir Thomas Edylyne described a denizen in these terms:

> an alien born, but who so obtained, *ex-donatione regis*, letters patent to make him an *English* subject; a high and incommunicable branch of the royal prerogative. A denizen is in a kind of middle state between an alien and natural-born subject... He may take lands by purchase or devise, which an alien may not... no denizen can be of the privy council, or either house of parliament, or have any office of trust, civil or military, or be capable of any grant of lands, etc. from the crown.

Thus a denizen was usually denied political rights, but was granted designated economic rights as well as the citizen's normal civil rights.

In British colonies, the governor was empowered to grant letters of denization to foreigners if they arrived with letters of recommendation from the relevant British secretary of state. Or they could petition the governor, who could submit their names to the secretary of state for approval. Denizens had to swear the oaths of Allegiance and Supremacy, disavowing the Pope's temporal authority, abjuring the claims to the English throne of descendants of the Pretender, and affirming the Declaration against Transubstantiation. While Catholics were exempted from the last of these, they were restrictions on 'cultural deviance'.

Thomas Hammar (1994) is credited with the modern reintroduction of the term denizen, to refer to migrant workers who came to Western and Northern Europe from the 1960s onwards and became long-term residents. They were granted negative freedoms, including access to the labour market, and gained some positive social security rights. But denizenship remained an 'in-between' concept (Oger 2003; Walker 2008).

This idea of denizenship as an 'in-between' status has historically been one of *progress* for the person involved. A denizen was someone who moved from being an outsider to a partial insider, with some rights. But denizenship should be seen as *regress* as well. In the globalization era, while the rhetoric of rights gained force and popularity, the reality has been the conversion of more people into denizens, denied certain rights or prevented from obtaining or retaining them. This does not affect only migrants. If Hannah Arendt's idea of citizenship is 'the right to have rights' (Arendt [1951] 1986), today it would be better to think of citizenship as a continuum, with many people having a more limited range of rights than others, without any simple dichotomy of citizen and non-citizen.

Until the 1980s, the conventional view was that over the long run, in a democratic society, residence and citizenship should coincide (Brubaker 1989). This would not be true today. Many residing in a country never obtain citizenship or the rights attached to it; others who have resided since birth lose rights that supposedly go with citizenship.

Many denizens not only have limited rights but also lack 'the right to have rights'. Asylum seekers denied refugee status are an example; migrants who cannot practise the occupation for which they are qualified are another. Often, they do not have the means or the procedural avenues to contest their marginal status. Many lack the capacity to claim or enforce rights, or fear that the act of asserting a claim right would have a high probability of retributive consequences or disastrous costs. Others have no avenues at all for pursuing nominal rights.

Historically, a denizen was granted citizenship rights on sufferance, on demonstration of worthiness, which was a matter of discretion by or on behalf of the ruler. Modern denizens are in a similar position. A denizen can also be seen as someone subject to 'unaccountable domination', that is, domination by others whose conduct cannot be held to account. This is contrary to the republican ideal of non-domination, meaning subject only to accountable legitimized power.

There are six ways by which people can become denizens. They can be blocked from attaining rights, by laws, regulations or non-accountable actions of state bureaucracies. The costs of maintaining rights can be raised. They can lose rights due to a change in status, as employee, resident or whatever. They can be deprived of rights by proper legal process. They can lose rights *de facto*, without due process, even though they may not lose them in a *de jure* (legal) sense. And they can lose them by not conforming to moralistic norms, by having a lifestyle or set of values that puts them outside the range of protection.

One egregious path to denizenship is the loss of rights due to growing criminalization. This is partly because governments have made more activities into crimes. The UK's New Labour government passed 28 criminal justice bills in its 13 years in office, adding the equivalent of one new offence a day to the statute book, many of them trivial (Birrell 2012). The prison population nearly doubled. And digital technologies have also increased the long-term costs of being criminalized, making it harder to wipe the record and exposing people to discrimination long after what may have been a minor misdemeanour.

In sum, denizenship can arise not just from migration but also from an unbundling of rights that removes some or all of the rights nominally attached to formal citizenship. The neo-liberalism that crystallized in the globalization era has generated a 'tiered membership' model of society. Worst of all, the unbundling of rights has gone with a class-based restructuring of rights. This is the ground on which the precariat must make demands.

The right to work and 'labour rights'

Let me start with the importance of work. As I have said before: Labour – the party of work – the clue is in the name.

Ed Miliband, Leader of the UK Labour Party, June 2013

We must insist on a distinction between 'work' and 'labour', and recognize its implications for the 'right to work', a concept that has caused confusion ever since it was first asserted. While central to citizenship, it is only meaningful if all forms of work are treated with equal respect. Labour is only part of work.

Every age has had its stupidities about what is work and what is not. The twentieth century was the most stupid of all. As argued in *The Precariat*, and in an earlier book (Standing 2009), we should return to the insights of the ancient Greeks, who had a better conceptualization of work, despite their sexist and slave-based system. Labour was not done by citizens; it was done by slaves, *banausoi* and *metics*. Work was what the citizen and his family did around the home; it was reproductive activity done in civic friendship, *philia*. Play was for recuperation and a balance of life.

The main aim of a citizen was to free up time for leisure, for *schole*, which was understood as the time and space to participate in the life of the *polis* (community), in the *agora*, the commons, the open social spaces. *Schole* was a combination of learning and public participation; it was intrinsically political. It was also a vehicle for moral education, through watching and participating in the great theatrical tragedies, where empathy was learned.

Flash forward through the centuries, through the nonsense of Adam Smith and Emmanuel Kant, who both dismissed as unproductive anybody doing what we call 'services', to the triumph of labourism and the male-breadwinner model in the twentieth century. For the first time, all those doing work that was not labour disappeared statistically. As Arthur Pigou famously said, if he hired a housekeeper or cook, national income and employment went up. If he married her and she continued to do the same work, national income and employment went down. This folly persists, in policy and statistics.

In the speech cited above, Miliband went on to say: 'Our party was founded on the principles of work. We have always been against the denial of opportunity that comes from not having work.' This is the Labour Party's problem. Only work done for bosses, in subservience, in master-servant relations, as labour law has put it, counts in this vision of society.

The first batch of Labour MPs in 1906, when asked what book had most influenced their political thought, cited John Ruskin's *Unto This Last* ([1860] 1986). The theme of that elegiac essay had been the need to struggle for the values of work against the dictates of labour. Interpreted for today, his argument was that only creative, ecological, reproductive work done in freedom should count. Alienated resource-depleting labour should be resisted. This inspired William Morris, another contemporary voice shouting against labourism. He would have been horrified at the labourist trap into which Miliband fell when going on to justify workfare, forced labour for the unemployed.

As explained elsewhere (Standing 2009, 2013a), we should define the 'right to work' as the right to pursue an occupation of one's choice, where occupation comprises a combination of work, labour, leisure and recuperation that corresponds to one's abilities and aspirations. While that will never be fully realized, policies and institutional changes should be judged by whether they move towards or away from it for the most deprived in the community.

The emerging class structure

Each epoch and productive system spawns its class system. As argued in *The Precariat*, globalization, starting in the 1980s, has generated a class structure, superimposed on earlier structures, comprising an elite, a salariat, proficians, an old 'core' working class (proletariat), a precariat, the unemployed and a lumpen-precariat (or 'underclass'). A group of scholars has since come up with a variant of this classification, though it differs in significant respects (Savage et al. 2013).

Class can be defined as being determined primarily by specific 'relations of production', specific 'relations of distribution' (sources of income), and specific relations to the state. From these arises a distinctive 'consciousness' of desirable reforms and social policies.

Starting at the top of the income spectrum, the elite or plutocracy consists of a tiny number of individuals who are really 'super-citizens'; they reside in several countries and escape the obligations of citizenship everywhere while helping to limit the rights of citizens almost everywhere. They are not the 1 per cent depicted by the Occupy movement. They are far fewer than that, and exercise more power than most people appreciate. Their financial strength shapes political discourse, economic policies and social policy. Thus the Koch brothers in the USA have spent billions in funding Republican congressional candidates, conservative think tanks, and groups opposing action on climate change.

In *Superclass* (2009) and *Power, Inc.* (2012), David Rothkopf has argued that a global elite of 6,000 runs the world without regard to national allegiance. These super-citizens include corporations, whose influence over US policy has been reinforced by the 2010 Supreme Court ruling that they have the same rights of free speech as individuals and can spend what they wish to promote their views. In a study of corporate networks, a mere 147 entities (mostly financial groups and mostly owned or run by the elite) were found to control 40 per cent of the value of the world's multinationals; 737 entities controlled 80 per cent (Torgovnick 2013).

In some respects, the elite coalesce with senior corporate citizens belonging to the salariat. This class consists of those in long-term employment or with contracts that promise permanency, if they adhere to conventional rules of behaviour and performance. They receive extensive non-wage enterprise benefits and all the forms of labour security outlined in the earlier book.

The salariat has been the primary beneficiary of twentieth-century social democracy. Its members come closest to having all the rights associated with being national citizens. Most are also corporate or occupational citizens, or both, in that they receive benefits and rights granted to members of these club-like entities. What puts them in a distinctive class position is that they receive much of their income from profits and shares, often indirectly through company or private pension plans, and benefit from generous tax breaks (subsidies) on their spending – housing, insurance, pensions, charitable donations and so on. This inclines them to support a market society and neo-liberal individualism, an orientation reinforced by the trend to a commodified education system, deprived of much of its enlightenment content.

Alongside the salariat in income terms are proficians, consisting of a growing number of people, often youthful, who are mobile self-entrepreneurs, wary of salaried employment, flitting between projects and occupational titles. Some hope to enter the plutocracy, most live a stressful life, subject to burn-out and nervous exhaustion. But most like their bank balances.

Below the salariat and proficians in terms of income is the old working class, the proletariat. Here we plunge into treacherous conceptual waters. The proletariat still exists, but it is not a majority anywhere and is shrinking. It was never a homogeneous class. But it could be defined by several modal characteristics, notably by its 'relations of production' and its 'relations of distribution'. The working class was expected to supply stable labour, even if its members were subject to unemployment. The term that characterized their working lives was proletarianization, habituation to stable full-time labour. Even their representatives, trade unions and labour parties, preached a doctrine of disciplined labour.

Their relations of distribution meant their income came mainly from wages, supplemented by enterprise benefits provided to raise labour productivity. Outside the workplace, income was supplemented by transfers from kin and the community, and income-in-kind from public services and 'the commons'. So, the proletariat was defined by its reliance on mass labour, reliance on wage income, absence of control or ownership of the means of production, and habituation to stable labour that corresponded to its skills.

From the nineteenth century up to the 1970s, the representatives of the proletariat – social democratic and labour parties, and trade unions – strove for labour de-commodification through making labour more 'decent' and raising incomes via a shift from money wages to enterprise and state benefits. The normal 'consciousness' was a desire for more secure employment, to increase the ease of subordinated labour.

All labour and communist parties, social democrats and unions subscribed to this agenda, calling for 'more labour' and 'full employment', by which was meant all men in full-time jobs. Besides being sexist, this neglected all forms of work that were not labour (including reproductive work in the home, caring for others, work in the community, and other self-chosen activities). It also erased a vision of freedom from labour that had figured powerfully in radical thinking in previous ages.

The precariat

As that labourist agenda ran out of steam, a new group – the precariat – began to emerge. Rather than repeat a description of its evolution, we may just note its defining characteristics. Many are perceived as negative. But there are also positive features, which are what make the precariat a potentially transformative 'dangerous class'.

Distinctive relations of production

First, consider its relations of production. The precariat consists of people living through insecure jobs interspersed with periods of unemployment or labour-force withdrawal (misnamed as 'economic inactivity') and living insecurely, with uncertain access to housing and public resources. They experience a constant sense of transiency.

The precariat lacks all seven forms of labour-related security that the old working class struggled to obtain, and that were pursued internationally through the International Labour Organization (ILO). Of course, there have always been workers with insecure conditions. That alone does not define today's precariat. But the precariat has distinctive relations of production because the new *norm*, not the exception, is uncertain and volatile labour. Whereas the proletarian norm was habituation to stable labour, the precariat is being habituated to unstable labour. This cannot be overcome simply by boosting economic growth or introducing new regulations.

Labour instability is central to global capitalism. Multinational capital not only wants flexible insecure labour but can also obtain it from any part of the world. In a global market economy, trying to curb labour instability in any one country would fail. This is not a counsel of despair; it is a call for an alternative approach.

Put bluntly, the proletariat's representatives demand decent labour, lots of it; the precariat wishes to escape from labour, materially and psychologically, because its labour is instrumental, not self-defining. Many in the precariat do not even aspire to secure labour. They saw their parents trapped in long-term jobs, too frightened to leave, partly because they would have lost modest enterprise benefits that depended on 'years of service'. But in any event, those jobs are no longer on offer to the precariat. Twentieth-century spheres of labour protection – labour law, labour regulations, collective bargaining, labourist social security – were constructed around the image of the firm, fixed workplaces, and fixed working days and work-weeks that apply only to a minority in today's tertiary online society. While proletarian consciousness is linked to long-term security in a firm, mine, factory or office, the precariat's consciousness is linked to a search for security outside the workplace.

The precariat is not a 'proto-proletariat', that is, becoming like the proletariat. But the centrality of unstable labour to global capitalism is also why it is not an underclass, as some would have it. According to Marx, the proletariat wanted to abolish itself. The same could be said of the precariat. But the proletariat wanted thereby to universalize stable labour. And whereas it had a material interest in economic growth and the fiction of full employment, the precariat has an interest in recapturing a progressive vision of 'freedom from labour', so establishing a meaningful right to work. The precariat should be sceptical about growth, seeing the downside in terms of social externalities, ecological destruction and loss of the commons.

Distinctive relations of distribution

Second, the precariat has distinctive relations of distribution, or remuneration. Rather than compressing income into capital (profits) on the one hand and wages on the other, the idea of 'social income' (Standing 2009) aims to capture all forms of income that people can receive – own-account production, income from producing or selling to the market, money wages, enterprise non-wage benefits, community benefits, state benefits, and income from financial and other assets.

In early industrial capitalism, it was unusual for workers to receive only money wages (McNally 1993). But during the twentieth century, the trend was away from money wages, with a rising share of social income coming from enterprise and state benefits. What distinguishes the precariat is the opposite trend, with sources of income other than wages virtually disappearing.

This is a structural change. The precariat lacks access to non-wage perks, such as paid vacations, medical leave, company pensions and so on. It also lacks rights-based state benefits, linked to legal entitlements, leaving it dependent on discretionary, insecure benefits, if any. And it lacks access to community benefits, in the form of a strong commons (public services and amenities) and strong family and local support networks. This has been under-emphasized in labour-process analysis.

The enclosure movement, precursor of the Industrial Revolution, created conditions conducive to proletarianization. With twentieth-century capitalism, community systems of reciprocity and solidarity fell into decay, as social functions were taken over by the state and corporations. Then, in the globalization era, commodification and privatization of social amenities and services completed the dismantling of what had been a vital component of social income throughout history.

Another distinctive aspect of the precariat's relations of distribution is that it has no access to income from profits or rent, whereas groups above it have been gaining capital income in some form or another. It does not make sense to divide people into 'capitalists' and a unified 'working class' when the salariat receives a large and growing part of its income from profits. This is a greater source of inequality than commonly appreciated, since it provides higher-income earners with a share of global capital income. It has accompanied a regressive shift in the functional distribution of income, from wages to profits. The salariat's material interests have become more unlike those of other workers.

STRENGTH OF RIGHTS BY CLASS

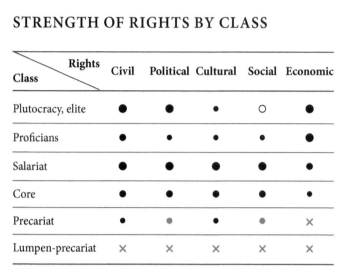

Class \ Rights	Civil	Political	Cultural	Social	Economic
Plutocracy, elite	●	●	●	○	●
Proficians	●	●	●	●	●
Salariat	●	●	●	●	●
Core	●	●	●	●	●
Precariat	●	●	●	●	✕
Lumpen-precariat	✕	✕	✕	✕	✕

FIGURE 1: *Matrix of strength of rights by class*

Note: ● weak ● quite strong ● strong ● doubtful, under attack ✕ absent ○ not needed

Political rights: The precariat is relatively disenfranchised, as its members are less likely to have a vote (e.g. migrants) or less likely to exercise it (e.g. youth, minorities). As long as the precariat remains a minority or stays divided, politicians have little electoral incentive to promote policies in its favour.

Civil rights: The precariat is losing rights to due process, especially in the areas of employment and social benefits.

Cultural rights: Governments are demanding more conformity to societal norms and majoritarian institutions, intensifying a cultural marginalization of minorities.

Economic and social rights: The precariat is losing economic and social rights, notably in the spheres of state benefits and the right to practise an occupation.

Distinctive relations to the state

A *third* feature of the precariat is its distinctive relations to the state. The state is not the same as government. It consists of the institutions and mechanisms that determine how society is ordered and how income and assets are distributed. As will be argued later, the precariat lacks many of the rights provided to citizens in the core working class and salariat. Members of the precariat are denizens.

The word precarious is usually taken as synonymous with insecure. But being precarious also means depending on the will of another. It is about being a supplicant, without rights, dependent on charity or bureaucratic benevolence.

The precariat is confronted by neo-liberal norms, in state institutions, conventional political rhetoric and utilitarian social policy, which privilege the interests of a perceived 'middle class', alongside the plutocracy. The state treats the precariat as necessary but as a group to be criticized, pitied, demonized, sanctioned or penalized in turn, not as a focus of social protection or betterment of well-being.

While we might say that political parties of the right look after their middle class, as consisting of the salariat and proficians, along with parts of the plutocracy they wish to cultivate, social democratic parties look after their middle class, as consisting of the lower rungs of the salariat and the proletariat, along with liberal members of the elite. It has served the interest of both sides to ignore or disparage the predicament of the precariat, as long as it was a small minority. This will change.

Lack of occupational identity

A *fourth* feature of the precariat is lack of an occupational identity or narrative to give to life. This is a source of frustration, alienation, anxiety and anomic despair. Recognizing this does not imply a romantic view of the past, since throughout history many people have had to survive through myriad unpredictable activities. Nevertheless, the turmoil in occupational communities is pervasive in the globalization era and has created trauma in the precariat. Even many who manage to enter a profession or craft feel uncertain about their future, unsure about what they are doing or about having a ladder to climb. The guild traditions that guided occupational life for two millennia gave people an anchor, a code of ethics, status, feasible lifetime trajectories and communities of practice.

Much of an earlier book (Standing 2009) was devoted to analysing how the neo-liberal strategy set out to dismantle occupational communities, largely unnoticed by commentators. In so doing, governments eroded the ethics of reciprocity and solidarity that had been an integral part of occupational life. Social democrats were as remiss in rejecting the positive aspects of the guilds as the political right. In the UK, guild life has virtually disappeared, leaving just the pantomime of the City of London's livery companies, an excuse for the elite to dress up in funny togs and have lavish get-together dinners. But the precariat has no occupational trajectory by which to define life.

Lack of control over time

A *fifth* feature of the precariat, again distinguishing the precariat from the proletariat, is that its members must undertake a great deal of work that is not paid labour. They are exploited and oppressed by a squeeze on time unlike the past. We may call the phenomenon 'tertiary time' to distinguish it from 'industrial time', the underpinning of industrial capitalism (Standing 2013b). The precariat cannot demarcate life into blocks of time. It is expected to be available for labour and work at all times of the day and night.

This is epitomized by the growing phenomena of crowd-labour and zero-hours contracts; millions of people (the statistics do not tell us) are hired without specified hours of labour, but are required to be on standby for moments of activity. Others are expected to flit between activities, to network constantly, wait, queue, retrain, fill in forms, do a little of this, a little of that. It all goes with the precariatized mind, a feeling of having too much to do at almost all times. It is corrosive, leaving people fatigued, stressed, frustrated and incapable of coherent action.

The pressure extends from reproductive work, with pressure to prepare for some mirage of a tomorrow, through rounds of retraining and résumé-refreshing, to work on personal financial management, juggling debts and ways to make ends meet. To take 'time out' is to risk missing opportunities and falling behind, although it is never clear behind whom. For the precariat a high ratio of work to labour is a norm.

Detachment from labour

A *sixth* feature underlines why the precariat should not be seen solely as victim or vulnerable, terms taken too much for granted. Those in the precariat are more likely to have a psychological detachment from labour, being only intermittently or instrumentally involved in labour, and not having a single labour status – often being unsure what to put under 'occupation' on official forms. This makes them less likely to develop the false consciousness that the jobs they are doing are dignifying.

They are therefore more likely to feel alienated from the dull, mentally narrowing jobs they are forced to endure and to reject them as a satisfying way of working and living. Do not tell me I am being a responsible citizen in doing this lousy job of packing shelves, serving drinks, sweeping floors or whatever it is today! Detachment in this sense is potentially liberating. Do not say my job must be satisfying or a route to 'happiness'. I do it for the money. I will find my life and develop outside it.

Low social mobility

A *seventh* feature is one the precariat shares with many in the prole-tariat, though not with the salariat and proficians. It emphasizes why it is unhelpful to compress all 'workers' into a single 'working class'. It is that the precariat has a very low probability of social mobility. The longer a person is in it, the lower the probability of escape. In most of Europe and North America, social mobility has declined, alongside growing income inequality, since the start of the globalization era (Blanden, Gregg and Machin 2005; Sawhill 2008; OECD 2010). Ironically, this has emerged during a period in which governments have claimed to be promoting meritocracy and social mobility.

Over-qualification

An *eighth* feature is over-qualification. For the first time in history, the mainstream worker – or what Marxists call 'labour power' – is over-qualified for the labour he or she is expected to undertake. As a society, we have yet to come to terms with this, and so far the political response seems to be the wrong one.

In early industrial capitalism, most workers were expected to learn a trade that conformed to the skills practised in their labour. Today, it is rare for people to use more than a fraction of their skills or qualifications in a job. 'Credentialism' rules. Having high-level qualifications is just enough to enter the labour market lottery. For many jobs, candidates must have either a well-connected parent or qualifications greater than could possibly be used by the job in question. This leads to an epidemic of status frustration and to stress from 'invisible underemployment', having underemployed skills. For the precariat today, there is nothing invisible about it.

Uncertainty

A *ninth* feature is that the precariat is subject to a peculiar combination of forms of insecurity. The labourist model of industrial capitalism was based on the norm of a nuclear family in which the male 'breadwinner' was expected to earn a 'family wage', enough to keep a dependent wife and several children in subsistence. In the twentieth century, 'fictitious' labour decommodification took place through the construction of enterprise and state benefits supposed to cover what economists call contingency risks, those that arise from what one is doing. These were wrongly depicted as labour 'rights'. They were acquired for specific groups who struggled to secure them, but they were never universal or unconditional.

Besides being mostly sexist and patriarchal, as befitted the labourist model, compensatory benefits were constructed on the premise that one could, in principle, calculate the probability of a risk coming about (unemployment, illness, pregnancy, retirement, etc.). Thus for the proletariat in stable labour, contingency risks could be covered by social insurance. The interests of the 'rough' minority were of less concern.

However, in a tertiary open market economy, social insurance systems cannot give strong social protection. The precariat faces uncertainty, 'unknown unknowns'. With uncertainty (as distinct from risk), a person cannot calculate the probability of an adverse event. Today there are far more spheres of uncertainty, due largely to economic liberalization and a market system based on competition and created scarcity. The probability of adverse shocks and hazards is higher, the cost of adverse events is greater, and the ability to cope with and recover from them is lower. This is more worrying than suggested by the term 'risk society'. And not only is the precariat exposed to more spheres of uncertainty than other groups, it is also less resilient, having fewer resources to deal with them. So the impact of adverse events is more severe.

Poverty and precarity traps

This leads to the *tenth* feature of the precariat, which no other group experiences – a combination of poverty traps, exploitation and coercion outside the workplace, and precarity traps that amounts to a tsunami of adversity. The welfare state, in all its variants, was built for and by the proletariat. It was based on national or social insurance, with benefits tied to regular contributions by or on behalf of regular employees. As the precariat has grown, this model has decayed. All welfare states have moved towards means-tested social assistance, supposedly targeting help on 'the poor'. In the past, the poor were the 'rough', outside the mainstream of society. Now social policy is geared to identifying the poor through means-testing.

For the precariat this creates severe poverty traps. Anybody receiving means-tested benefits who then takes a low-wage casual job can face a marginal 'tax' rate close to 100 per cent. Since going from benefits to labour costs time and money, there is no incentive to labour at all. Though governments have introduced tapers in the form of 'in-work' benefits and tax credits, they have failed to overcome the poverty trap. Millions in industrialized countries face an effective tax rate of over 80 per cent, double what the salariat is expected to tolerate, and treble what multinational corporations are supposed to pay when they are not siphoning off profits to overseas tax havens.

As there is no incentive to take low-paying jobs, poverty traps have led predictably to state coercion in the form of 'workfare', whereby youth and others are obliged to take low-wage jobs or do unpaid 'work experience', on pain of being penalized and demonized as 'scroungers', 'skivers' and the like.

There has also been a growth of precarity traps, situations where taking low-paid jobs can be expected to lower income subsequently (see Article 17 of the Charter). The state requires the precariat to undertake a lot of work to try to gain entitlement to benefits, through numerous steps of personal action, each a barrier to be overcome, a trap for the unwary, nervous, ignorant, frail or short-tempered. Life is built around queuing, form-filling, providing extensive documen- tation, frequent reporting for interviews, answering 'trick' questions, and so on. The process becomes harder, more humiliating and prolonged. Taking a low-wage job that could end at any moment would risk being back at the beginning of this benefit-claiming process within weeks. No rational person would take such a job in these circumstances. Yet the precariat is being forced to do so.

This form of precarity trap is widespread in the countries of Northern Europe, including the UK, where wages at the lower end of the labour market and state benefits are chasing each other downwards. Elsewhere, other precarity traps are more common. They include the situation where taking a low-status low-wage job lowers the probability of obtaining a career job later, a trap made worse by the threat of benefit sanctions if the low-wage job is refused. Another precarity trap arises from the difficulty of moving in search of employment. In many countries, youths, in particular, cannot rent an apartment because without a 'permanent' job they are not accepted as tenants.

In sum, the precariat is defined by ten features. Not all are unique to it. But taken together, the elements define a social group, and for that reason we may call the precariat a class-in-the-making. Critics may claim the notion is too vague, as if that were not true of 'the working class' or 'the middle class'. However, two questions remain. Is the precariat a single group? And is it the new dangerous class?

Varieties of precariat

The precariat is not homogeneous. There is nothing unusual about this. All classes have had fractions, especially during their evolution.

But the precariat is divided to such an extent that one could describe it as a class at war with itself. This may change sooner than some observers imagine.

In *The Precariat*, the precariat was divided into 'grinners' and 'groaners', those who accepted the status with equanimity and those who felt frustrated, angry and desperate. A complementary way of looking at what has been happening is to identify three varieties of precariat.

The first consists of people bumped out of working-class communities and families. They experience a sense of relative deprivation. They, their parents or grandparents belonged to working-class occupations, with status, skill and respect. Looking back to an imagined or real past, they become atavistic, asking why life cannot be as it was. They are also relatively uneducated, and so more likely to listen to populists peddling neo-fascist agendas. People in this part of the precariat typically blame the 'other' for their plight and are keen to punish others in the precariat by cutting 'their' benefits, even when they are receiving benefits themselves or face the prospect of needing them.

The second variety consists of traditional denizens – migrants, Roma, ethnic minorities, asylum seekers in limbo, all those with the least secure rights anywhere. It also includes some of the disabled and a growing number of ex-convicts. This group too experiences relative deprivation, comparing current experience with 'home' or a previous world lost to them. The nostalgia may be delusional, but anger is likely to be combined with a pragmatic need to survive. This part of the precariat may be detached from the political and social mainstream. They keep their heads down. That should not be mistaken for lack of resentment or readiness to become active if a vision emerges to energize them.

Their anger may feed into a willingness to labour hard, to offer a high effort bargain. It is not surprising that migrants are preferred as labourers, or that, in a number of OECD countries, the majority of new jobs in recent years have reportedly been taken by migrants. That is why the first variety of the precariat is so easily mobilized against the second.

However, there is a third, rapidly growing variety. It consists of the educated, plunged into a precariat existence after being promised the opposite, a bright career of personal development and satisfaction. Most are in their twenties and thirties. But they are not alone. Many drifting out of a salariat existence are joining them.

The defining feature of this part of the precariat is another form of relative deprivation, a sense of status frustration. They are not doing what they set out to do, and there is little prospect of doing so. But because of their education, and awareness of the drabness or absurdity of the labour they are expected to accept, they are well placed to appreciate the delusion of labourism and the need for a new progressive vision. We should not be surprised to find a new youthful romanticism, a flour-ishing artistic outbreak, analogous to what happened two centuries ago (Hobsbawm [1962] 1977). Perhaps the biggest challenge for this part of the precariat is to induce the other varieties to share a common vision. There is no reason why that cannot happen, just as craftsmen and intel-lectuals acted as educators and leaders of 'the working class' in the late nineteenth and early twentieth centuries. But it is a challenge.

In sum, we can say that the first part of the precariat experiences deprivation relative to a real or imagined past, the second relative to an absent present, an absent 'home', and the third relates to a feeling of having no future. But enough of the three groups must find a common identity, for the precariat must form a class-for-itself, if only to have the strength to seek to abolish itself.

Why the precariat is 'a dangerous class'

The precariat is a class-in-the-making, in that those in it have distinctive relations of production, relations of distribution (sources of income) and relations to the state, but not yet a common consciousness or a common view of what to do about precarity. While many understand the precariat and what it means to be in it, some scholars reject the concept as describing a class (e.g. Braga 2012). One understands the reluctance of Marxists to dispense with the dichotomy of capital and labour, though while they dismiss ideas of a new class they often talk of 'the middle class', a most un-Marxian concept. But their desire to compress the precariat into old notions of 'the working class' or 'the proletariat' distracts us from developing an appropriate vocabulary and set of images to guide twenty-first century analysis.

To say the precariat is 'dangerous' is to make the point that its class interests are opposed to the mainstream political agendas of the twentieth century, the neo-liberalism of the mainstream 'right' and the labourism of social democracy. However, as of 2013, the precariat was still not a class-for-itself; while all three varieties were aware of what they were against – insecurity, impoverishment, debt, lack of occupational identity and multiple inequalities – they were not yet agreed on, or perhaps even aware of, what they needed or wanted. The precariat was still in the 'primitive rebel' phase, like the Luddites of the early nineteenth century or others that have emerged in the disembedded phase of transformations.

The precariat is dangerous for another related reason, because it is still at war with itself. If populist demagoguery had its way, the first variety would turn vicious towards the second, as has been happening in Greece, Hungary and Italy. It is also dangerous because, as predicted in *The Precariat*, the combination of anxiety, alienation, anomie and anger can be expected to lead to more days of riot and protest. And it is dangerous because stress, economic insecurity and frustration can lead and are leading to social illnesses, including drug-taking, petty crime, domestic violence and suicide.

Finally, the precariat is dangerous because it is confronted by a strident divisive state. Many in it feel commodified, treated as objects to be coerced to labour, penalized for not labouring, exhorted by politicians to do more. Nobody should be surprised if they react anomically. But since the precariat is emotionally detached from the labour it is expected to do, it is less inclined to imagine that jobs are the road to happiness or that job creation is a sign of social progress. The precariat pins its hopes and aspirations elsewhere. Quite soon, it will echo a slogan of 1968: 'Ça suffit!'

2

The austerity era

The neo-liberal ideology that guided governments from the 1980s onwards ushered in what we now call globalization. Economies, firms and individuals were urged to become more 'competitive' in order to succeed in a global market economy. Governments re-regulated labour markets to make them more flexible, dismantled institutions of social solidarity, rolled back mechanisms of social and economic security, and commodified education to serve the interests of business. These changes expanded the number of denizens, while the precariat took shape.

Loss of rights was scarcely noticed at the time, because a 'Faustian bargain' created a false mood of boom and prosperity. Governments disguised falling real wages – needed to compete with the workforce of emerging market economies and brought about by flexible labour policies – with a combination of easy money and labour subsidies. Growing inequalities, and the emergence of a plutocratic elite, were seen as the corollary of competitiveness. After 2008, all that changed.

The subsequent austerity era has exposed and exacerbated the trends unleashed by globalization that governments had concealed.

Inequalities have grown; wages have fallen further; unemployment, poverty and homelessness have risen. Governments have cut support for the precariat, while increasing subsidies for the rich. More people are losing rights; more are joining the precariat.

Meanwhile, a Great Convergence is gathering pace; wages in emerging economies are rising while those in industrialized countries are falling, a process that still has many years to run. Rich countries have become 'rentier' economies, receiving increasing income in profits and dividends from overseas operations and investments. This serves to enrich the plutocracy and elite, with good pickings for the salariat and proficians. There is a way out. But it depends on understanding what has been happening.

End of the Faustian bargain

When the neo-liberal project took off, the defining features were liberalization, which meant opening up national economies to global competition; individualization, which meant re-regulation to curb all forms of collective institution (notably trade unions and occupational guilds); commodification, which meant making as much as possible subject to market forces (notably through the privatization of public services); and fiscal retrenchment, which meant lowering taxes on high incomes and capital.

Liberalization opened up a global labour market, trebling the world's labour supply; two billion extra workers became available, habituated to labour for incomes one-fiftieth of those in the rich countries. With capital and technology highly mobile, productivity began to rise rapidly in emerging market economies. The mantra of 'competitiveness' became the guide to economic and social policy, as every country tried to cut labour costs.

The Chicago school of law and economics that underpinned what became known as the Washington Consensus argued that policies and regulations were justified only if they promoted growth. But it was obvious that liberalization globally would lead to a long-term convergence of incomes, with wages rising slowly in developing countries while they fell more quickly in rich countries. Neo-liberal economists also knew that what they were unleashing would increase inequality; the returns to capital would soar while wages and employee benefits in rich countries would come under downward pressure.

Two courses were open to governments and the financial agencies guiding them. As their reforms automatically boosted the incomes of those in finance and export-oriented multinationals, one option was to oblige the fortuitously well-placed beneficiaries to pay more to the public coffers, for society's benefit. After all, their vastly higher incomes were not due to any new collective brilliance but to rule changes in their favour. Inequality could have been limited by a compact to share the gains across society.

Sadly, that road was not taken. Instead, governments made a Faustian bargain with their populations while engaging in a fatal embrace with financial capital. In illustration, in the 1960s, bank assets equalled 50 per cent of US national income; by 2008, they totalled over 200 per cent. In 1982, none of the 50 richest Americans was a financier; by 2012, 12 of the 50 were financiers or asset managers. Yet no government that wished to be re-elected could allow wages to plunge. So, as policy and institutional changes were made in pursuit of flexibility, and as real wages stagnated, governments propped up the incomes of the emerging precariat through cheap credit, lax fiscal policy and labour subsidies, including tax credits. This Faustian bargain ushered in an orgy of consumption and dissaving.

The USA set the pattern. It printed dollars freely to cover rising current account and budget deficits. Meanwhile, the propensity to save rose in the emerging markets of south-east Asia following the Asian crisis of 1998; they accumulated many of those dollars (and euros), allowing the USA and Europe to spend lavishly. But that left the US economy exposed. By the time of the crash in 2007–8, the USA owed a net $2.5 trillion to foreigners, whereas China had accumulated net foreign assets of $1.8 trillion.

By then, a global market economy had emerged. Labour market institutions had been transformed, with labour flexibility, wage system flexibility and a restructuring of the social security system (Standing 1999, 2002). Multinationals had become established in emerging market economies, shifting investment and employment, and unbundling themselves in a new model of shareholder capitalism. Labour markets changed radically. Though some denied that fundamental change was occurring (e.g. Doogan 2009), this view is hard to sustain. Labour insecurity became the norm.

Manufacturing production and employment in OECD countries fell, notably in the USA (Pierce and Schott 2012). The jobs lost should not be romanticized as 'good' in the sense of being better than in services. But they had been mostly full-time stable jobs, with extensive non-wage benefits, labour protection and collective bargaining.

The Great Convergence started slowly. Between 1960 and 2000, about 20 low-income countries grew faster than the USA and Western Europe. After 2000, 80 did so, narrowing the gap in living standards (Subramanian 2011). China, with over a billion people, emerged as a global giant. Manufacturing expansion coincided with growth of 145 million in its huge labour force between 1990 and 2008. Productivity grew annually by over 9 per cent. Output that took 100 workers to produce in 1990 required fewer than 20 in 2008, according to the Asian Productivity Organization. In 1999, China's exports were less than a third of the USA's. By 2009, China was the world's largest exporter.

Investment flooded into emerging market economies. Corporations became global in character: sales of multinationals' foreign affiliates rose sixfold between 1990 and 2010, their assets rose twelvefold, their exports quadrupled, and employment in affiliates more than trebled to over 68 million workers (UNCTAD 2011). The share of employees in US multinationals working for subsidiaries abroad rose from a fifth in 1989 to a third in 2009. These figures understate the changes, since they do not include the growing use of foreign sub-contractors.

Workers in rich countries were in trouble. Real wages for middle-income and lower-income labour declined. In OECD countries overall, the share of labour income dropped by five percentage points between 1980 and 2008 (OECD 2012). In the USA, before the crash, the wage share of national income had tumbled from its 1970 peak of 53 per cent to just above 45 per cent, its lowest level in modern history. By the end of 2012, the wage share was down further to just 43.5 per cent. Some economists attributed this to technological change (Brynjolfsson and McAfee 2012), but this is simply a variant of 'the lump of labour fallacy', a familiar refrain since the Luddites. Although technological change played a part, policy and institutional changes were mainly responsible, along with workers' weakened bargaining strength. The fall in wages was associated with globalization, not induced by digital technologies.

The trend was global. According to the Asian Development Bank, between the mid–1990s and the mid–2000s, labour income as a share of manufacturing output fell from 48 per cent to 42 per cent in China and from 37 per cent to 22 per cent in India. These were enormous shifts, and surely reflected labour surplus conditions and the power of capital.

In another indicator of structural change, the close positive relationship between productivity and wages stopped in the 1980s and the gap widened after 2000, producing a graph dubbed 'the jaws of the snake'. This was reneging on an implicit social compact of the post-war era, by which real wages moved in parallel with productivity growth. In a globalizing economy, capital no longer needed to make that compromise.

As wages fell, and as labour flexibility made life for those living off labour more insecure, the Faustian bargain was kept going through cheap credit and subsidies. A defining moment came in 1992 when the US government made housing loans cheap and easy to obtain. It brought short-term political advantage to then President Bill Clinton, but was unsustainable. By 2007, total credit had passed $50 trillion, fifty times greater than in 1964. The explosion of asset prices was aptly described by one economist as 'creditism' (Duncan 2012).

Other countries followed. In Europe, millions were enabled to acquire housing beyond their sustainable means. The share of households in England owning their homes rose from 57 per cent in 1981 to 71 per cent in 2003, at a time when earnings of lower-income groups were stagnating or falling. In Spain, banks were encouraged to lend 100 per cent mortgages to low-income workers, including migrants. In Ireland, banks rushed to grant 115 per cent loans in a building boom that nearly doubled the housing stock; fancy houses sprang up everywhere, many soon to become sad derelict building sites.

Like all Faustian bargains, the orgy had to end, which duly happened in 2007–8. But while the media focused on the greed of bankers and financial markets, attention was diverted from the structural features of the global market system and the related 'crises' that had been nurtured by the neo-liberalist strategy.

The *first* was a fiscal crisis. When the financial system went into meltdown, governments rushed to 'rescue the banks'. It was the greatest give-away to the rich the world had ever seen. It was also a missed opportunity to redistribute income. Governments, central banks and international financial agencies fed the banks gluttonous amounts of money, generating more government debt.

The *second* was a distributional crisis. Inequality had become greater than at any time since the 1920s. That was due to the Faustian bargain, to the strategy of weakening workers' bargaining strength and to the restructuring of social protection. It was to worsen when governments addressed the fiscal crisis; they gave more subsidies to the affluent, while cutting benefits and services for others.

The *third* was an existential crisis. The neo-liberal model was a crude version of Darwinian competition, based on 'winners' and 'losers'. It eschewed values such as compassion, empathy and solidarity, and preached individualism, competitiveness, meritocracy and commodification. This ideological break, initiated by Ronald Reagan and Margaret Thatcher, created an epidemic of stress, fear and insecurity among the precariat and those close to it. At the same time, the drive for 'competitiveness' encouraged unbridled opportunism, cheating and criminality, especially among the plutocracy. Bernie Madoff, who managed to defraud others of $65 billion, was only the most vivid example of the plutocracy's venality.

Fourth, an ecological crisis built up through the globalization era. Although there were other causes as well, pursuit of economic growth brought disregard for the externalities that were exacerbating the environmental threat. Governments and corporations looked to the short term, four or five years in the case of most politicians, fewer for most chief executives looking to the bottom line and their bonuses. Proposals to curb, or impose costs on, polluting activities were thwarted by commercial interests and their pet politicians, with job generation often cited as a higher priority. The austerity era intensified the policies of giving subsidies and tax breaks for dubious production, while paying lip service to environmental needs.

Fifth, a 'rights crisis' waited in the wings. A democratic deficit has opened up, due to the commodification of politicians, many of whom are using politics as a 'stepping-stone occupation' enabling them to go on to money-making careers. This has been happening almost everywhere, including the UK. Many people have lost faith in the 'post-truth' version of electoral politics, knowing it is shaped by money, mainly from the plutocracy, with presentational skills, slogans and buzz words dominating substance. The democratic deficit is compounded by the growth of surveillance that is curtailing rights to privacy and freedom. The 'panopticon state' is a threat to civility and equality. We will return to the rights crisis. But first we must consider the orthodox reaction to the end of the Faustian bargain.

The austerity era

Such is the scale of the global adjustment required that the generation we hope to inspire may live under its shadow for a long time to come.

Mervyn King, Governor of the Bank of England, October 2012

After a period of fiscal and monetary stimulus following the 2007–8 crash, a new orthodoxy crystallized. Governments, backed by international financial agencies, decided to impose 'austerity' on their populations to pay for the profligacy they had promoted. Ironically, the International Monetary Fund (IMF) and financial groups that had promoted the liberalization agenda became overseers of the strategy intended to clear up the mess. Many of the top policymakers to emerge after the crash were alumni of Goldman Sachs, including so-called technocratic prime ministers of Italy, Greece and Spain, the head of the European Central Bank and the new Governor of the Bank of England. It was a case of poachers turned gamekeepers, epitomizing what even *The Economist* (2012c) has called 'the rise of the financial-political complex'.

Reducing debt became the mantra of all governments, which later justified big cuts in public spending and living standards with research claiming that debt of more than 90 per cent of GDP reduced economic growth (Reinhart and Rogoff 2010). Three years later, it was shown that the data and methodology behind this claim were dubious (Herndon, Ash and Pollin 2013; Pollin and Ash 2013). But by then, the policy of rapid debt reduction had become entrenched. The original paper had been accepted simply because it accorded with the ideological paradigm. That can be contrasted with indifference to research showing that reducing inequality would raise growth. As summarized by Berg and Ostry (2011a), in both rich and poorer countries, inequality was correlated with shorter economic expansions and lower medium-term growth.

The rationale for austerity was that high debt slows growth. But, as has become only too evident, the causation can run the other way, with slow growth leading to higher debt. By dampening growth, cutting public spending can increase debt rather than reduce it, creating a vicious circle of decline. It is harder to cut budget deficits during recessions, when living standards are falling and unemployment rising. Some expenditure, on benefits for example, rises automatically while tax revenue falls. Yet governments have responded to persistent debt with further cuts in benefits and services, including public goods, public spaces and the commons, thereby impoverishing more people, leading to more 'dependency' on benefits, and more pressure on health services.

Although debt in industrialized countries was substantial before the crash, it was swollen by the financial crisis itself. The average ratio of government debt to GDP, 74 per cent in 2007, surged by over a third to 101 per cent in 2010, and continued to rise subsequently in some of the hardest-hit countries. In Ireland and Portugal, debt rose to over 100 per cent of national income *after* the crash. In Spain public debt, just 36 per cent of GDP before the crisis, was close to 100 per cent by 2013. According to the IMF, the main culprit was falling revenues, as austerity measures, intensified by external pressure, drove incomes down. Growth stagnated, yet governments continued to try to reduce debt by cutting the incomes of the majority, with empty promises that short-term pain would lead to long-term gain.

In Ireland, which in 2013 was being touted as a success story, a new government imposed austerity on lower-income workers while cutting corporation tax to 12.5 per cent to draw investment from elsewhere. By 2012, household debt exceeded 200 per cent of disposable income. Living standards tumbled, while foreign capital made more profits. As *The Economist*, an austerity advocate, ruefully admitted: 'That widening shortfall reflects the fact that the Irish people have fared much worse than the Irish economy' (Economist 2013a).

Elsewhere too, post–2008 policies were savagely deflationary. The debt ogre was used to justify plans to slash public spending and accelerate privatization, while huge hand-outs were given to banks by way of 'quantitative easing' in an effort to recapitalize the financial sector and induce investment lending. The outcome was more fat bonuses for bankers, while those relying on state benefits and social services suffered most.

Countries at the forefront of the crisis, such as Greece, Ireland, Portugal and Spain, paid a terrible price. Spanish households lost 20 per cent of their wealth, and Irish households 36 per cent, between 2007 and 2012. Greece's economy shrank by a quarter in that period and more spending cuts were planned, while in Portugal, higher income taxes and cuts in benefits led to big falls in national income and soaring unemployment, with more austerity measures on the way.

The Eurozone crisis may have been the precipitating factor. But the main problem was the neo-liberal model that had allowed levels of inequality unimaginable at the start of the globalization era. Put bluntly, if more income goes to a tiny elite, the world economy becomes hostage to a 'money strike': the financial elite can withhold their money, just as workers can withhold labour in a labour strike, to force governments to entice them with more tax breaks and subsidies. The burden of cuts is then borne by everyone else, especially those most reliant on social spending and benefits – the precariat.

The Great Convergence

While austerity spluttered, the Great Convergence accelerated. Average living standards in emerging economies are rising, although many have suffered from austerity (Ortiz and Cummins 2013). While growth stalled in OECD countries, it remained buoyant in most emerging market economies. And the Great Convergence has been accompanied by 'structural decoupling'. Whereas before the crash cyclical patterns in OECD countries were matched by similar changes in emerging economies, now most of the latter grow even when OECD countries are in recession. And the most successful have relied on state capital to do so.

In rich countries, the crash slowed potential as well as actual growth. The IMF concluded that the Group of Seven biggest industrial economies would grow at most by 2 per cent per annum between 2012 and 2017, compared with 4 per cent in the recovery from recession in the 1980s (1983–8) and 3 per cent in the 1990s recovery (1994–9). At 2 per cent a year and falling, the US economy's potential growth rate has slowed to half what it was in the late twentieth century.

By contrast, although China's government orchestrated a slowdown in its hectic growth, partly in response to signs of a property 'bubble', real wages and benefits rose faster after the crash just as they fell more sharply in OECD countries. In 2012, China's dollar GDP, measured at purchasing power parity, overtook the USA's. India struggled, but its economy still grew at 5 per cent a year. The convergence promised by globalization was gathering pace.

Much has been made of rising wages in China and it is true that, in one year alone, the minimum wage in some provinces rose by 30 per cent. But as productivity has also risen sharply, labour and production costs are still well below those in the OECD, and will remain so for years. Talk of a roll-back of manufacturing jobs and production to OECD countries is wishful thinking. Instead, investment and production shifted to other emerging market economies, such as Vietnam, Indonesia, Bangladesh, India and Cambodia. While manufacturing output and profitability picked up in the USA, aided by subsidies and shrinking wages and employee benefits, there was no strong revival of manufacturing jobs.

Above all, the Great Convergence involves a global shift of capital. The World Bank (2013) concluded that by 2030 half the global stock of capital will be in today's developing countries, compared with under one-third in 2012. Compared with 2000, their share of global investment is projected to triple to 60 per cent. China and India together will account for 38 per cent of global gross investment.

Growth in capital mobility also reflects the new global model of shareholder capitalism, in which corporate unbundling has gone with a shift of trade from finished goods to tasks and parts of goods. More corporations are integrated globally, able to switch production and employment according to market and cost changes. For instance, Boeing's Dreamliner, a midsize jet, involves 43 suppliers spread over 135 sites around the world; 70 per cent of its components are produced abroad. In Sweden, Ericsson's mobile phones have 900 components from 60 suppliers in 40 countries, which are shipped to customers in 90 countries. A typical Swedish car is only 50 per cent Swedish.

The global restructuring of investment has accelerated. Between 2007 and 2011, private investment in the 27 countries of the European Union fell by €350 billion, 20 times the fall in private consumption, four times the fall in real GDP. Including the USA and Japan, the fall in private investment was $1 trillion. Foreign direct investment (FDI) into developed countries fell in 2012 to its lowest level for almost ten years, while for the first time FDI into developing countries accounted for more than half the global total (UNCTAD 2013).

The rush of multinationals to emerging market economies accelerated. Although many complained about rising anti-business sentiment in Europe, their motive was to boost profits. American firms led the flight, with Ford, General Motors, GE (General Electric), Dow Chemical, HP (Hewlett-Packard) and others closing European plants. Financial services firms followed.

Big corporations are blossoming in what are now dynamic members of a global market system. At the pinnacle in terms of labour impact is the Taiwan-owned Foxconn, electronics workshop of the world, dubbed the champion of flexible manufacturing. By 2013 it employed 1.4 million people in China alone, up from 100,000 in 2003 and more than twice as many as when the global shock struck. In 2012, it announced plans to double in size again by 2020. Indicative of its global ambitions, it has become the Czech Republic's second largest exporter, is expanding in Mexico, Brazil, Turkey, India and Indonesia, and in 2013 was setting up its first US operation, in California, to manufacture Google Glass. Alibaba, a Chinese internet firm, plans to become one of the world's most valuable companies soon. Others are following.

China used the austerity era to buy the technology of high-profile European corporations, its state enterprises gaining control of private, often privatized, firms with the aid of subsidies, cheap credit and tax breaks. Chinese enterprises invested $12.6 billion in Europe in 2012, 21 per cent more than in 2011. German manufacturing firms were again a favoured target, while China Investment Corporation took minority stakes in London's Heathrow airport and Thames Water. When Portugal privatized its power industry, China's Three Gorges took a 21 per cent stake in the largest power company. There is more to come.

Employment restructuring

The global restructuring of employment has also accelerated. Between 2008 and 2010, US-based firms cut 2.9 million jobs in the USA and expanded jobs outside the USA by 2.4 million, while leading French firms in the CAC–40 stock-market index cut employment in France by 4 per cent but increased global employment by 5 per cent. By 2012, one-fifth of Japanese manufacturing took place outside Japan. For electronics it was over 30 per cent, for cars over half. Toyota's boss lamented: 'Industry and employment are on the verge of collapse' (Economist 2012d). Japan has become a 'rentier' economy, relying on investment income from overseas, which keeps the yen strong, impeding exports.

Some still believe the USA is an industrial country. But its leading firms have been shifting more jobs abroad. Apple, then the biggest US corporation by value, had only 43,000 employees in the USA in 2012. Outside, it employed directly just 20,000 people and contracted out another 700,000 manufacturing jobs, mostly in Asia. In 2011, Steve Jobs famously told President Obama that 'those jobs aren't coming back.' Apple's shift abroad, which only began in 2004, was due not just to labour costs but also to the availability of skilled flexible labour and the ability to scale up and down rapidly in response to demand and technological change.

By 2012, China had 34 million urban factory workers earning on average $2 an hour, while a further 65 million in town and village enterprises earned 64 cents an hour, with 675 million workers available elsewhere. Talk of the labour surplus drying up is delusional. If the Chinese authorities wished, they could raise the retirement age, now 60 for men and 55 for women, low by international standards. The number of Chinese aged over 60 is expected to rise from 181 million in 2012 to 390 million in 2035. If the retirement age was raised by just one year, it would unleash additional labour equivalent to the total labour force of an average EU country.

However, perhaps the outstanding feature of the labour market restructuring is the continuing rise of labour migration, including rural-urban migration in emerging market economies, which is swelling the global labour supply. When commentators ruminate about the ending of labour-surplus conditions – called the Lewis tipping point, after a famous paper written in 1954 – they focus on shrinking additions to the adult population. More important is the loosening of people from rural pursuits as they flood into globalizing labour markets.

Globalization of migratory labour

The Great Convergence is linked to the changing pattern of migration, unique to the Global Transformation. Migration is now global, with flows of people in all directions. More countries have high emigration as well as immigration. And more migration is circulatory and short-term, rather than for settlement, unlike the previous surge in the movement of people before the First World War.

Since 2008, emigration from Europe's most crisis-hit countries has soared. The number of Greeks and Spaniards moving to other European Union countries, notably Germany, doubled between 2007 and 2011. In 2007, 300,000 migrants came to Spain from Latin America; in 2010 the number leaving Spain for Latin America overtook total immigration. The Portuguese too flooded to former colonies, Angola, Mozambique and Brazil. The number of Portuguese living in Brazil rose from 276,000 in 2010 to 330,000 in 2011. More than 100,000 people, many of them young university graduates, were estimated to have left Portugal in 2012, a bigger outflow than at any time since the mid–1960s. Ireland's central statistical office estimated in 2012 that since 2008 50,000 people had left the country, and the exodus was gathering pace.

The migration of highly educated people also accelerated after 2008. In the five years following the crash, a third of new migrants to OECD countries had tertiary education. On average, immigrants in rich countries are more educated than the native-born and the gap is widening, reflecting inflows from North America and Eastern Europe. In Canada, over half of immigrants have tertiary education; the proportion is over 40 per cent in the UK and Ireland, and about 30 per cent for the OECD as a whole.

A growing number of people migrate within multinational corporations and multilateral agencies. Many are in the salariat, but there is also more movement by proficians as consultants, short-term contractors and freelancers. And student mobility has grown as part of the global commodification of education. Not only have the numbers risen, but the mobility has become global, with students going to more countries, and the USA shrinking as a destination.

There has also been feminization of migration, with more women than men moving, usually for employment. The proportion of women migrants who are highly educated is higher than for men. Migrants have a higher fertility rate, and the fertility rate of citizens in rich countries has dropped below the natural reproduction rate. So, the share of children whose parents are migrants has risen.

Much migration is undocumented, which is transforming labour markets in a number of rich countries. Of the estimated 232 million migrants around the world, about 30 million may be undocumented.

Almost a third of migrants in the USA are thought to be 'illegals'. Migrants lost jobs in droves in the post–2008 recession, but most did not show up in the unemployment count or claim benefits. They just slipped into the shadow economy. Tight border security deterred illegals from leaving, for fear of being unable to return.

There are also more refugees and asylum seekers than ever. Their treatment has grown more punitive and exclusionary, often designed to deter them coming to that particular country. And there is an impending disastrous development of growing 'environmental migration', due to global warming and related ecological trends.

A new phenomenon is the migration of labour without migration of workers. Call centres may turn out to be a transitory phase in a broader trend, involving telecommuting and the extraordinary rise of 'crowd-work'. The old image is of people moving to look for economic opportunity. But migration of labour without the migration of workers poses challenges to economic analysis, labour statistics, fiscal policy and social protection policy.

Another new migration trend consists of elderly Europeans going into long-term care institutions in lower-income countries. This is topical in Germany, and is attributed to rising care costs as well as ageing. Instead of people from Eastern Europe or Asia going to Germany to care for the elderly, families are sending their old people to those countries. Elderly care is profitable. And although EU law currently prohibits state insurers from signing contracts with overseas homes, pressure is building to change that. Old-age migration, for retirement or care, will grow.

Meanwhile, internal migration has grown in emerging market economies, notably China, while it is falling in the USA, possibly because information and cheap travel have allowed more to seek jobs without relocating (Kaplan and Schulhofer-Wohl 2012).

Rich countries as 'rentier' economies

Appalled by austerity, some social democratic economists have called for a Keynesian response (boosting spending). But the OECD countries are not in a Keynesian world. They are becoming 'rentier' economies, drawing in foreign capital with subsidies and tax breaks, and gaining more income from repatriation of profits and dividends by multinationals, thereby benefiting from rising sales and investment abroad.

In 2012, US profit margins were higher than at any time in the previous 65 years; corporate profits as a percentage of national income reached 13.6 per cent. Yet this did not lead to a surge of domestic investment or employment. Not only did full-time jobs not return to their pre-recession level but wages remained below the starting level of previous recessions. The foreign share of profits was a third of the total, more than double the proportion in 2000.

The USA tried to increase manufacturing exports. But creating manufacturing jobs by this route is becoming ever harder. According to the US Department of Commerce's Office of Competition and Economic Analysis, each billion dollars of manufacturing exports generated 14,000 jobs in 1993, but only 5,350 by 2012. Most of that decline was due to productivity growth. Although workers in export-oriented manufacturing earn nearly 20 per cent more than their peers, goods exports supported just 7.3 million jobs in 2012 and the evidence of previous years suggests that roughly half of these may have been in services rather than manufacturing. Improving export competitiveness will only make a modest change.

As for the UK, the BBC's presenter Evan Davis summarized its future as 'butler to the global super-rich', serving visiting plutocrats and depending on the City of London to bring in income from financial services. In contrast, Peter Marsh (2012), manufacturing editor of the *Financial Times*, wrote a bullish book claiming that the rich countries will not lose production because a 'fifth industrial revolution' will rescue them. Whatever that might be, there is no reason to think it will restore production or manufacturing jobs in those countries.

The trend towards rentier economies has implications for the precariat's response. But as the Great Convergence gathers momentum and OECD countries adjust to their new status, the devastation produced by the austerity era will surely only worsen.

3

The precariat grows

On its narrow terms of preserving the economic structure of inequality, the austerity strategy may have modest success for a while. But those who have had their lives devastated should neither forget nor forgive. This chapter traces some of the consequences in expanding the precariat and tipping more people into a denizen status of one sort or another.

Poverty and homelessness

Poverty and economic insecurity grew sharply in the austerity era. In the European Union, after declining in the early 2000s, the number of people at risk of poverty rose to 120 million in 2011, a quarter of the population, though this was reduced to 17 per cent after social transfers. 'At risk' was defined as those earning less than 60 per cent of average disposable income (the poverty line), plus those in jobs of less than 20 per cent of standard weekly hours, and those in 'severe material deprivation', defined as unable to afford four or more of nine items considered indispensable (such as rent, a one-week holiday a year, a car, a washing machine and a nutritionally adequate meal every other day). The number deemed 'severely deprived' rose by 5 per cent between 2009 and 2011 to nearly 42 million.

More than a quarter of all children were in households at risk of poverty. As a UNICEF report (Ortiz, Daniels and Engilbertsdóttir 2012) makes clear, child poverty is primarily linked to the distribution of income and consigns many to a lifetime of social and economic insecurity via educational underachievement, ill health and lower life expectancy.

In Britain, an inter-university study (Gordon et al. 2013) found that in 2012 a third of households lacked at least three basic necessities, compared with 14 per cent in 1983. Basics included heated homes, eating healthily and properly fitting shoes. The Institute for Fiscal Studies reported that the number of children in poverty in the UK would rise from 2.3 million in 2011 to 3.4 million by 2020, affecting nearly one in four of all children. And a majority of poor children are now in households where adults are in jobs, a pattern found in most OECD countries. In New Zealand, two in five poor children live in households with at least one adult in a full-time job.

In the USA in 2012, over 46 million people were officially below the poverty line, more than at any time since the early 1960s. According to UNICEF, nearly a quarter of American children were living in poverty, defined as in households with incomes half the median; this was a higher proportion than in any of the 29 ranked rich countries except Romania (UNICEF Office of Research 2013). The Pew Charitable Trusts estimated that nearly a third of Americans who as teenagers in 1979 were in what Americans call 'the middle class' (between the thirtieth and seventieth percentiles of the income distribution) had slipped into lower-status situations as adults by the mid–2000s.

Across America and Europe, growing poverty went with more precarious housing. In the UK, where ownership has been the desired norm, the share of households owning homes fell from over 70 per cent before the crash to 64 per cent in 2009–10, and was forecast to drop to below 60 per cent by 2025. By 2012, an estimated 1.6 million people aged 20 to 40 were living with their parents because they could not afford to rent or buy a home, according to Shelter, a housing charity. For those under 45, home ownership in 2012 was lower than in 1960.

By 2013, one in every 12 families in England was on a waiting list for social housing, homelessness had soared by a quarter in two years, and private rents had jumped 37 per cent from 2007. Almost half a million more people in jobs had become reliant on housing benefit, unable to afford to pay the rent.

Across Europe, banks foreclosed on homeowners unable to pay even the interest on their mortgages. In Spain, banks had inflated property prices through reckless lending, but even after they received more than €40 billion in government aid, they continued an aggressive programme of evictions. By 2013 Spanish courts had issued a quarter of a million expulsion orders since 2008 and 80 families a day were still being evicted from their homes. A spate of suicides by people about to be evicted even led to a strike of locksmiths, so ashamed at what they were being asked to do that they refused to take jobs for the banks. Campaigners formed human barricades outside homes to prevent evictions. The precariat was stirring.

While homelessness mounted, so did the number of empty or

unused houses. In Spain, as of 2011, some 3.5 million homes – 14 per cent – were empty, with almost every city affected. In England in 2013, the number of empty homes was over 700,000. Over a third of all houses in Greece are vacant. The system was in shambles. Everywhere, the social right to decent housing was in retreat.

Inequality unbound

For two decades, politicians made little fuss over rising inequality, many reasoning that voters were unconcerned with or hostile to a redistributive agenda. When Raghuram Rajan, a former chief economist of the IMF, reiterated what numerous others had shown, Martin Wolf of the *Financial Times* commented: 'Thus, Prof Rajan notes that "of every dollar of real income growth that was generated between 1976 and 2007, 58 cents went to the top 1 per cent of households". This is surely stunning' (Wolf 2010). It was only stunning if one had ignored what had been well known for a long time.

In the austerity era, nominally independent central banks worsened inequality, notably by pushing down interest rates for corporations and buying up corporate debt. Governments too continued to act in ways that increased inequality.

In the USA, profits soon rebounded. By 2013, they accounted for the highest share of national income since 1950, while the share going to employees was at its lowest since 1966. The shift of income from labour to capital was accelerating. Prominent banks announced that it was a golden age for profits. It was a leaden age for personal incomes, which had been falling since 1980. In the top corporations

(S&P 500), the average pay of chief executives was 204 times the average employee's wages, up from 170 times in 2009, 120 times in 2000 and merely 42 times in 1980.

In the five years after the crash, the top 1 per cent of earners took 93 per cent of US income gains (Saez 2012) while their share of national income in 2012, at 19 per cent, was the highest since 1928. Even the IMF felt it politic to groan: 'When a handful of yachts become ocean liners while the rest remain lowly canoes, something is seriously amiss' (Berg and Ostry 2011b).

In the UK, while the government claimed that all must share cuts to living standards, inequality rose further. Between 2008 and 2012, the richest 1,000 people increased their wealth by £155 billion, more than enough to pay for the government deficit of £119 billion. The number with salaries over £1 million a year almost doubled, to 18,000, between 2010 and 2012, compared with 4,000 in 2000, and more people were paid between £500,000 and £1 million. The Boston Consulting Group estimated that 1,000 British households had net financial assets of more than £100 million, excluding property. In 2013, those earning above £1 million received a tax cut of over £42,000 a year – much more than the total income of anybody in the precariat. And the Resolution Foundation, a think tank, showed that any gains from economic growth between 2012 and 2020 would all go to upper-income groups.

Meanwhile, 19 US-owned multinationals were shown to be paying an effective tax rate of 3 per cent on profits in the UK, compared with the corporation tax rate of 26 per cent. Tax-cutting competition between countries made tax avoidance an easy game. And while the British government tightened checks on benefit cheating by the poor, it cut the tax inspection workforce, making it easier for the affluent to evade and avoid tax.

While most OECD countries stagnated, stock markets thrived. Those earning income from capital made the gains. In 2012, the average value of equities rose by 25 per cent. Pay and bonuses of financiers boomed again, even though the renewed profitability had been made possible by government bailouts. Having stayed high throughout the crisis, Wall Street bonuses in 2012 totalled $20 billion; profits of the US financial industry tripled in a year to $24 billion while it went on making job cuts. In 2012, according to Forbes, the world's top 40 hedge-fund bosses earned $16.7 billion. A former Goldman Sachs trader, David Tepper, received $2.2 billion.

As inequality grew, the plutocracy took advantage of light regulation and showed contempt for the law. Banks were at the forefront. For instance, two British banks that had to be rescued by 'the taxpayer' were found to have acted recklessly. Their managers went on blithely paying themselves huge amounts. At the end of 2012, after Barclays had just been caught rigging interest rates, inducing the resignation of its chief executive, it reported that 600 of its UK staff had earned over £1 million that year. In 2011, Barclays had 238 staff paid on average £1.2 million, while the Royal Bank of Scotland, the other offender, had 386 staff earning on average £820,000.

In sum, the plutocracy and elite were allowed to operate under different rules from everybody else. They have been fed by politicians eager to receive some of their largesse and influence. It is a corrupt system. One event captured its venality. In August 2013, Carl Icahn, a plutocrat, tweeted that he held a lot of shares in Apple and believed the company was undervalued. Within hours, he had made $50 million. Not bad for 20 seconds of tweeting. Why should the precariat respect such a system?

Debt and the precariat

Austerity has exacerbated personal debt built up in the Faustian bargain era, threatening the precariat with permanent insecurity. While governments' debt reduction strategy focused on helping banks and corporations, personal debt rose, against a background of falling wages and falling taxes on the rich and capital.

In the UK, household debt rose from 57 per cent of GDP in 1987 to 109 per cent at the start of the recession in 2008, and was still close to 100 per cent in 2012. Bank of England figures published in December 2012 showed that 3.6 million households – 14 per cent of the total – were spending more than a quarter of their income on debt repayment, including mortgages. Some 1.4 million households were in special measures with their banks. The poorest 10 per cent on average spent 47 per cent of their income on debt repayments. And this was at a time when interest rates were close to zero.

The state is creating a begging society by shrinking social provision and leaving charities to fill the gap. The number of people in the UK forced to rely on charitable food banks rose from 41,000 in 2010 to over half a million in 2013. Even that was a tiny proportion of those in need; there were 13 million people living below 'the breadline' at the time.

One outcome is the flourishing 'payday loan' industry. Payday loans are a way by which the precariat is pushed into deeper insecurity. Wonga, the UK's biggest payday loan company, claims on its website to be 'very, very selective' and to lend only to good-risk clients. Yet in 2011, it wrote off £76.8 million because numerous loans proved 'uncollectable', equivalent to 41 per cent of Wonga's annual revenue. In that year, it provided 2.46 million short-term loans, at a 'representative' annual interest rate of 4,214 per cent. In 2013, Wonga took over as shirt sponsors of Newcastle United Football Club.

In the USA, the payday loan industry is also booming. Online companies operate even in states where payday loans are banned. Banks have allowed loan companies to take money from clients' accounts without their approval or even knowledge. Bank chiefs expressed horror when this was exposed. They must have been asleep.

Low-income earners induced to overspend in the Faustian bargain era were punished by dispossession and the prospect of interminable debt. Those who had acted prudently and saved were hit too, by low interest rates. Trying to boost growth, the US Federal Reserve cut interest rates to near zero in 2008, promising to keep them there while unemployment remained high. Interest income for small US savers plunged 30 per cent between 2008 and 2012. Those saving for future security reacted by reducing their propensity to spend. Raghuram Rajan, the former IMF chief economist, said this amounted to 'expropriating responsible savers in favour of irresponsible banks' (Economist 2012e). Far from boosting growth, businesses were reluctant to borrow, while households cut spending.

In the UK, lower rates redistributed income from pensioners – who had paid off mortgages but received less on their savings – to the salariat who benefited from low interest rates on their mortgages. Lower interest rates also boosted equities, held mainly by the wealthy. Monetary policy was regressive.

The debt that has become a structural feature of market economies is linked to their growing rentier character. They have been turned into 'plutonomies', a merger of 'plutocracy' and 'economy', which is not a name devised by some radical, but by strategists at Citigroup, a finance multinational. Once an economic system is dominated by a plutocracy and elite, rental income from the precariat's indebtedness adds to their wealth. Citigroup did not put it in those terms. But the economic interests of the salariat and elite are enhanced by that debt. Income from interest on payday loans and student debt goes into financial institutions whose profits yield share income, bonuses and dividends. The income does not come from labour or investment. It is a rent.

One might say lenders provide a service. But they gain from debt generated by structural changes and a meaner welfare system. When a government cuts benefits, it increases inequality directly and indirectly by pushing more of the precariat into debt, lowering their social income. In sum, the rentier economy is parasitic.

The accelerated commodification of education

The austerity era saw an acceleration of what had been happening to education for many years. Education ceased to be a right; it became an entitlement, which can be bought and sold. The Chicago school's concept of 'human capital' crystallized in the 1970s. But as education was converted into a global industry, the loss of a right to education became clearer.

Education has always had a dialectic character, with schooling implying disciplining and preparing people for roles, and education implying liberation of the mind. In the neo-liberal model, the functionalist agenda for the masses triumphed.

Every aspect of education has been commodified, made subject to market forces, driven by profit making. Cuts to public education in the austerity era accentuated the trend. The long-term developments are clear. Even in emerging market economies, commercial schooling has been gaining, alongside private tuition. In India, over a quarter of pupils now attend private schools, and in cities the proportion is much higher. Private schooling is spreading in China as well, aided in part by its migration policy that has created a huge precariat consisting of millions of workers without the *hukou*, the residence permit required for their children to attend state schools.

Cramming has become big business, sold as giving children a competitive advantage for the best schools, universities and jobs. In Japan, a rising proportion of children, including pre-schoolers, attend cramming schools, known as *juku*. Nearly two-thirds of middle-school students attend them, at a cost to their parents of thousands of dollars a year. Cramming is also widespread in South Korea, where education accounts for nearly 12 per cent of all consumer spending.

In addition, there is ideological detachment from public schooling by upper-income groups, aided by state subsidies. In the USA, fewer than 15,000 children were taught at home in 1975, but by 2012 there were about 2 million, the same number as attending charter schools. A majority were from Christian families; the main motivation was religious, followed by dislike of the school environment. But whatever the reason for withdrawing children from public schools, the public ethos of education is jeopardized.

Above all, the commercialization of schooling is manifested in the growth of multinationals selling schooling services, while aggressively lobbying for state subsidies and opportunities to displace a shrinking public provision. The neo-liberal state has been only too willing to comply. New Labour led the way in the UK, setting up so-called academy schools, welcoming Swedish commercial firms and encouraging state schools to form alliances with private companies.

The education industry is being driven by a growing number of students. Global student numbers rose from 50 million in 1980 to 170 million in 2009. Emerging market economies are multiplying their educated at a rate that will soon dwarf numbers in the rich countries and are sending huge numbers into the international education market. The growth of highly educated Chinese is remarkable. In 2002, 1.5 million graduated; in 2012, 7 million did.

In the battle to turn these numbers into profit, the education industry has become an aggressive zone of competition that has diverted resources from education to branding, selling, campaigning and lobbying. Public universities are following suit. 'Credentialism' holds sway as more and more qualifications are demanded to obtain a job. Schooling for jobs is more blatantly an investment in human capital. The multiplication of testing and grading, and the stress induced in both teachers and students, contributes to the precariatized mind (Standing 2011). Students soon work out that they are being dumbed down and required to learn by rote to game a system designed to process them. And when the schooling is over, it beckons them back to redress the disadvantages.

The austerity era has strengthened other dangerous trends as well. The education industry has fuelled the rentier economy. While secondary and even primary schooling have increased the indebtedness of many families, tertiary schooling has almost guaranteed it for a majority. More people are emerging from school, college and university with huge debt burdens. Student debt has exploded almost everywhere.

In the 15 years to 2012, student debt in the USA nearly tripled to $1 trillion, according to the Consumer Financial Protection Bureau (CFPB). Between 1980 and 2012, the inflation-adjusted cost of a four-year college education (including fees, room and board) increased by over 130 per cent for both public and private colleges, while median family income increased by just 11 per cent. One in ten households with student debt owed more than $62,000 in 2010, while the CFPB estimated that 10 per cent of recent graduates of four-year degree courses faced monthly repayments for all education loans amounting to more than a quarter of their income. Not surprisingly, default rates have soared since the crash. Many have left college laden with debt only to find themselves in precarious low-paid jobs, facing payment defaults and ruined credit ratings. Precarity breeds precarity.

In Italy, in 2012 only 60 per cent of teenagers with high school diplomas enrolled in an Italian university, the lowest rate for 30 years. Many youths thought it better to take a job without doing a degree, given the cost and prospective debt. Universities were also losing more students. Italy has a dropout rate of 45 per cent. In France, it is 48 per cent in the first year alone and just 38 per cent finish their degree.

Since the crash of 2007–8, students have faced a cruel dilemma. The probability of acquiring a job with career prospects for any level of schooling has declined. This leads some to embark on yet more education or training, and yet more debt, to try to make themselves more 'competitive' (McGettigan 2013). It leads others to abandon education altogether as the threshold for probable success recedes. Which course is taken depends not simply (or at all) on capability but on such factors as appetite for risk, ability to sustain debt and access to alternative opportunities. Having a salariat family background is almost vital.

There are commercial interests waiting to take advantage of either choice. For the first, high-interest lenders are waiting. For the second, there is already an industry preaching a modern philistinism – that life is about making money, for which extra schooling is not needed. In the USA, 'millennials' are being encouraged to see themselves as entrepreneurial and pragmatic, with books such as Michael Ellsberg's *The Education of Millionaires: Everything You Won't Learn in College about How to be Successful* (2012). There are also the 'anti-school' activities of Peter Thiel, billionaire co-founder of PayPal, who in 2010 set up the Thiel Fellowship programme that pays $100,000 to students under age 20 to drop out of college and set up commercial ventures. The anti-schooling movement also includes 'hackademic camps' – lower-cost informal activities supposedly preparing people for technology jobs. These surely reflect a system under strain.

Meanwhile, teachers are being pushed into the precariat in droves. More are engaged without secure contracts, deprived of autonomy in what they can teach, without mobility channels, feeling their fellow teachers are not in control of the curricula or educational practices, and feeling that they do not belong to a community of solidarity and empathy. They epitomize supplicants. Governments rush to grade them, set league tables, and devise targets, sanctions and other infantilizing procedures. Stressed and disillusioned, labouring in acute uncertainty and insecurity, teachers are unable to fulfil their great roles of imparting values and individuality. It is de-professionalization.

That is made easier by the growing state control of education itself. Critical, non-conformist and innovative education is under threat. Many governments, as in the UK, are tightening control over curricula to incorporate commodified values, to the extent of telling schools what they must and must not teach. They are also tightening control over the content of university research and the orientation of research, notably by constructing and legitimizing grading of institutions, by directing money to where they claim there is 'value for money' and by evaluating institutions by how much commercial money they attract.

Status frustration is becoming a pandemic. Many emerging from education cannot practise what they are qualified to do. By 2012 nearly half of employed US college graduates were in jobs that did not require a degree. In Europe, the situation is similar. Only 77 per cent of Italian university graduates find any job within a year, below the EU average of 82 per cent; many of those jobs are below what they are educated to do. Educated Poles accept underpaid, unstable jobs just to obtain another line on their CV (Kozek 2012). In the UK, more than a third of employed new graduates in 2012 were in 'non-professional' jobs for which a degree was unnecessary, while 6 per cent, nearly twice as many as in 2007, were in 'elementary occupations', such as cleaning, road sweeping, labouring, schools meals services and hospital portering. Status frustration is global. In South Korea in 2012, the Samsung Economic Research Institute estimated that 42 per cent of the 500,000 college graduates were jobless or overqualified for their jobs. With a college diploma seen as a ticket to social mobility, the share of high-school graduates entering university rose to 84 per cent in 2008, the highest in the world, though it has since declined somewhat. This compared with 36 per cent in Germany, 48 per cent in Japan, and 64 per cent in the USA. Moreover, many Korean parents finance their children's education by going deep into debt. This represents a large chunk of household debt, which averaged 164 per cent of disposable income in 2011, more than the 138 per cent US average before the crash. And the graduate wage premium in Korea has fallen, to the extent that the McKinsey Global Institute calculates that lifetime earnings no longer justify the costs of a university degree.

In sum, the combination of educational commodification and the post–2008 crisis has created a dysfunctional system, with a growing educational precariat wondering about their role, more families sucked into long-term debt, more ex-students looking at a lifetime of debt, more without hope of an occupation or proper career. It is a situation demanding radical change.

Labour market outcomes

France has an unemployment problem; the solution is greater growth, and the solution to greater growth is competitiveness.

Pascal Lamy, Director General of the World Trade Organization,
March 2013

This simplistic statement from a social democrat is a typical response to the labour market chaos in the austerity era. The result has been accelerated growth of the precariat, as governments rushed to erode remaining labour protections, cut unemployment benefits, increase means-testing, tighten conditionality for benefits and liberalize more occupations.

Casual or temporary jobs have become the norm for new jobs throughout the OECD countries. Dead-end jobs have proliferated, giving their temporary occupants little reason to want to stay in them. While the true size of the precariat remains a guess, in many countries the number in contingent or insecure labour statuses can be estimated. In Poland, to take just one example, 27 per cent of all adult workers – and 65 per cent of those under 30 – were in the 'junk jobs sector' in 2011 (Kozek 2012). A growing part of the precariat consists of the so-called self-employed. In Australia, 'independent contractors' made up 10 per cent of the labour force in 2012, when the number in non-permanent jobs was about 40 per cent. A report on insecure work in New Zealand estimated that at least 30 per cent of the workforce was affected (New Zealand Council of Trade Unions 2013).

According to the US Government Accountability Office (GAO), 42.6 million contingent workers – contract workers, temporary workers, self-employed contractors and part-time employees – made up more than 30 per cent of the total labour force in 2005, and the proportion has risen since the crash. The US Department of Labor suggests that as many as one-third of firms routinely misclassify regular employees as independent contractors in order to avoid paying them benefits.

Labour flexibilization has generated strange phenomena. They include unpaid interns labouring for free, employees on zero-hours contracts who have no labour and no income, permanent temporaries who stay in the same job for years, independent contractors who are dependent on a single employer, dependent contractors who are wage workers in disguise, crowd-work done online by huge numbers of isolated individuals, and so on.

Many of these contracts are simply devices to lower wages, avoid benefits or bypass regulations. Much of the growing part-time employment is part-time pay for longer-than-part-time labour, without commensurate benefits or employment security. In many countries, temporary contracts are rolled over into further temporary contracts, while many who are really employees are disguised as 'independent contractors'. In 2012, according to CGIL (*Confederazione Generale Italiana del Lavoro*), the largest Italian trade union federation, there were 46 types of labour contract in Italy, which it proposed reducing to five; only 18 per cent of new jobs offered permanent contracts. In 2010, 40 per cent of the employed aged under 45 had non-permanent job contracts and a shrinking proportion was moving on to permanent contracts. In Poland and Spain one in four of all employees are on temporary contracts, and in Portugal the figure is more than one in five. In Japan, once the home of 'salaryman', 38 per cent of all workers were classified by official statistics as flexible or non-regular workers in 2012.

The internship craze

In a twinkle, internships have become a global phenomenon. Ross Perlin (2011) estimated there were 1–2 million interns in the USA. In

Europe there may be substantially more, with some 600,000 intern-ships undertaken every year in Germany alone, according to the Institute for Employment Research. However, contrary to popular imagery, China is the leading exponent. Pun and Chan (2013) estimate that China has anything from 7 million to over 10 million student interns. Although regulated by a 2007 law that requires employers to pay them, the minimum wage does not apply. They are blocked from insurance benefits and union membership, must work long days for 6–7 days a week and cannot have a pay rise while on internship contracts.

The Chinese government fosters internships. For instance, the Education Department cooperates with Foxconn to ensure its 'student labour quota' is met. Schoolteachers are dispatched to co-supervise interning students, and receive two paychecks, one for their day job, one for their supervisory role in the factory. Foxconn operates the world's largest intern programme – accounting for 15 per cent of its labour force, roughly 150,000 workers, during peak production in 2010. Its production system allows quick shifts of production between factories, making interns a flexible labour pool.

Internships are an exploited form of flexible easily disposable labour, used to displace others doing similar labour. A Precariat Charter must address them.

Zero-hours contracts

In *The Precariat*, zero-hours ('standby' or 'on-call') contracts were called 'a wheeze'. In the austerity era, they have become pervasive, and more widely recognized. According to the trade union UNISON, the number of such contracts, which oblige firms to pay wages only for hours employees are asked to do, usually at short notice, quadrupled in the UK between 2005 and 2012. By 2013, more than a quarter of UK companies were reported to be using them for at least some of their employees, while another survey suggested that they were even more widespread in the voluntary and public sectors than in the private sector. In 2013 they were used by more than half of all UK universities; National Health Service (NHS) hospitals employed over 100,000 workers on zero-hours contracts, a jump of a quarter in two years; and a majority of care workers – over 300,000 on official figures – were on such contracts.

Almost certainly, the numbers and growth have been under-estimated (Pennycook, Cory and Alakeson 2013). The Office of National Statistics revised up its estimate of the number of people on zero-hours contracts to a quarter of a million, but admitted this understated the position, because many workers were unaware they were on such contracts. The Chartered Institute of Personnel and Development put the number involved at about 1 million or 3–4 per cent of all employees. The trade union Unite said the figure could be as high as 5.5 million. UK employers using zero-hours contracts in 2013 included McDonald's (nine in ten McDonald's employees were on them), retailer Sports Direct, Amazon, pub chain JD Wetherspoon, cinema chain Cineworld and Buckingham Palace.

Although most of those on zero-hours contracts are workers who receive low earnings at the best of times, the trend has spread up the professional – or profician – scale. The chief executive of Adecco, the biggest recruitment firm in the UK, said that professional and financial services were using zero-hours contracts to be more 'agile and competitive' (Kuchler 2013).

Zero-hours contracts have been particularly invidious for paid domiciliary care providers, a vulnerable part of the precariat. In the UK, many receive less than the minimum wage for the hours they put in because they are paid only for actual 'care minutes' with a client and not for their time in travel to and from those requiring care – work-for-labour. Nearly three-quarters of all paid care workers now face this situation, up from one-third in 2008.

Zero-hours contracts are a way of disguising unemployment. Thus there should not have been much surprise that, in the wake of uproar over public revelations of the extent of them in the UK, the government merely launched a leisurely low-level enquiry.

Agency labour and brokers

This leads to what is probably the major long-term trend, the shift to agency labour, by which corporations and government agencies are contracting out their employment function. Many of those engaged by employment agencies are in effect on zero-hours contracts. As many agencies blur into old-fashioned labour brokers or labour-only sub-contractors run as work gangs, the 'modern' part of the industry is an underestimate of its size or growth. Nevertheless, the International Confederation of Private Employment Agencies (CIETT) estimated that the industry's global sales revenue increased from €83 billion in 1996 to €259 billion in 2011, while the number of agency workers more than doubled to 46 million.

Employment agencies will continue to expand. The biggest are major global players, with Adecco, Manpower, Randstad and a few others sending out hundreds of thousands of temporaries every day all over the world. One result is that many workers are never sure who is employing them. The agencies are setting up training and qualification schemes, and boast that they are giving people security and careers. But this is unlikely to benefit the majority. The growth of employment agencies is also one more reason for scepticism about conventional labour statistics.

Crowd-labour

Many millions of people around the world are now doing 'crowd-work', a form of labour without parallels in labour history. Crowd-work is transforming and globalizing the labour market in unprecedented ways. The crowd-sourcing industry estimated that over 6 million people were doing crowd-work in 2011, compared with 1.3 million in 2009, and the number was set to double in 2012. According to crowdsourcing.org, nearly half these workers had a college degree and nearly a quarter had a master's degree, with about 40 per cent based in North America and another 35 per cent in the Asia-Pacific region, notably in India and the Philippines.

Crowd-work is online labour in which designated 'requesters' post jobs available for what amounts to a global, on-demand, 24/7 labour force. Requesters, who are not employers but modern labour brokers, are appointed by firms that coordinate crowd-work on online piecework platforms. Armed with a computer or smartphone, people can bid online for tasks advertised by requesters, who name the tasks, the maximum price and the deadline for completion. Successful bidders commit to what is called a 'hit' (human intelligence task). It is piecework, in a form that is conducive to extreme 'sweating'. It is the ultimate zone of the precariat, in which workers are supplicants, without rights or security.

Although there are exceptions, the labour is usually split into tiny, narrowly defined tasks, giving modern meaning to Adam Smith's division of labour in pin making. Remuneration is very low, taking advantage of the extreme flexibility of home-based workers. One researcher has described it as 'a system that doesn't talk back' (Hodson 2013). Requesters can decide on whom to give contracts and can then decide whether to accept or reject tasks done. Rejected tasks are not paid. It is a phenomenon that will transform labour regulations and influence social protection reform in profound ways.

Crowd-work has produced big profits for online piecework platforms such as Amazon's Mechanical Turk, CrowdFlower, CloudCrowd, oDesk and eLance. A growing number of companies are outsourcing tasks in this way. IBM has announced it is cutting its regular payroll by a third and outsourcing to a 'liquid community'. One industry insider guesstimated that by 2020 one-third of the global workforce could be hired online (Vanham 2012).

Mechanical Turk engaged over half a million crowd-workers in 2012, about 70 per cent of them women, in more than 100 countries, although half were in the USA and 40 per cent in India. The apparent market leader, oDesk, estimated that by 2012 it had contracted 18 million hours in the Philippines, nearly 14 million in India, and millions more in the USA, Bangladesh and elsewhere. Half a million Filipinos were registered on its freelance website, more than were employed in the country's growing business process outsourcing industry, which crowd-labour is bypassing. Overall, oDesk had 2.4 million registered freelancers and over 480,000 client companies;

eLance claimed to have clients in 180 countries and registered freelancers in 155 of them, with 226,000 in India alone.

Governments in emerging market economies have been promoting crowd labour. Bangladesh, for example, has provided subsidies, and has declared online earnings to be tax-free. Although the growth is global, Europe has lagged behind the curve perhaps because the payments have been extremely low. But the austerity era will no doubt change that.

Flexible careers

Another aspect of the precariat is loss of career paths. It goes high up the scale. A poll conducted by Berlin's Trendence Institute in 2013 found that among business graduates, hardly the least employable, most expressed worries about having a career – 92 per cent in Greece, 89 per cent in Spain, 88 per cent in Italy, 66 per cent in the UK, 54 per cent in France and 42 per cent in Germany.

One factor has been offshoring, since middle ranks of professions are mainly being transferred. The number of occupations that are offshorable or tradable has been multiplying, accentuating occupational uncertainty and creating disruptions to career opportunities and social mobility. Examples include high-paying tasks in accountancy, financial analysis and computer programming. This is tending to fragment professions, generating an elite and salariat in rich countries alongside a precariat dealing with 'customers', while middle ranks are exported.

Offshoring has been facilitated by occupational re-regulation that removed guild control of mobility channels, the essence of occupational liberalization. Alan Blinder made a distinction between personal and impersonal services, claiming that only the latter were offshorable (Economist 2011). *The Economist* gave examples: 'A contract lawyer or radiologist is vulnerable to offshoring; a divorce lawyer or family doctor isn't.' But the latter are just as subject to task standardization. There is no limit to offshoring or fragmentation.

Interim managers

In the heyday of industrial capitalism, the manager was the power in the corporation. In the emerging shareholder model, where financial capital dominates, managers themselves are exposed to flexibility and insecurity. The average time an executive holds a position has dropped considerably. And a body of interim managers has grown, consisting of people, often former members of the salariat, who hire themselves out for short periods to companies or government departments to do a particular managerial job and then move on.

That interim managers exist at all is testimony to the change in global capitalism. Mainstream economics literature regarded managers as pivotal figures in national capitalism in the twentieth century. Now management functions are being outsourced and subject to division of labour, such that it is scarcely an exaggeration to say that the class structure is reproduced inside management, with an elite, proficians, a salariat and a precariat. An elite is paid large sums for each day's work and has more jobs than it can handle; middle-ranking proficians do well enough but have irregular jobs; and those verging on the precariat, with short-term jobs, are struggling to stay in business.

The trend contains multiple dangers. Those brought in to restructure companies are typically paid for a job, which they may be expected to complete in three or six months. They do not have to bear the personal consequences, either inside the firm or in the wider community. As such, they can be pitiless, neatly captured by the film *Up in the Air* starring George Clooney. Interim managers are under pressure to be ruthless, typically being called into a firm to make unpopular changes and sack many who have been loyal staff.

Unemployment and underemployment

In 2013, there were over 26 million recorded unemployed in the European Union, including nearly 6 million youths, one in four of all those under 25. The numbers around the world were many times that, though labour statisticians should admit we do not know how many. In Europe and elsewhere, a large proportion had exhausted unemployment benefits or had never gained them. Long called a social right, unemployment benefits have been denied to most of the unemployed.

Five years after the start of the Great Recession in the USA, the unemployment rate was still over 7 per cent, a record worse than in all recessions since the Great Depression. The youth (under age 25) unemployment rate was 16 per cent. According to one study (Shierholz, Sabadish and Finio 2013), high-school graduates under age 25 had an unemployment rate of 30 per cent and an underemployment rate – including those discouraged from jobseeking and those employed for fewer hours than they wanted – of 51 per cent.

The corresponding rates for young college graduates were 9 per cent and 18 per cent. The number of 'disconnected' or NEETs (not in education, employment or training) had also grown sharply.

By 2013, the youth unemployment rate was over 50 per cent in Spain and Greece and more than 40 per cent in Italy. In the UK, Italy, Norway and New Zealand the rate was three times the rate for prime-age adults; in Sweden it was over four times. And in many countries, unemployment has hit highly educated youths almost as hard as others, giving a lie to old claims that 'education' is the way to avoid unemployment. Youth unemployment also has 'scarring' effects, raising the probability of later unemployment and lowering lifetime earnings by as much as 20 per cent compared with peers who find jobs quickly (Morsy 2012). This is a precarity trap, a cycle of unemployment and short-term jobs.

Nevertheless, a feature of the post–2008 labour market is that much of the slack shows up in underemployment rather than unemployment. This is mainly due to flexible labour relations that enable employers to bump full-time employees down into part-time work, put more on zero-hours contracts or furloughs, and hire workers disguised as apprentices or interns. The term underemployment was long used in developing countries where unemployment is an unreliable measure of labour underutilization. Now, because services account for most jobs and because of flexible labour relations, more workers in industrialized countries are recorded as employed rather than unemployed, even when they are doing (and earning) little or nothing in their jobs.

Some years ago, this author devised a measure for labour slack that combined several measures of underemployment: part-time working, whether voluntary or involuntary; short-time working and lay-offs; those employed but without doing any hours of labour (e.g. on zero-hours contracts); discouraged unemployed who are available for labour but are not actively seeking it; and the recorded unemployed (Standing 1999, 2002). The measure was applied to as many EU countries as had suitable data in Eurostat's Labour Force Survey. The results show that labour slack is much higher than the unemployment rate and that the divergence has generally widened – see Figure 2 for the UK.

Blanchflower and Bell (2013) took another approach for the UK, by adding to the unemployed those working fewer hours than they wanted. This too showed underemployment growing relative to unemployment. Another UK indicator was the number in jobs dependent on tax credits, which rose by more than half between

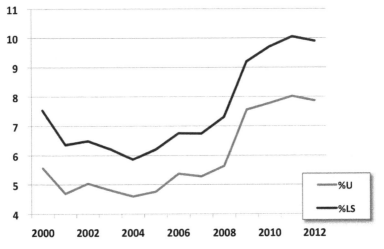

FIGURE 2: *Unemployment and labour slack, all adults, United Kingdom, 2000–12*

Source: Eurostat Labour Force Survey data. Methodology available at http://www.guystanding.com/files/documents/Labour_Slack_Estimates.pdf

2003 and 2012, to 3.3 million, according to the Joseph Rowntree Foundation. By 2012 61 per cent of children in low-income households had at least one parent in a job, the highest proportion recorded. Much the same was happening across Europe. In Italy in 2011, the CGIL estimated that 8 million people were unemployed, working part-time involuntarily or temporarily laid off under the *cassa integrazione* scheme, living on an average of €600–700 a month.

Visible underemployment is accompanied by invisible underemployment – people doing labour beneath their qualifications or skills, a feature of the precariat. In Italy, the biggest job losses after 2008 were in technical, scientific and specialized occupations. Many have been bumped into low-level jobs. In the USA, by 2013 a uniquely high proportion of young graduates were in jobs not requiring degrees. Even in 2000, when the labour market was tight by American standards, with an unemployment rate of 4 per cent, 40 per cent of employed college graduates aged under 25 were in jobs not requiring a degree. By 2007, that was 47 per cent; by 2012, 52 per cent. In 2013, according to another survey, 41 per cent of Americans who had graduated from college in the previous two years were in jobs that did not require a degree.

As low-level jobs are increasingly taken by those with high-level qualifications, people with less education are being doubly squeezed. In the 1960s and 1970s, high-school dropouts could obtain a factory job and expect some upward mobility. Those jobs have largely disappeared, and for low-skill jobs in services this group is now competing with high-school and even university graduates.

Morbid symptoms have sprouted everywhere. In 2012, the labour market chaos took on tragicomic dimensions in Alameda, Spain, where a lottery for menial public service jobs was instituted. The unemployed signed up for jobs as cleaners and every month eight were selected randomly to take public service jobs. In addition, four men were selected for construction jobs, while 200 men and women competed for three road sweeping posts. These 15 survived on about €650 a month, but the other 5,000 unemployed had to sit it out with nothing.

The wage plunge

During the Faustian bargain era, a rising share of the employed in industrialized countries earned wages that kept them in poverty or would have done without a state top-up, mainly in the form of tax credits and targeted benefits, such as SNAP (Supplemental Nutrition Assistance Program) food stamps and housing vouchers in the USA (Ehrenreich 2001). After the crash, this came much more into the open. 'Jobs' were not the route out of poverty for a large and growing proportion of the population in OECD countries.

In 2011, 10.4 million Americans were recorded as working poor, defined as spending at least 27 weeks a year in the labour force but still having an income below the poverty line. This largely reflected a decline in hourly wages. After stagnating for two decades, average hourly wages fell between 2007 and 2011 for the bottom 70 per cent of American workers, with the steepest drop for the lowest quintile. As the *State of Working America 2012* (Mishel et al. 2012) showed, the first decade of this century saw no growth in income, wealth or wages for most Americans.

Schooling was no protection. Between 2000 and 2012, real wages fell by 12.7 per cent for US high-school graduates and by 8.5 per cent for college graduates, accentuating the long-term decline. They also lost enterprise benefits. The proportion of high-school graduates with health care insurance fell from 23.5 per cent to 7.1 per cent; for college graduates it fell from 60.1 per cent to 31.1 per cent. Pension coverage dropped from 9.7 per cent to 5.9 per cent and from 41.5 per cent to 27.2 per cent respectively (Shierholz et al. 2013).

Wage stagnation occurred in almost all industrialized countries. Real wages fell in the UK by more in the five years following the shock than at any time in recorded history, more than in the Great Depression. There is little prospect of much revival. The Resolution Foundation in 2012 forecast that real wages would not return to their 2000 level until at least 2017. The average worker was £4,000 worse off in real terms in 2012 than in 2009. And because of flexible labour markets, the brunt of income insecurity has been borne by those in low-paying jobs or flitting in and out of such jobs. Of the 11 million in poverty in the UK, more than half were in jobs. This has enormous implications for a progressive counter-strategy.

The secular decline in wages in OECD countries has coincided with a decline in their share of national income. UNCTAD (2012) estimated that the wage share globally in 2012 was at its lowest since the Second World War, while unemployment was at its highest. The trouble is compounded because erosion of wages dampens aggregate demand for goods and services, pushing up unemployment and thus putting more downward pressure on wages.

As wages are more flexible, they fall in recessions by more than they used to do. That does little to raise labour demand, since workers with declining or more insecure incomes spend less, leading firms to shift their locus of activities to where demand is rising. UNCTAD recognized the dilemma. But there is a problem with its prognosis – that governments should resist the mantra of 'flexible labour markets' and that nominal wages should rise at the same rate as average productivity. In an open economic system, that would require internationally coordinated policies unimaginable in a system based on pursuit of national competitiveness.

There is no reason to believe the parallel relationship between wages and productivity will return. According to the *State of Working America 2012* (Mishel et al. 2012), productivity grew by more than 80 per cent from 1973 to 2011, but median wages grew by less than 11 per cent. In Germany, productivity rose by a quarter in the two decades after 1991 while real wages stagnated. In Japan, much the same happened. Even in fast-growing Poland, wages stagnated while productivity rose. The ILO reported in 2012 that labour productivity in developed countries increased twice as fast as wages between 1999 and 2011. This is a global trend, and there is no reason to think it will be reversed. It stems from workers' weakened bargaining position.

Another trend is the growth of wage and salary differentials. There are competing explanations (trade, technology, bargaining, flexibility, etc.), but the fact is that differentials have soared. In the past three decades, US CEO pay rose by 725 per cent compared with 6 per cent for the average employee, with CEOs paid 210 times more than the average wage in 2011 compared with 26.5 times in 1978 (Mishel and Sabadish 2012). It was a similar, if less extreme, story in almost every country in the industrialized world, including the UK, Canada, Australia and Germany.

In sum, wages at the lower end of labour markets have dropped considerably, and differentials have grown. In that context, it was bizarre that the European Commission joined a chorus demanding that, in the interest of international competitiveness, French wage cuts negotiated in early 2013 should be matched in Spain, where it said nominal wages should be cut by a further 10 per cent. Beggar-my-neighbour wage cuts are surely the wrong answer to the wrong question.

Stratification of non-wage benefits

A key to understanding the restructuring of social income is the erosion of non-wage forms of remuneration, which had provided some labour security and helped in the decommodification of labour. While the salariat has continued to gain non-wage benefits, those further down the income spectrum have been losing them, a trend that has helped define the precariat.

Nowhere captures what has happened more starkly than Detroit, epitome of the American dream, heartland of its industrial prowess, Henry Ford and industrial citizenship. When globalization deindustrialized places like Detroit, job losses meant a rising share of labour costs went on 'legacy costs', benefits for ex-employees. In its heyday, the city grew in the car industry's shadow, building up a public sector with pensions and medical entitlements to match the industry. But city revenue fell as manufacturing declined, as property values flattened and as better-off residents fled to the suburbs.

When the crisis hit, the Obama administration rescued the car industry with $80 billion in subsidies. That did not stop what was happening to workers' social income. A restructuring of the remuneration and contract system of car-industry employees, with two-tier wages and loss of benefits, was accompanied by swingeing cuts in public services. When the city eventually filed for bankruptcy in July 2013, its emergency manager said he would aim to cut health care and unfunded retirement benefits for city workers, accounting for half Detroit's $18 billion long-term debt, while already poor public services will be reduced further. Both industrial and public service workers lost most of their non-wage benefits; declining wages were only part of a collapse in social income.

What happened in Detroit is mirrored in former industrial areas in many countries. By 2011, only a third of the UK's private-sector workers had an employer-sponsored pension scheme. Only 10 per cent of private-sector employees had a defined-benefit (relatively secure) pension scheme, down from 30 per cent in 2001. Under half of all private-sector workers had entitlement to any pension beyond the meagre state pension. Low interest rates also increased the deficits in company pension schemes by lowering bond yields, which accelerated the decline of occupational pensions. By 2012, US defined-benefit pension plans had a deficit of $619 billion, and could meet only 72 per cent of future obligations. The salariat was facing an uncertain future too.

Legislative changes are making it easier for firms to cut benefits. Under the US Affordable Care Act (ACA) of 2010 ('Obamacare'), new employees who average under 30 hours a week do not have automatic entitlement to health care benefits. Walmart, one of America's biggest employers and supporter of the Act, promptly subjected all part-timers hired in the previous year to an 'annual benefits eligibility check', put more people on short hours and hired more part-timers. Non-wage benefits were lost, underemployment jacked up.

Others have followed suit, in both the private and public sectors. Youngstown State University in Virginia limited the hours of non-union part-time employees, including faculty. Department chairs were instructed to cut part-timers to less than 24 hours a week. Showing how civil, social and economic rights were eroded, part-timers had to sign a form acknowledging that the employer had informed them they were not public employees – even though they were working in a public university – and so not eligible to join the Virginia state pension scheme. And whereas many, as academic nomads, had taken multiple teaching assignments, Virginia is now deemed to be the employer at all state university campuses, so that faculty cannot combine jobs on separate campuses if this would break the part-time threshold of 29 hours a week.

The ACA has also encouraged cost shifting onto the precariat. Some firms are allowing workers to work longer than 29 hours a week but only if they pay higher health care premiums or accept co-pay arrangements. Many firms have stopped health care benefits. In 2013, the Congressional Budget Office raised its estimate of those losing employer-provided insurance from 4 million to 7 million. Social income was cut. Taxpayers are also footing more of the bill for health care, amounting to a subsidy to corporations. The ACA expands eligibility for Medicaid to anyone with an income up to a third above the federal poverty level. So a low-wage firm like Walmart can reduce labour costs, while public spending is raised, distorting fiscal policy by increasing pressure to cut other spending in compensation.

While the precariat has lost non-wage benefits, the salariat has gained them, increasing the income and psychological distance between them. In the USA, the salariat has increasingly benefited from equities, which derive from profits, rather than wages or salaries. One-third of American workers derive part of their income from shares. About half the American population has a financial interest in Apple shares, as they have investments in broad index and mutual funds. Between 2005 and 2011 Apple's share price rose nearly tenfold, and in fiscal 2011 the company's employees and directors received stock worth $2 billion and exercised stock options worth $1.4 billion. A related trend is that many firms have converted themselves into worker-owned businesses. About one in ten workers partly owns the firm for which they labour, and the number is rising. To classify these workers as in the proletariat would be misleading, as would calling them 'capitalists'.

Other countries may not be so extreme, but the trend to receiving more from non-wage sources is the same. It applies in Germany, where regular employees have been gaining more from shares than from wages. As this trend becomes more pronounced, the salariat will become more detached from the precariat beneath it.

Fragmentation of state benefits

Labour costs reflect a combination of wages and non-wage payments. To the extent that firms can reduce these costs, they can become more 'competitive' and make higher profits. For workers, income security depends on wages, enterprise benefits and state benefits. These constitute the main components of social income. The precariat has lost in all respects.

China has been reconstructing its workforce's social income. By 2012, 326 million rural residents had been enrolled in a public pension scheme, joining 300 million urban workers. This released enterprises from making pension payments, lowering labour costs at a time of rising wages. Other emerging market economies, such as Indonesia, have also shifted part of the social income onto the government, helping to keep labour costs down.

Meanwhile, in OECD countries, governments have responded to globalization by cutting benefits and making them harder to obtain. This has increased inequality, since the benefits cut most are for low-income groups, and since benefits comprise a higher share of their social income. Famously, in 2011, Newark's mayor set out to live on the weekly SNAP food stamps. He failed. Yet over 47 million Americans, many in jobs, have to rely on them. Meanwhile, millions have lost social rights by being put in flexible labour statuses. Thus, in Japan the big shift of the workforce to temporary status has been associated with a decline in the proportion of the unemployed entitled to unemployment benefits.

Every OECD country is experiencing similar trends. To appreciate the unfolding tragedy, we should recall what the pursuit of flexibility has unleashed. If labour is made more insecure, fewer workers can make regular contributions to social security. Without contributions, they cannot obtain insurance benefits in times of need. Social rights are lost. This is what has happened. In the UK, a committee to review the tax system reported in late 2011 that national insurance had lost its purpose.

In response to the collapse of social insurance, governments in OECD countries have had to raise more of the money needed to pay benefits from taxation. They have also had to use alternatives to contribution records to determine eligibility, which has reinforced the shift to means-testing. When social assistance was a residual form of social protection, means-testing was based on subsistence needs and measures like a percentage of average wages. But as wages declined, and as the precariat's wage income became more volatile and harder to calculate on a longer-term basis, assistance benefits based on subsistence tended to rise as a percentage of earnings. So, in a warped use of words, politicians justified benefit cuts by saying they wished to 'make work pay'. State benefits fell along with wages.

In 2013, justifying cuts to working-age benefits, the UK's Work and Pensions Secretary of State, Iain Duncan Smith, said:

> Working people across the country have been tightening their belts after years of pay restraint while at the same time watching benefits increase. That is not fair. The welfare state under Labour effectively trapped thousands of families into dependency as it made no sense to give up the certainty of a benefit payment in order to go back to work.

But benefits had not risen; real wages had fallen. Profits and salariat income had risen in real terms. There was no belt-tightening there. As for benefits being a 'certainty', a majority of the unemployed were not receiving any unemployment benefits at all.

However, the new cuts in state benefits hit middle-income earners as well as those in and below the precariat. The Children's Society calculated that planned reductions in benefits would cut the incomes of 40,000 soldiers, 300,000 nurses, 150,000 nursery and primary schoolteachers, 510,000 cashiers, 44,000 electricians, and over a million secretaries and administration assistants. While the government claimed to be aiming the cuts at 'scroungers' and 'skivers', they were set to hurt many people labouring hard for low incomes.

Tax credits, a defining feature of the globalization era, have posed a particular problem in the austerity era. Their fiscal cost rises as downward pressure in the labour market intensifies. Much of the welfare system, far from subsidizing 'idleness', has been geared to 'making work pay' in a more direct sense. Over a range of benefits, cutting their cost means reducing the income associated with labour. In the UK, the squeeze on the precariat has been intensified further because the government has pledged to protect state pensions, which account for over half of social spending. A commitment to cut state benefits overall has meant putting more of a squeeze on workers, including cuts in tax credits.

In sum, social income has been restructured, while wages are increasingly insufficient to escape from economic insecurity. For the precariat, income from labour will be inadequate for a dignifying standard of living. Wage income will have to be supplemented by state, private or community benefits. But at present, essential state benefits and community benefits are being taken away. This will not change until the precariat acts to change it.

Concluding reflections

The Faustian bargain postponed the decline in wages and social income that is part of the Great Convergence. The austerity era has accelerated it, through beggar-my-neighbour cuts in wages and benefits coupled with tax cuts and more subsidies for capital. There will be no recovery of living standards and economic security for the precariat until a new progressive strategy is devised to redistribute income and the key assets of modern society.

The second decade of the twenty-first century is the endgame of the neo-liberal experiment. The plutocracy – and the elite feeding off it – is falling into arrogant criminality and political manipulation. The salariat has done well, but many in it find they must put more aside to support adult children and grandchildren. Further down, the precariat is expanding. As it and the underclass grow, so governments will try to control their anomic protests while penalizing them.

Two points are clear. Raising employment does not necessarily lead to less poverty, as even Germany has found, with its rising number of 'working poor' (Seils 2013). And average wages are unlikely to rise in OECD countries, and will not rise for the precariat. Those claiming jobs are the route out of economic insecurity are defying the logic of globalization, or are being naïve or dishonest. Wages for the precariat will continue to fall.

The social situation is increasingly ugly. That should erode any residual confidence that the neo-liberal project can be sustained. Among the warning signs has been a rise in social protests, including riots. Populist politics should give more concern. The atavistic part of the precariat has been drawn into supporting neo-fascist agendas in countries like Greece and Hungary. And the far right has drawn others to the right. It is creating a bitter divisiveness. It is generating more denizens, and demonizing more people: migrants, welfare claimants, the disabled, minorities, youth… the list grows longer. We need a counter-strategy oriented to the needs, aspirations and insecurities of the precariat. What is blocking that from emerging?

4

Confronting the utilitarian consensus

There are two great traditions of thinking about social policy, which may be called utilitarian (or majoritarian) and progressive (or egalitarian). In the globalization era, utilitarianism triumphed; standard-bearers of the progressive tradition mostly deserted to the neo-liberals, leaving a vacuum on 'the left', possibly for the first time in history.

This chapter briefly reflects on the values that have shaped the utilitarian rhetoric and agenda, and compares them with what have guided the progressive tradition through the ages. A polemical approach is chosen to sharpen the debate, recognizing there are shades of grey in the spectrum of opinion. It draws most of its examples from the UK, where the utilitarian agenda has perhaps gone furthest. But the drift is global.

The neo-liberal model that has guided politicians, policymakers and mainstream academics and commentators is simple. It believes in a competitive market economy, regulated to ensure market forces operate, with due rewards for the fittest, the most competitive. It follows that there must be winners and losers. The latter must be convinced that losing is their fault, for not being competitive enough.

The economic model has fostered commodification of politics and a 'thinning' of democracy. Instead of being class-based and value-driven, political parties have become vehicles for competition only loosely related to old traditions. This has fostered a crude utilitarianism – pursuit of the happiness of a majority. And if governments focus on satisfying a majority with benefits, tax cuts and subsidies, a minority will be disadvantaged. Strengthening entitlements of privileged citizens turns others into denizens and pushes more into an insecure precariat. This is roughly what has happened.

The micro-politics of regressive reform

One of the dark arts of politics is to change structures in order to make people think what the politicians want them to think. In the UK, Margaret Thatcher and her advisers did that explicitly in devising the micro-politics of privatization: first, starve public services of funds, making it harder for them to operate; then report on public dissatisfaction; then point out that private services are better; then privatize services to accord with people's 'needs', in the avowed interests of efficiency and delivery.

Governments have refined that technique. The latest variant goes under the disarming name of 'libertarian paternalism', drawing on ideas of Jeremy Bentham, the founding father of utilitarianism in the late eighteenth century. The essence of libertarian paternalism is that people must be steered to 'make the right choice'. This perspective has been influenced by *Nudge*, a book by two Americans, Richard Thaler and Cass Sunstein (2008), which used Benthamite language, without attribution. They also failed to mention Bentham's panopticon, an all-seeing surveillance device initially designed for prisons that aimed to identify for punishment those 'not making the right choice'. Sunstein was later appointed by President Obama as chief regulator, with an office in the White House, while Thaler became an adviser to the newly elected UK Prime Minister David Cameron. Cameron promptly set up a Behavioural Insight Team in Downing Street, soon nicknamed the Nudge Unit.

Techniques of altering opinions and steering behaviour have been strengthened further by the plutocracy's control of mainstream media, enabling them to assert untruths with impunity and reinforce prejudices, using the modern device of opinion polls to show that prejudice plays with 'the public'. It is an era of 'post-truth' media and politics.

Religification of social policy

Since the 1980s, social protection reform in the UK and USA has been driven by religion and finance. In the UK, the figures shaping it have been Tony Blair (a convert to Catholicism), Gordon Brown (a man of Christian convictions), Frank Field (ditto), Iain Duncan Smith (a practising Catholic), and an ex-merchant banker, David Freud, ennobled by New Labour for his services to social policy, who switched to David Cameron when he saw which way the political wind was blowing and became Minister for Welfare Reform. Duncan Smith's special adviser, Philippa Stroud, belongs to an evangelical church that preaches that women are inferior to men.

The religification has been led by Catholicism, drawing on Pope Leo XIII's encyclical, *Rerum Novarum* of 1891, which asserts that the poor have a duty to labour. Tony Blair's favourite theologian, Hans Küng, regarded laziness as a sin. Duncan Smith, the UK Work and Pensions Minister, has said it is a 'sin' not to take up jobs; just after taking office he made the eerie statement, 'Work actually helps free people', reminiscent of words etched in our collective memory emblazoned on a gate to a hell on earth, the entrance to Auschwitz. The allusion was no doubt unintentional. But his remark reflects the naiveté of equating labour with work, and imagining that jobs liberate. He should explain how litter clearing or graffiti cleaning for pitiful wages (the activities he set as mandatory labour) enhances freedom.

Catholics see 'the poor' as 'fallen', to be pulled up by charity and the benevolence of the church and state. The doctrine accords well with a stratified society, with images of 'natural orders'. The moving sentiment of the religious conservative is *pity*. And as David Hume pointed out, pity is akin to contempt. Losers are failures, worthy of help as long as they show gratitude and earnest endeavour. If they do not follow our guidance, they should be persuaded to mend their ways, and failing that should be coerced or penalized. The road from one thought to the next is well trodden.

By contrast, a progressive starts from a sentiment of *compassion*. That could be me over there if I made a couple of bad calls or had an accident. That man or woman should have the same security as anybody else. Only then can they make something of themselves. But I do not know what they want. That should be up to them. I have no right to force them one way or the other. This is where the progressive takes a stand.

Faith-based social policy leads to faith-based assessments. In 2013, Duncan Smith stated his 'belief' that a cap on the amount of benefits any family could receive had led more people to find jobs, despite lack of any supporting evidence.

The moralizing is based on blaming the victims as responsible for their unemployment or poverty. As a general rule, that is untrue. The unemployment rate is determined by economic forces and policies. Governments deliberately run the economy with slack. Neo-liberals argue there is a natural rate of unemployment ground out by institutions and macro-economic policy. If unemployment is pushed below that, through macro-economic policy, inflation will accelerate. So, unemployment must exist, rising in recessions or periods of restructuring. All reputable economists accept a version of this account. And in the austerity era, it was risible to claim unemployment was the fault of the unemployed.

Nevertheless, a judgemental perspective prevails. The poor are not us. They are deserving, undeserving or transgressing, the last being not just undeserving by habit but lawbreakers as well. This is consistent with the Americanization of social policy, where the poor are not seen as our brothers or sisters but as subjects for reform, for treatment, retraining or therapy.

In the UK, both major parties looked to the USA for their welfare policy, and in the Conservative case rushed in two paternalist American advisers within weeks of taking office. One, Lawrence

Mead, an evangelical Christian, has said that Jesus gave no preferential treatment to the poor, has called theologians 'unacknowledged
social legislators' and has written that the unemployed must be
induced to 'blame themselves'. In 2010, he expressed pleasant surprise
at how his advice had been welcomed in Downing Street. The other
was Thaler, who became adviser to the Nudge Unit, the task of which,
according to Deputy Premier Nick Clegg, was to make people make
better decisions. That would make the great liberal, John Stuart Mill,
rage in his grave.

The religious bent and the paternalists have made social policy
moralistic, directing people to behave in ways deemed by the policymakers as best for themselves and for society. But if you are told what
to do, you cannot be moral. This classic liberal principle was nicely
captured by the philosopher T. H. Green in 1879 (1986):

> The real function of government being to maintain conditions of
> life in which morality shall be possible, and morality consisting
> in the disinterested performance of self-imposed duties, 'paternal
> government' does its best to make it impossible by narrowing the
> room for the self-imposition of duties and for the play of disinter-
> ested motives.

Besides religion, social policy has been dictated by utilitarianism,
in which the pursuit of the majority's happiness allows a different
attitude to the 'persistently misguided' minority. Another who
influenced Labour's social policy was Richard Layard, also ennobled
for his endeavours, an avowed admirer of Bentham. Layard helped
shape Labour's various New Deals, and became its 'happiness and
therapy czar', inducing the government to coerce youths into jobs

and provide cognitive behavioural therapy for the unemployed. The New Labour government also introduced snooping on the homes of benefit claimants, dressed up as a device to 'help' the unemployed.

Dividing society into 'Them' and 'Us'

Growth of more flexible labour relations went with abandonment of models of social solidarity built up in the twentieth century. Deconstruction of the welfare state was part of the strategy, as not corresponding to the open flexible labour process being constructed.

Although varying from country to country, the welfare state consisted of a mix of universal or citizenship-based social rights, a contributory social or national insurance system, and means-tested social assistance for those on the edge of society. It drew on principles of solidarity. While sexist and labourist (linking entitlements to the performance of labour), it provided a framework for limiting inequalities and for legitimizing reciprocities, on top of a floor of basic rights. But from the 1980s onwards, this framework was dismantled by both neo-liberal and social democratic governments. In shifting to means-testing, they abandoned the solidaristic basis of social protection. Respect for universalism – rights for all – was tossed aside. Values of compassion, empathy and reciprocity were replaced by pity, contempt and individualism.

This shift was at the heart of Margaret Thatcher's infamous war cry that there was 'no such thing as society'. It also influenced New Labour's Third Way, with its simplistically appealing view that there are 'no rights without obligations', and Conservative Prime Minister

David Cameron's insistence that nobody has a right to receive 'something for nothing'. Of course, this ignores the fact that wealth inheritors receive a lot of something for nothing.

The twentieth-century progressive agenda had been to extend universal rights, as our due as human beings, not the result of privilege, contributions or prior obligations. But the routes chosen by social democrats ultimately ran into contradictions; they linked entitlements to old notions of the working class and ignored the rising precariat.

Social policy became dominated by 'targeting' on 'the poor', an amorphous category that assumed the character of a sub-species. The argument that benefits should go only to the poor was inevitably followed by distinctions between the 'deserving' and 'undeserving'. This meant policymakers had to make rules for entitlement and disentitlement. They then had to make more rules for punishing those deemed to have broken entitlement rules. Arbitrary judgements are required at every point. The system generates unfairness.

There is also a contradiction between guaranteeing everybody the right to subsist and the right to a life of dignity, and the belief that those in need of support should conform to state-set norms of behaviour. Ironically, those who claimed to believe in curbing the role of the state led the way in demanding more state regulation of those in need of support.

The drift to means-testing and 'targeting' inevitably created poverty traps – situations where many faced losing benefits that exceeded the income they could gain from available low-paying jobs. Poverty traps lead to more rules of disentitlement and penalties to combat the inevitable moral hazard – deciding not to take a low-paying job

– and the inevitable immoral hazard – concealing small additions to income in order not to lose benefits. An edifice of arbitrary decisions and moralistic judgements is constructed, creating an increasingly complex barrier to full citizenship.

Mainstream politicians have posed the issue as one of a 'hardworking Us' versus 'Them', an undeserving, lazy, state-dependent bunch living off benefits paid for by 'Us', or unwelcome outsiders intent on stealing 'Our jobs'. Many who preach this dualism may do so cynically, perhaps telling themselves that it is necessary to avoid being outflanked by others who not only believe it but who would also drag the public further to the right. Few politicians have had the political courage and morality to challenge the hardening utilitarianism.

Modern utilitarianism has several guises, but each seems to justify actions in favour of a majority and against a minority, even to the extent of rationalizing a form of collective punishment, beyond the rule of law. Let us consider a few topical examples.

'Our culture' and 'liberal values'

The most blatant is playing the cultural card. In 2011, following a speech condemning 'multiculturalism' by German Chancellor Angela Merkel, the Council of Europe's Secretary General, Thorbjørn Jagland, said: 'Multiculturalism allows parallel societies to develop within states. This must be stopped. It is also clear that some parallel societies have developed radical ideas that are dangerous. Terrorism cannot be accepted' (Hollinger 2011). He claimed multiculturalism posed a threat to security.

Besides earning Merkel's approval, Jagland was also in tune with French President Nicolas Sarkozy, who said that encouraging diverse cultures to live together had damaged national identity. What does damaging national identity mean? A society contains numerous identities. One could say that letting Old Etonians or financiers run a country damages its identity. They are scarcely in any majority. But note how Jagland elided from multiculturalism to 'parallel societies' to 'terrorism', as if the first causes the third.

Instead of supporting a system to combat individual acts of violence, there is a veiled threat of collective punishment of minorities deemed to have separate cultures. The enemy is particular 'cultures'. It is relevant that shortly afterwards Sarkozy expelled from France thousands of Roma, although they had not broken any law, let alone indulged in terrorist acts. Unwittingly, the person representing the body that defends the European Convention on Human Rights had contributed to the condemnation of political and cultural denizens.

A second example is as menacing. In the UK, in the early days of his government, Cameron advocated a 'new muscular liberalism', a term hardly suggesting gentleness. He argued that benefits should be denied to those who did not show British liberal values, thereby combining jingoism with a sinister utilitarianism and a disregard for liberal values and due process. Who decides what are and are not 'liberal values', and who decides whether someone holds them? Unless someone is charged with a specific offence that is on the statute books, and is found culpable in a procedure respecting due process, it is illiberal to take rights away – and all the more so from any group, which amounts to collective punishment.

Migrants, 'illegal, dirty, alien, terrorists'

In recent years, across the world, the group most singled out for demonization has been 'migrants', a term laden with innuendo. In the UK, as in many countries, the main narrative has been a drive to withhold benefits, although doing so has been made harder by the liberalization of labour markets (including free movement within the European Union) and by the shift from social insurance to means-tested benefits based on 'need'.

Study after study show that migrants play a productive role in society and contribute more to national income than they 'cost' in public services and benefits. They tend to work hard and do jobs others do not wish to do, including in vital social services. They often have higher education than natives and tend to be more innovative. Yet they are demonized as 'taking Our jobs', 'living on benefits paid for by Us' and 'threatening Our culture'. They are easy targets for utilitarians, at the top of a slippery slope. 'National identity' and 'muscular liberalism' rhetoric, advocating denial of rights to those who do not share 'liberal values', easily slides into a darker version of utilitarianism that justifies penalizing all non-conformists disliked by the political establishment.

In 2013, the British government stepped up spot checks in a search for illegal migrants, sending squads of immigration officials and police wearing stab-proof vests into train stations at rush hour and taking off people for questioning. Then, in what was described as a pilot scheme that could be extended nationally, the Home Office sent vans into ethnically mixed areas of north London displaying a picture of handcuffs and the message: 'In the UK illegally? Go home or face arrest.' Liberals were shocked, but that was surely factored into the action, to give added publicity. The vans experiment was later abandoned as ineffective. But it was an example of thin democracy, utilitarianism and the new technique of 'wedge' politics associated with Lynton Crosby, the Conservatives' electoral strategist – appealing to a group that traditionally supported Labour, low-educated whites from the old core working class who make up the first variety of the precariat. Sadly, opinion polls suggested that 47 per cent supported the campaign while 41 per cent opposed it. Other similar actions of this type will follow, unless more people stand up for a position based on values rather than opportunistic posturing.

The Precariat ended by citing the famous chilling admonition attributed to Pastor Martin Niemöller on the rise of the Nazis in 1930s Germany, to the effect that by not standing up for one targeted minority after another, no one will be left to stand up for you when it is your turn. The targeting of 'illegal migrants' – 'undocumented' or 'without papers' – is a reminder of that dark time. Those arrested were denizens, denied the rights of citizens. We must resist.

Strivers versus skivers

Utilitarianism has given the political mainstream a narrative to justify taking away social rights from the precariat. Thus benefit recipients are characterized as 'Them' – 'scroungers', 'dependent on welfare', 'idle' or 'not doing the right thing'. As such, they must be deprived of entitlements due to citizens, because they do not meet their 'obligations'.

In a speech in June 2012, David Cameron listed 17 ideas for reforming the welfare system, designed – he claimed – to save £10 billion from the welfare budget. The media reported 'Downing Street sources' as saying the speech was 'pitch rolling – preparing public opinion for future reforms'. Cameron began by reiterating a dualistic distinction between 'those who work hard and do the right thing' and those on benefits. He did not mention that a majority – 60 per cent – of people receiving benefits are in jobs, presumably working hard to survive on low earnings.

He asserted that benefits had encouraged people to have children and not to work. 'If you are a single parent living outside London, if you have four children and you are renting a house on housing benefit, then you can claim almost £25,000 a year. That is more than the average take-home pay of a farm worker and a nursery nurse put together.' He did not demand that employers raise the low wages of farm workers and nursery nurses. Instead, he set up a straw woman to condemn, juxtaposing the image with two types of well-liked worker.

The speech was designed to justify benefit cuts and pressure people to take low-paying jobs. Labour's then spokesman Liam Byrne criticized the speech solely on the grounds that cutting tax credits was the wrong way to achieve Cameron's target, adding that he agreed that 'work should be encouraged'. The speech had not been about encouragement; it had been about cutting benefits and coercing people to labour.

The manipulation of public opinion, aided by a pliant media, into thinking that most benefit recipients are lazy and dependent on the state has had success. According to the British Social Attitudes survey by NatCen Social Research, a majority believe most unemployed could find a job 'if they really wanted one' and say unemployment benefits are 'too high and discourage work'. When the Chancellor of the Exchequer announced more benefit cuts in late 2012, a poll showed that 52 per cent thought the cuts were reasonable. As *The Economist* (2012f) observed:

> In a speech delivered at the Tory party conference in October, the chancellor painted a sympathetic portrait of a fictive blue-collar striver, rising early for work only to see the drawn curtains of his neighbour 'sleeping off a life on benefits'. Nasty as that may sound, it is probably as good a way as any to go about slashing the welfare budget at a time of economic hardship.

The imagery was a gross distortion of reality, appealing to prejudice to justify cutting benefits. How could dishonesty be a 'good way'?

Youth, 'lazy and non-contributing'

Modern utilitarianism has seen a demonization of youths and erosion of their rights. In that 2012 speech, Cameron drew an image of youths on housing benefits:

> For literally millions, the passage to independence is several years living in their childhood bedroom as they save up to move out; while for many others, it's a trip to the council where they can get housing benefit at 18 or 19 – even if they're not actively seeking work.

To end this 'culture of entitlement', he said housing benefit should be denied to anyone aged under 25, who should not be entitled to any benefits until they had paid contributions.

The reality is that millions of youths cannot 'save up to move out' because they are in the precariat, with intermittent jobs and interrupted benefits. Many cannot live with parents, including those with families of their own. Denying them benefits would also worsen a poverty trap as youths could not afford to move in search of low-paying jobs. As it is, they experience the highest unemployment and most precarious existence. In 1990 youths were 50 per cent more likely than others to be unemployed; by 2013 they were three times more likely.

Cameron then foreshadowed tougher rules for the young jobless, noting that in some countries claimants were made to undertake work in return for benefits within six months of becoming unemployed. Not to be outdone, Labour announced that it would introduce a 'compulsory jobs guarantee', forcing all youths who were unemployed for over 12 months into low-paying jobs. Youths in the precariat were henceforth to be treated as denizens, denied the rights of citizens.

Cameron's speech coincided with publication of a study by the Intergenerational Foundation showing that the young's living standards had deteriorated since 2008, and that the intergenerational gap was 28 per cent wider than a decade earlier, due to higher unemployment, increased housing costs, stagnant wages and greater university costs. The proposed policies would increase intergenerational inequality, while Cameron's rhetoric created a false imagery of youthful sloth.

The disabled, 'faking it'

The disabled are another target. Many of us are disabled in some way, or will be. But in a society based on competitiveness and flexibility, impairments become more stratifying and stigmatizing. Disadvantages accumulate. In the austerity era, politicians and commentators have created a new caricature, the 'undeserving disabled'.

In his June 2012 speech, after disparaging youth, Cameron turned on the disabled. Referring to the disability living allowance (DLA), he said: 'It is not right that someone can get more than £130 a week DLA simply by filling out a bit of paper. But on the other hand, it is not right that those with serious disabilities have nightmare 38-page forms to fill in.' This is the logic of the witches' ducking stool. The 'bit of paper' is that 38-page form. How is it simple for fraudsters and a nightmare for others? In fact, £131.50 was the highest someone 'virtually unable to walk' and needing care or oversight day and night could obtain, if they received both care and mobility components of the DLA. In 2005, the latest data at the time, only 36,000 were awarded the high rate for both components, less than a fifth of all DLA awards and less than a tenth of all DLA claims.

Cameron said he was aware of incapacity benefit claimants being fit for work, implying this was widespread, and that it might be necessary to make those on sickness benefits do more to improve their health, implying people want to be sick. In the post-truth utilitarian mood, the Prime Minister was suggesting there were numerous undeserving benefit claimants, without any evidence, fanning hostility towards the disabled. Disability 'hate crime' has doubled since the start of the financial crisis, with disabled people increasingly subject to insults and assault.

The 'fitness for work' tests introduced by the Labour government have been tightened further, resulting in more disabled people losing social rights despite evidence that the assessment methods are unreliable and unfair. Collective punishment has led to loss of civil and social rights.

'Welfare queens living in mansions'

Another imagined minority to be targeted consists of people living in subsidized council or social housing, depicted as unemployed and unwilling to 'work', claiming housing benefit to occupy spacious dwellings, with rooms to spare and luxuries the average worker cannot afford. Although the number corresponding to this caricature is negligible, the imagery helped legitimize a cap on benefits that households could claim, irrespective of need, and a cut in housing benefit for those deemed to have 'spare bedrooms' – the 'bedroom tax'.

In his June 2012 speech, Cameron proposed that councils should give priority in waiting lists for social housing to those 'in work' rather than to those in most need. The Labour leader made the same proposal shortly afterwards. The precariat, at most risk of unemployment, would be hit hardest. Such a move would deny a social right to those already denied economic rights. In fact, only one in eight drawing housing benefit was unemployed. Higher benefits were needed, as a housing shortage had forced up rents, which had risen faster than earnings. Cameron's plan to peg housing benefit to wages rather than prices will hit the precariat hard. Wages are falling, housing costs are rising, so cut benefits! It is unjust.

Squatters as enemies of the public

In the unequal society of the neo-liberal state, homelessness has become commonplace, its extent only partly captured by the numbers sleeping rough, in bus shelters, train stations, parks, special hostels and so on. Many cadge a spot with friends and relatives. Many squat. Squatting has become a mass reaction by the precariat in some countries, such as Italy. In Rome, a thousand people, many of them migrants from the south of the country, some from Africa and Latin America, took over a disused army barracks and converted the rooms into makeshift apartments. Such was the popularity of this action with Rome's wider precariat that the mayor decided to leave them alone.

However, the state understands that unrestricted squatting breeds civil disobedience and rejection of respect for private and state property. So, rather than tackle the causes of squatting, most governments target squatters, penalizing the victims. In the UK, it is now a criminal offence to squat in an abandoned house. Yet often the homeless have no real choice. Registered shelters are overcrowded and many face closure due to lack of funding, made worse by a court ruling that those using night shelters cannot claim housing benefit. Local councils, particularly rich ones, have lobbied the government to amend the 1986 Housing Act so as to make it easier for them to refuse to house young homeless people and remove the right of appeal against refusals.

In May 2013, police raided a disused building in Ilford, a London suburb, to remove a group of rough sleepers, confiscating their sleeping bags and food, which had been donated by charities and individuals. The chief inspector in charge said: 'The public rely on police to reduce the negative impact of rough sleepers' (Fogg 2013) So, squatters are not members of the public; they are denizens in every sense.

'Philpotts'

In early 2013, an odious man, Mick Philpott, who had fathered 16 children by three women, was convicted of murder after intentionally setting fire to his council house, killing six of his children. In the coverage of this shocking crime, the media latched on to the fact that Philpott had been unemployed and receiving benefits. The Chancellor of the Exchequer seized on this to say the murders raised questions about the welfare system; the Prime Minister agreed. The message was that benefits had enabled Philpott to live in depravity, showing that benefits were depraving, requiring reforms of the welfare system. The crime was depicted by *The Economist* (2013d) as 'a signal crime' that would shape public opinion and policymaking.

A. N. Wilson, a prominent literary figure, wrote in the *Mail on Sunday*, a popular newspaper, that Philpott epitomized what was wrong with the welfare system (Wilson 2013). He claimed the case 'lifted the lid on the bleak and often grotesque world of the welfare scroungers – of whom there are not dozens, not hundreds, but tens of thousands in our country', suggesting this unique case was typical of those living on benefits. He gave no evidence. He just asserted that the system encouraged Philpott to live in a threesome with his wife and another woman, to maximize child and other benefits. In support of the government's reforms, Wilson added:

> The government argues calmly that what is immoral is leaving families such as Michael Philpott's to languish on benefits for generations. Indeed, Philpott never even attempted to find a job. The children owed their existence to his desire to milk the welfare system.

As it happens, Philpott had been in the British army. While in it he was charged with attempted murder, years before he started to receive any benefits. Why did Wilson not attribute his violent behaviour to his being in the army? Instead, with prose clearly intended to inflame emotions, Wilson went on: 'Those six children, burnt to a cinder for nothing, were, in a way, the children of those benevolent human beings who, all those years ago, created our state benefits system.'

Wilson then attributed the London riots of 2011 to 'the perversion of our benefits system'.

> We have turned into a country where ordinary morality – the simple concept that you do not take what is not yours – does not seem to register in whole rafts of society. Many of the looters were in full employment, many were grown-ups, but they still had the Philpott morality – they had been programmed into believing they

were entitled to 'something for nothing'. What the Philpott trial showed was the pervasiveness of evil caused by benefit dependency.

What Wilson did not wish to contemplate was the possibility that the riots stemmed from a society based on commodification and unprecedented inequality that was generating deep tensions, anomic alienation and status frustration. Those riots were sparked by the police shooting of a young man in murky circumstances that were still awaiting elucidation more than two years later.

Moralizing on benefits ill becomes those who accept the inequality, much due to inherited privilege. Wilson, like Cameron and Osborne, was brought up in privilege, with all the benefits that come from affluence and high status. Iain Duncan Smith, the minister praised by Wilson for welfare reforms, was living on a 1,500-acre estate inherited by his wife – 'something for nothing' – which received over a million pounds in farm subsidies from the European Union over a decade, for which he had done nothing. Wilson did not claim that these larger unearned benefits had led to a 'pervasiveness of evil'.

Articles such as his, fanned by casual comments of senior politicians, create caricatures that help in the construction of a utilitarian dystopia. The Philpott story was indeed a parable for the age, but not the one Wilson asserted.

The elderly, 'your turn to come'

The elderly have become a vociferous part of the utilitarian majority. In Britain, as in some other countries, old-age pensioners were the one group protected in the austerity era and were excluded from Cameron's plans in his June 2012 speech. Again, this was utilitarian politics, since the elderly are a rising share of the population, have an above-average propensity to vote, and are relatively likely to vote Conservative. However, pensioners, particularly those experiencing economic insecurity, should beware. Proposals in the air involve means-testing certain benefits they receive, such as free bus passes. One can anticipate that will be followed by images of deserving and undeserving pensioners.

Strikers as 'skivers'

In June 2012, the UK government found another minority to target, proposing to cut entitlement to benefits by low-paid workers on strike. Under rules derived from the National Assistance Act of 1948, workers who strike continue to receive housing benefit and working tax credits for up to ten days, as well as extra tax credits if they lose pay. But Duncan Smith said that with the planned universal credit (which consolidates various benefits into a single payment), these entitlements would end. Justifying the measure, the minister said:

> It is totally wrong that the current benefit system compensates workers and tops up their income when they go on strike. This is unfair to taxpayers and creates perverse incentives. Striking is a choice, and in future benefit claimants will have to pay the price for that choice, as under universal credit, we no longer will (Peev 2012).

This argument presumes that somebody striking does so voluntarily and without just cause. The move restricts the hard-won right to strike by depriving strikers of social rights. Over a million UK workers went on strike in 2011, most of them low-wage public sector workers, such as nurses, teaching assistants, cleaners and transport workers. Many were in the precariat. They will be doubly penalized by the new rules, through loss of benefits as well as earnings. It is class-based utilitarianism.

A utilitarian check-card

In sum, the tendency of utilitarian politics is to create minorities, each targeted for denial of rights, transformed into denizens, approved by a citizen majority. Each minority is painted in some way as 'undeserving'. In the neo-liberal state, the overlap between them and the precariat is considerable.

The state is becoming more directive and punitive towards minorities, proposing forms of collective punishment justified by caricature. In 2013, the UK government proposed that mothers with children aged three should be required to prepare résumés for jobs or lose benefits; the Labour leader said the same, adding that under a Labour government 'workless' parents of pre-school children would be required to attend 'regular interviews in the Job Centre, undertaking training, finding out what opportunities exist' in preparation for a requirement to 'go back to work' when the youngest child turns five (Miliband 2013). Duncan Smith is reportedly considering denying child benefits for children after the second. Why should people be subject to such paternalistic dictates? They encroach on freedom.

Neo-liberal utilitarians are moralistic paternalists, wishing to cut benefits for minorities so that taxes for the majority can be reduced. This is why they draw a dualism between 'taxpayers' and 'claimants', even though taxpayers are the main beneficiaries of benefits.

The progressive instinct

What is the alternative to utilitarianism? Progressives start from a premise that inequalities are accentuated by market forces, competition and exploitation, are morally unacceptable and can be reduced. Seeing society in class terms, not just an aggregation of individuals, they believe policy must respect principles of compassion and empathy.

Compassion is a feeling of concern for others that prompts a desire to alleviate their suffering. It inspires altruism. Compassion requires empathy, the ability to imagine oneself 'in the shoes of' the other. Instead of dividing people into 'Them' and 'Us', an empathetic imagination recognizes all as worthy of support and dignity, appreciating that we too could be in the position of the disadvantaged. It also allows the other to be different. Karl Polanyi ([1944] 2001) made the point when he wrote, 'Socialism is the right to be a non-conformist.' He meant that institutions should preserve the space to be different. Forcing everybody to be 'normal' is anathema.

Celebration of empathy is linked to a tradition going back to Aristotle, and brought to modern form by Hannah Arendt, that we realize freedom in association, because only by acting in concert can we find out what full freedom means. This is republican freedom. Empathy and compassion mean that, while perhaps not understanding or liking your views or actions, I have no right to condemn or punish unless you do harm to others. Even then, a progressive should accept that penalties are justified only if someone is found to have violated a democratically approved law by a procedure that respects due process.

The difference between a utilitarian and a progressive can be highlighted by the role of empathy in attitudes towards unemployment. A neo-liberal sees unemployment as the person's fault, or as 'voluntary', or as due to the person being uncompetitive or not sufficiently 'employable'. There is a strong moralistic tone. A progressive sees unemployment as mainly the outcome of market malfunction, government mistakes, deliberate maintenance of labour slack to hold down inflation, and misguided incentives. In these circumstances, the fortunate owe a right to compensatory benefits to those who are unlucky enough to be the ones unemployed.

The role of empathy in that reasoning is clear. Empathy is what divides progressives from utilitarians. Some believe history is marked by spreading empathy – from family to tribe to nation (Rifkin 2009). But simply enlarging a circle of contacts does not strengthen empathy. It may dilute it. Indeed, a wider market society penalizes empathy in favour of selfishness and competitive opportunism. Social empathy is weakened by inequalities and social stratification; fewer find it easy to imagine themselves in the position of others. A number of psychology studies (e.g. Kraus, Côté and Keltner 2010) have found that the rich have less empathy and compassion than others. And if there is low social mobility, people tend to rationalize discarding empathy. As long as the elite, salariat and core workers have no exposure to the insecurities of the precariat, they will have little empathy with it. So they can be easily persuaded to support policies that hit the precariat.

In one egregious example of lack of empathy, Lord Freud, the UK Minister for Welfare Reform and former merchant banker, claimed that the reason why more people were resorting to food banks was the chance to obtain free food, as increased supply of 'a free good' created its own demand. The reality is that many desperate people, on the wrong side of changes in benefit rules, would go hungry without the rations food banks provide. To suggest they are just after 'a free lunch' shows an extraordinary insensitivity to hardship, made worse coming from someone overseeing welfare reform.

Loss of social empathy in the neo-liberal dystopia has been fostered by other developments too. Schooling has become more functionalist, given to preparing 'human capital' for jobs at the expense of the liberating disciplines of moral education. Exposure to the great realist literature of the world, for example, instils empathy, developing the capacity to understand the complexities of the human condition. The ancient Greeks devoted a great deal of time to the theatre, which was part of *schole* and helped reproduce empathy. The neo-liberal model rejects such time use; it does not add to growth or competitiveness.

Empathy has also been eroded by the drift to means-testing, the shrinkage of universalism and the privatization of public social services. The economically successful obtain a better service than the precariat and those on the edge of it. A true public sector is ruled by an ethos of universalism and empathy. All are equal, and come as citizens. Privatized services become vehicles of inequality. Those who pay demand and expect better and quicker treatment than those reduced to being supplicants.

Perhaps the most ignored factor in the erosion of empathy has been the dismantling of the occupational guilds (Standing 2009). They were vehicles for the intergenerational transfer of codes of ethics, standards and reciprocity. Whatever their flaws as rent-seeking institutions, they provided a work-based framework by which ethics and reciprocity were reproduced. In dismantling them, governments killed a major source of social empathy.

While the progressive's challenge is to revive empathy, that is also the case for another progressive value, social solidarity. We need institutions to defend our commonality. Solidarity can only be sustained by big and little 'platoons', recognizing that every interest must be represented in them. In the neo-liberal model, such bargaining bodies are rejected as distorting the market. The plutocrats, elite and salariat do not need them; they can hire lawyers and accountants.

Social democrats' other Faustian bargain

In the 1990s, social democrats made their own Faustian bargain. To gain credibility with their version of 'the middle class', and potential backers, they abandoned solidarity principles in the briefly popular Third Way and opted for labour market flexibility and means-tested targeting of welfare, with a hard edge of workfare. This was epitomized by US President Bill Clinton's 1996 pledge to 'end welfare as we know it'. Others followed suit.

In doing so, they surrendered the space traditionally occupied by progressives, since means-testing necessitates distinctions between the deserving and undeserving poor. The poor once again became a social category, with emphasis on reducing their number. Principles of compassion, empathy and solidarity were abandoned, and social democrats helped to legitimize a mood swing in the way of looking at society. No mainstream party kept faith with progressive values.

In the UK, this Faustian bargain ended with the General Election in 2010, by which time many Labour supporters had come to believe in the dichotomy of deserving and undeserving. They were convinced Labour had not done enough to stop the undeserving from gaining benefits while they themselves had been denied them. In 2013, the Joseph Rowntree Foundation found that even Labour supporters no longer believed social injustice was the main cause of poverty – only 27 per cent thought so, compared with 41 per cent in 1986. Instead, 22 per cent of Labour supporters said laziness and lack of willpower were the main causes, compared with 13 per cent who said that in 1986.

Labour was hoist by its own petard. But it ploughed on, trying to present as hard a line as the government. At a time when reforms were worsening poverty, Labour's then work and pensions spokesman, Liam Byrne, said benefit cuts were a 'strivers' tax' and that Labour would attack 'the great evil of benefit dependency'. In that case, why did he not focus on the subsidies going to the elite and salariat? If social democrats play to prejudices, they help legitimize them. Instead of challenging these prejudices, and trying to draw people away from them, Labour has tried to court popularity by going along with what it thinks is majority opinion. In wanting to avoid criticism from the right, it betrayed the progressive heritage. The progressive has always risked short-term unpopularity by challenging established ways of thinking.

Social justice principles

The progressive agenda is in disarray. A counter-movement for the Global Transformation is needed. In the second half of this book, some elements are proposed. However, we may set the scene by suggesting five justice principles (developed in Standing 2009) by which any proposal should be judged.

The *first* is the Security Difference Principle. It derives from the seminal work of John Rawls (1971), a progressive liberal. Put succinctly, a policy or institutional change is socially just only if it improves the security of the most insecure groups in society. Numerous utilitarian measures fail this principle. Basic security should be a human right.

The *second* is the Paternalism Test Principle. A policy or institutional change is socially just only if it does not impose controls on some groups that are not imposed on the most free groups in society. Paternalism is a pervasive outcome of neo-liberalism and utilitarianism. Neo-liberals claim to believe in a free unregulated market. But they have devoted an extraordinary amount of effort to building a tighter regulatory framework for directing the behaviour of those in and around the precariat. Unless the same rules apply to the idle rich as to the idle poor, they must fail the Paternalism Test. Unless all of us are enabled to pursue our idea of freedom without state direction, the principle is disregarded.

The *third* is the Rights-not-Charity Principle. A policy or institutional change is socially just only if it strengthens *rights* and does not increase the discretionary and unaccountable power of those dealing with citizens. Charity is welcome, but it must be marginal. Giving bureaucrats and their agents discretionary power, domination that is unaccountable and arbitrary, is clearly a regressive move, chipping away at freedom and doing so for vulnerable groups much more than for others. Policies that require people to show deference and grateful humility are offensive.

The *fourth* is the Dignified Work Principle. A policy or institutional change is socially just only if it promotes the capacity to pursue work that is dignifying and rewarding in other ways. This requires respect for all types of work, not just labour in subordinated activity.

The *fifth* is the Ecological Constraint Principle. This is critical today. A policy or institutional change is socially just only if it does not impose ecologically damaging externalities. For instance, a job creation scheme that results in more pollution or environmental degradation is unacceptable. Jobs are instrumental, not an end in themselves. Of course, there are trade-offs. But respect for the principle requires constant search for alternatives to activities that jeopardize today's and tomorrow's environment and the sustainability of species.

Where do these five principles lead? They should lead to a demand for social protection to be reframed from a progressive perspective, with the precariat's insecurities at the forefront of consideration. We might call this a 'social empathy' strategy. And the elements of the Precariat Charter outlined later should be assessed by all five principles.

Concluding reflections

Utilitarianism could lead to something close to neo-fascism, with authoritarian control over minorities. The austerity era has created a perfect storm of adverse outcomes: economic stagnation, chronic insecurity, rising inequality and commodified politics of dubious morality. The utilitarian way of thinking sets up dichotomies. When a prime minister divides people into those who 'do the right thing' and those who do not, he means those not doing the right thing should not have the rights afforded to those who do. To translate that into policy, you must define, measure and monitor rules. Once on that path, directive regulations and state control grow. The outcome is loss of freedom for the precariat.

The unemployed are told they must search for jobs every day and be on permanent standby. They must be prepared to move home and go to where they have no friends, relatives or support system. They must give up housing if they have one room not currently in use. This is not freedom. This is the moralistic and coercive Big State.

One interpretation of what is happening is that 'society' is shrinking, in that the share of the population with full citizenship rights is falling. But a lesson of history is that as outsider groups grow, so does the perceived illegitimacy of the structures that make them outsiders. At some point, the edifice becomes unmanageable, since too many people are being hurt. The opportunity that moment provides for a radical change in a progressive direction must not be missed.

5

Towards a
Precariat Charter

No mainstream political party has adequately picked up the mantle of the precariat. In Italy's general elections in February 2013, it was left to a populist movement, ostensibly anti-political, to pick up the threads and set the scene for a transformative dismantling of the twentieth-century political establishment. Coming from nowhere, it gained more than a quarter of the popular vote and 163 elected representatives in a hung parliament.

The discordant noise of the Five Star Movement (*MoVimento 5 Stelle* (M5S)), fronted by Beppe Grillo, a comedian, showed that a new progressive utopianism was still in its infancy. It was nevertheless a significant moment; it was almost political genius to unite enough of the first and third groups in the precariat (those fallen out of the core working class and educated youth) around an incoherent agenda based on a simple rejection of old centre-left and centre-right politics. It signalled the fragility of those bastions of privilege.

What the M5S lacked is a set of policies that could meet the precariat's needs and aspirations. Such policies must rest on a vision of a feasible Good Society. To help identify them, we can envisage a charter of demands that recognizes the precariat's insecurities and deprivations, and that provides a reinterpretation of the great trinity of liberty, fraternity and equality.

The charter as unifier

The idea of a people's charter has a rich history, going back to the Cyrus Cylinder of 539 BC, by which the Persian king freed slaves, allowed freedom of religion and established racial equality. It was the first charter of human rights. Of those that followed, most pertinent is the Magna Carta of 1215, signed by England's King John under pressure from his barons beside the River Thames at Runnymede.

The Magna Carta was remarkable for its detail – 63 numbered commitments – and for the fact that it was a class-based constitutional mechanism, reflecting the social and economic advance of a growing class whose interests were constrained by the social structure generated 150 years previously by the Normans. Less widely known is that the Magna Carta was followed in 1217 by a Charter of the Forests, a clarion call for preservation of the commons and reproduction of the environment through assertion of the rights of the common man. It deserves to be celebrated by environmentalists and the precariat today. It was a gesture towards the working class of the time.

The next leap forward was the English Bill of Rights of 1688–9, which again can be interpreted in class terms, reflecting the advance of the landed (Protestant) aristocracy and the rising bourgeoisie serving it. The Bill fed eventually into the American Declaration of Independence, the US Constitution, and the French Declaration of the Rights of Man and of the Citizen of 1789.

The charter form was entrenched. A line can be traced from the Magna Carta through the Bill of Rights to the UN's Universal Declaration of Human Rights of 1948 and the European Convention on Human Rights of 1950. The latter two can be interpreted as in part affirming the legitimacy of the proletariat and the labourism that was triumphant at the time, epitomized by Article 23 of the 1948 Declaration on employment and 'the right to work'.

In the centuries between the Magna Carta and the UN Declaration, the tide of rights moved forward through other declarations. In England, the most relevant follow-up to the Bill of Rights was the social agitation in the 1830s around the Chartists and the People's Charter, its six points, all political, drawn up by working-class radicals in 1838. The points were universal male suffrage, equal-sized electoral districts, secret ballots, an end to property qualifications for members of parliament, pay for MPs, and annual elections for parliament. Five of these (the exception being annual elections) are today taken for granted but in the decade after they were formulated, the Charter's leading proponents were imprisoned, deported or executed.

The Chartist movement was led by male artisans and craftsmen, and articulated by philosophical radicals. Although not a movement for the whole working class, it was a struggle against ruling class interests, in favour of emerging class interests. And the Charter helped to bring coherence to a mishmash of demands from a motley number of groups. As John Bates, an activist of the time, recalled:

There were [radical] associations all over the country, but there was a great lack of cohesion. One wanted the ballot, another manhood suffrage and so on… The radicals were without unity of aim and method, and there was but little hope of accomplishing anything. When, however, the People's Charter was drawn up… clearly defining the urgent demands of the working class, we felt we had a real bond of union; and so transformed our Radical Association into local Chartist centres (cited in Thompson 1984).

So, reaching the point of producing a common Charter took considerable time. Although the Chartists were then suppressed, their ideas took root, never to go away. Among their subversive demands was one for land redistribution. They also developed the tool of localized strikes and among their most radical and enduring principles was the demand for 'equality before the law'.

The event that has most resonance with contemporary developments was a mass meeting in Manchester in April 1848, called to establish a Chartist Convention, which fuelled riots in the streets, depicted predictably by the authorities as mob activity and violently suppressed. That could be said to have ended the movement. But the Chartists set the scene for a future forward march; they were a loose alliance of emerging class interests, asserting rights and expressing their insecurities and injustices. Soon their demands were to become new norms. We now vilify their suppressors.

Confronting the global transformation crisis

Perhaps those historical events will have their twenty-first century equivalents. A counter-movement is taking shape. And one does not have to be much of a futurologist to appreciate that government and international reactions to the multifold crisis following the 2007–8 crash were, and are, unsustainable in the medium term.

The biggest fear has been that political establishments would limp from one bout of austerity to another, and that years of divisive economic and social policies would usher in a drift to authoritarian coercion directed to the most insecure groups in society. Between 2008 and 2013, that is what happened. It is not hyperbole to talk of a neo-liberal state, consisting of institutions and policies geared to and supportive of economic liberalization, implemented by all mainstream political parties. But after 2008, the power exercised by dominant interests was a negative one, causing more misery to minorities, the precariat and denizens, but unable to offer an attractive vision of what was to come out of it all. A vague promise of renewed 'growth' and more 'jobs' was dangled before an increasingly sceptical populace.

Yet a progressive alternative is emerging. The challenge is to find ways of articulating it and to shape a strategy for realizing it. The word 'revolution' is too tainted by history to describe what is required. The word 'reform' is too tainted by the neo-liberal use of it, and is too weak. The essence is captured by the concept of 'trans-formation', associated with Karl Polanyi's Great Transformation, a progressive counter-movement to re-embed the economic system in society, with new mechanisms of regulation, social protection and redistribution.

Following the upheavals of 2007 and 2008, it was clear that the political parties described as 'left' were bereft of ideas. Most were guilty of having done as much to create the economic mess and the plight of the precariat as any on the 'right'. Others had imploded after the end of autocratic state socialism. And political parties had ceased to be regarded as vehicles for structural change. Most had become commodified, propped up by plutocrats and other rich donors, corporate largesse, celebrity cheques, fundraising dinners, or shrinking contributions from atavistic unions trying to resurrect labourism.

There was a failure to recognize that a crisis of the magnitude of the financial implosion of 2008 was an opportunity for a trans-formation of the political and economic landscape, based on three fundamental principles of political action.

The emerging class as vanguard

Defeat is the battle that isn't waged ... Lost battles are battles that are not fought.

Alexis Tsipras, May 2012

The first principle is that, while every successful transformation results from a struggle for more freedom and for equality, every new forward march in that direction is defined by the needs, insecurities and aspirations of the emerging class. In the early twentieth century, that was the proletariat. In the early twenty-first century, it must be the precariat. And just as the working-class struggle against industrial capitalism was led by the relatively educated craftsmen and those with access to the most modern forms of communication of the time, disseminating ideas through pamphlets and participation in workers' education, so one may anticipate that – if there is to be a new forward march – it will be defined by the educated and 'wired' part of the precariat, exploiting the potential of electronic communications.

It was no surprise to find that many of those who participated in the Occupy Wall Street movement in 2011 had university degrees (Milkman, Luce and Lewis 2013). As the occupation dragged on, the composition changed as more of the lumpen-precariat and those with social illnesses came in search of soup, sandwiches, medical help and sympathy. But the drive and energy came from the educated part of the precariat, not the bewildered and atavistic parts.

New forms of collective action

The second principle is that, for a new forward march, new forms of collective action are required. Historically, the form that makes the most progress or that has the most effect – for better or for worse – is unclear beforehand. For instance, a lesson learned only after welfare states had emerged was that working-class politics were defined and shaped through struggles and were not clearly perceived beforehand (Przeworski 1985).

Early trade unions were unlike the battalions that came to predominate in the mid-twentieth century. The craft guilds evolved into craft unions and were led and shaped by craftsmen and artisans, not proletarians. They owed their structures to guild traditions. The later industrial unions stood as much against craft unions as against employers and capital. To depict the 'union movement' as a united force is to ignore history. Indeed, one can argue that most twentieth-century unions were attuned to the needs of industrial capitalism, not to its overthrow.

Now, all we can predict with confidence is that new forms of collective action will be unlike what predominated in the past. That does not mean we should reject or ignore what the old model achieved. They were creations of their time, place, economic structure and possibilities, and modern society owes a lot to them.

Today, an associational revolution is taking place, in which old unions are failing, merging into more general bodies or trying to reinvent themselves, sometimes through incorporating non-union bodies. Meanwhile, the collective action in the streets and squares has been disjointed or what could be called the action of 'primitive rebels'. Protesters have been more united around what they are against than around what they have wanted instead.

The denunciation by the Occupy movement of the imaginary top 1 per cent captured the public imagination. But it did not address the class fragmentation or provide a political strategy. That is not a criticism. It is merely to recognize that mechanisms of protest crystallize by stages, beginning with a collective appreciation of a system of inequity, inequality and chronic insecurity.

This stage has been built up through the riots in the banlieues of Paris and in the cities of Sweden, the emergence of the EuroMayDay parades and then the Arab Spring, the Occupy movement, the riots in

English cities in August 2011 (following less chronicled antecedents), and the M12M (12 March 2011) protest in Portugal, when 300,000 people demonstrated against 'precariousness'. In Greece, there was the *den plirono* (refuse to pay) movement, when people refused to pay their utility bills or taxes, followed by the *aganaktismenoi* (the resentful), demanding accountability, but lacking a unifying agenda. The UK had the 'uncut' movement demanding that government should reverse cuts in social services spending. In Spain, there was the M15 movement or *los indignados*. And in Italy there was the Five Star Movement (M5S), which may have marked the next phase. Turkey saw mobilization in Istanbul, which was followed by spontaneous protests across Brazil. Many other countries saw similar demonstrations on a smaller scale. Everywhere, the mood was one of indignation, frustration and disgust.

Often these protests were partly motivated by nostalgia to the point of idealization, and by a mix of sentimentality, rage and impotence as protestors lashed out at the symbols of oppression and deprivation. Nobody should mock the primitive rebels of the age. The establishment wastes no opportunity to demonize them and manipulate 'middle-class' opinion through citing examples of excess. But the energy was surely forging a social force.

Mass protests are essential, but rarely strategic. They may even dissipate social and political energies, in the way that lifting the lid of a saucepan of boiling water reduces the pressure. In the wake of 2008, many protests had that letting-off-steam quality, particularly those organized by old structures trying to retain relevance. But collective protests enable the crowd to form alliances and crystallize ideas that can evolve into strategic action later.

In the stirring events of 2011, primitive rebels began to recognize each other as potential partners in a progressive force. A vital achievement was to induce more to join interest movements, whether oriented to environmental protection, the disabled, migrants and refugees, the unemployed, the homeless, interns, women's rights, rights of LGBT (lesbian, gay, bisexual or transgender) people, or other social issues. Most bear little relation to the movements that drew people into collective action in the Great Transformation era. The workplace is not seen as central to all of life and society, as labourists made it in their construction of 'breadwinner' welfare states.

It is hard for labour unions to adapt to this new reality, although some have tried with some success. Fairly or unfairly, unions are perceived as representing the interests of their older members, most of whom joined when young, and as intent on preserving the labour securities gained for their members for as long as possible. Collective agreements that preserve labour security are unlikely to appeal to the precariat. Those in it have little prospect of gaining those securities or the non-wage benefits won by the proletariat and salariat. Some in the precariat do not even seek them. They are unlikely to be impressed by union calls for such benefits to be 'extended' to the precariat.

Another contradiction arises from the fact that the unions have always promoted labour values over work values. Historically, they can be held partially responsible for entrenching the values of labour. They called for more people to be in 'jobs', were among the most vehemently opposed to a basic income, and never campaigned to transform labour statistics into work statistics. In the twentieth century, the unions' call for 'full employment' simply meant that as many as possible should be in subordinated labour. This may be unfair to individual unionists who worked tirelessly for improvements in the lives of 'workers'. But it is how labourism took shape. Today, labour unions are unlikely to overcome that legacy merely through a change of rhetoric and replacement of old-style union bosses.

The year 2011 was probably the pinnacle of the primitive rebel phase. Globally, the period afterwards may come to be seen as a lull before the storm, a period of darkness, when the wind died momentarily. Energies turned elsewhere, often to sheer survival in the face of deepening austerity. Nevertheless, the rebel sentiments fed into populist politics, displayed in the electoral success of Italy's M5S, which sent shivers of incomprehension down the backs of social democrats everywhere. Why had they not benefited from the backlash against globalization and austerity?

The reasons were clear. For two decades, labourist parties had opportunistically accepted the logic of the neo-liberal economic model. As enthusiastically as the political right, they went along with the Faustian bargain. They tried to ally themselves with occasional protests, but rarely took a lead or tried an alternative approach. Two examples from Italy of the leadership failure were the occupation of the Cinema Palazzo, a theatre in the San Lorenzo district of Rome, in defence of the arts, and the *beni comuni* (common goods) movement that led to the June 2011 referendum that resoundingly overturned the privatization of water given parliamentary approval a few months earlier (Mattei 2013). Such efforts took place outside the political mainstream. They were harbingers of a storm brewing.

Protest movements, rather than protest days of theatre epitomized by the EuroMayDay parades of a few years earlier, have displaced party and trade union action. Often they occur despite curbs on classic republican freedoms. A case is OUR Walmart (Organisation United for Respect at Walmart), in which employees who were banned from joining unions by the giant retailer nevertheless organized to protest at low pay, lack of affordable health benefits, unpredictable work schedules and refusal to recognize a union. Later, fast-food workers organized protests outside their workplaces. These social moves bypass barriers to collective action constructed by a state intent on limiting actions in favour of social solidarity.

Three overlapping struggles

The third great progressive principle that arises in a period of potential transformation is that every new forward march towards a more emancipated, egalitarian society is about three overlapping struggles. This does not mean they will take place, or that they will be successful. But if they do not occur, there cannot be a Great Transformation.

Struggle for recognition

The first struggle is for recognition. This is achieved mainly through collective action or protests that articulate an identity, in the streets, in cafes and bars, in workplaces, in novel mass media and in political debate. It is about recognizing oneself in others, about feeling a common need to overcome insecurity of identity that pervades a class-in-the-making. It is about recognizing the existence of a distinctive social group, and feeling that one can be part of it, without shame and with some pride.

Something like this happened during the nineteenth century. In the early decades, being 'in employment' was a badge of shame and stigma. As the proletariat took shape, as more were in full-time labour, landless and property-less, more identified with each other. And they came to have pride and dignity in their common circumstances. There had to be an emerging 'subjectivity', a realization that they were in a structural position in the socio-economic system and that they had a duty to support others in a similar position. It went with appreciation of the need to respect principles of reciprocity and solidarity, in struggling for others' dignity as well as for their own.

In such times, the emerging class must forge a distinctive social identity, to create the basis for collective action. This includes the vernacular creation of a new subversive discourse, altering images and the political language so as to highlight the tensions and challenges. It also requires acceptance that the old progressive vanguard of opposition to the structures of inequality and inequity can no longer play that role, and in some respects has become a reactionary impediment to a renewed struggle against growing inequality and the erosion of liberties or acquired rights.

This is where the precariat stood after the crash of 2007–8. The earlier EuroMayDay parades had set the scene. But awareness of precarious lives did not translate easily into recognition of a common identity. That required stories of common challenges to congeal into a common narrative. The mirror grew larger as people saw others nodding in recognition. Search for identity sprang from small-scale rumblings. In 2009, the self-designated 'Research and Destroy' collective of the University of California, Santa Cruz, issued a 'Communiqué from an Absent Future' that captured part of the emerging reality:

> 'Work hard, play hard' has been the over-eager motto of a generation in training... for what? – drawing hearts in cappuccino foam...We work and we borrow in order to work and to borrow. And the jobs we work toward are the jobs we already have. What our borrowed tuition buys is the privilege of making monthly payments for the rest of our lives.

Although somewhat self-pitying, it was the stirrings of a disillusion that must develop if recognition of the place of the emerging class is to crystallize.

The struggle took a great step forward during the upheavals of 2011. In all of them, perhaps above all in the movement of *los indignados* in Spain and parallel movements elsewhere, a sharpening of consciousness symbolized the emergence of the precariat as a social force. People all over the world could identify with it, seeing the energy of many thousands of others. We exist! It is not just me! And we can claim membership of the precariat with pride, without feeling shame, self-pity or personal responsibility for failure, however much utilitarian politicians tell us otherwise. We are here, and are not going away! Circumstances, institutions and processes create our realities. But we are prepared and able to struggle for rights, especially the right to develop our capabilities. There was an unintended meaning in the name of the Occupy movement, for it was not just about occupying spaces but also about forging an occupational identity.

These are not sentiments that come suddenly or that can be fully understood, even by those in the vanguard. But through 2011 more and more people seemed to understand the precariat and their relation to it. This fed into commentators' presentations and into blogs and public debate. Development of personal recognition as belonging to a growing group is a vital stage in overcoming the downside features that help to define it.

That recognition also goes with realization that old social labels are anachronistic. So, people with a university degree find it hard to identify themselves as part of the proletariat or even 'working class'. It seems even stranger to do so if their occasional income comes from sources other than stable wage labour. It is equally strange for people to call themselves 'middle class' – in either the American or European sense – when they have neither property nor salaried employment.

Gaining recognition ushers in collective sentiments. Labour unions reacted with confusion to the precariat, trying to show they were addressing labour insecurities and calling for more secure jobs, with decent wages. This failed to resonate, partly because of a failure to recognize that the radical part of the precariat is not wallowing in self-pity, but is challenging old norms. It rejects labourism as a model, and the proposition that all it wants is 'social integration' into the proletariat. In a wonderfully subversive statement of agency, of self-recognition, this was summed up by a graffito on a wall in Madrid: 'The worst thing would be to return to the old normal.' The progressive part of the precariat may want to abolish its current condition, but it is a transformative class, not one clinging to an imagined or real past.

Struggle for representation

Our dreams do not fit into your ballot box.

Los indignados, graffito

The next struggle is for representation. The events of 2011 did little for this, and policies and institutional changes in the austerity era weakened what little there was. Representation means the precariat must have an independent, distinctive and effective voice in every institution of the state, especially inside all institutions with which its members have to deal. The precariat needs forms of representation that relate to its interests, insecurities and aspirations. In the process, it will surely continue to reject mainstream political parties and professional politicians, because it cannot see itself represented in commodified politics. The word 'corruption' is a sloganized version of this idea. But it is the neo-liberal corrosion of politics that is being rejected.

The message of modern utilitarianism is that politicians and parties must be more competitive than others, and competitiveness must be achieved by repackaging and selling through more effective sound-bites, words and images tested through focus groups, clever advertising, presentational skills, physical beautification, and so on. The precariat, being disjointed so far, may not represent any majority in such utilitarian politics. But gradually the political establishment is being confronted by the awkward fact that while factions in it compete for some perceived majority, thereby splitting the majority, the precariat has been growing, to the point where it matches the split components of that middle. This was shown in elections across Europe in 2012 and 2013, most spectacularly in Italy.

Outside the political realm, representation must be meaningful, holding decision makers to account, ensuring due process at all levels at all times. Those in the precariat are supplicants, having to plead for fair treatment or benefits to unaccountable bureaucrats or agencies acting on behalf of the state. Representation is the only way to overcome this supplicant status, so as to restore and revive rights. Thus welfare agencies, which have become institutions for 'reforming' the behaviour, attitudes or capacities of 'clients', must have their discretionary power curtailed. This cannot happen unless those on the receiving end have an inside voice. It is not enough to have outside 'watchdogs' or ombudsmen set up with grand mandates to look after 'the public interest'. Those are valuable and should be strengthened. But there is no substitute for Voice (see Article 5). Only if the precariat is part of the governance of social and economic agencies will its interests be properly represented.

Strengthening and reinventing democracy is essential for re-legitimizing the forward march. In the struggle for representation, all spheres of policymaking must be democratized. A challenge will be to avoid the utilitarian trap.

Struggle for redistribution

The third struggle is for redistribution. Every transformation is about redistributing the crucial assets, or resources, of the era in favour of the emerging mass class. In feudal society, the struggle was primarily over land and water. In the era of industrial capitalism, it was over the means of production and profits from industrial production. The proletariat wanted to own the factories and mines. In the precariat's case, that form of socialism has little resonance. It is concerned about the inequalities that impede its liberation, related to the five key assets of today's tertiary market society.

First is security itself. The plutocracy, elite, salariat and even the old core working class have a number of sources of security; the precariat and the lumpen-precariat have only chronic uncertainty and hazards to overcome. The *second* key asset is control of time. Again, the upper groups have plenty of means to gain time for themselves, including access to expertise in dealing with all the complexities of modern life. The precariat has only more and more demands placed on its time, and suffers from the precariatized mind, having to flit between activities that eat up time, to little useful effect. A politics of time is required.

A *third* key asset is access to and control of quality space, which comes under the general term of 'the commons'. The neo-liberal onslaught on public spaces and services has depleted the commons, on which the precariat relies more than any other group. A *fourth* key asset is education, and here too the precariat has been disadvantaged, by its rising cost and by the commodification of schooling, which has weakened moral education and the vital ethos of empathy. A *fifth* key asset, financial capital, is crucial to progressive distribution. It has been the accumulation of financial gains from globalization by the plutocracy, elite and salariat that has driven the extraordinary growth of income and wealth inequality.

These are the assets that should be central to a Precariat Charter.

Italy's Five Star Movement: An interpretation

In Italy, the populist explosion in 2013 followed the nominally techno-cratic government of Mario Monti, on whose watch unemployment rose to 11 per cent, youth unemployment reached 37 per cent, and the number in poverty increased by a million to 9 million, in a population of 60 million. The social democratic Democratic Party had acquiesced in what the Monti government was doing, as had the ex-communists. Neither offered a realistic alternative. In this vacuum, the Five Star Movement (M5S) was gifted an opportunity. It appealed to the young 'Generation 1000 Euros', those in the precariat whose job opportu-nities at best offered sub-decent wages. In the election, most of the M5S' 163 senators and parliamentarians came from the precariat. Their average age was 37, 20 years younger than the rest of parliament.

It is doubtful whether the M5S was united in anything more than rejection of defunct political agendas. It encapsulated the dangerous nature of the precariat. We should hope that such movements at least do the essential job of clearing the decks of sterile labourism. Sadly, it did not offer a threat to neo-liberalism; its economic populism had more than a tinge of neo-fascism.

The M5S set out to appeal to several parts of the precariat. It presented an ecological position, calling for policies to cut greenhouse gas emissions. It demanded a halt to prestige mega-projects such as a bridge from the mainland to Sicily and the Turin-Lyon high-speed rail line, as well as penalties for motorized private transport in towns, and better provision for cyclists and public transport. It thus put itself on the side of the struggle for the commons.

However, its economic policies were incoherent. Leftist critics slammed them for being 'right-wing' and an assault on workers and the 'welfare state' (Wells and Schwarz 2013). One might depict them as neo-fascist rather than conventionally right-wing. They favoured a weaker administrative state coupled with freedom for capital. But they also offered the precariat what it most craves, basic security, via the promise of a basic income. This undercut the social democrats who were stuck with labourism, backed by their institutional support, the trade union body CGIL.

The M5S demanded sweeping cuts in public sector jobs, beyond what the technocratic right had demanded, and privatization of railways. It wanted to hollow out local government by abolishing small provincial bodies. So, its stance against public bureaucracies was neo-liberal. The diagnosis was valid, in that the bureaucracy had supported and benefited from old structures, and was filled by placemen from old political parties. Too many social democrats had failed to acknowledge the corruption of the state. Italy is notorious for its nepotistic system of job placement, notably in public services.

However, the prognosis was unattractive. A progressive agenda would have demanded democratization of state structures, so as to deliver public services needed by the precariat. Instead the M5S wanted privatization. It also wanted universities more integrated with business, again displaying neo-liberal instincts. Progressives would want to reverse the commodification of education and growing educational apartheid, with an elite university system for those with connections, alongside a job-preparing one intended to serve the needs of corporations.

A progressive response to the transformation crisis must be grounded in class tensions and objectives. Instead, Grillo resorted to dualist posturing. After the general election, he said that Italy was divided into Block A, which seemed to be roughly the precariat, and Block B, a ragbag of convenient villains, described as those backing the status quo, most public employees (i.e. everybody except M5S supporters), tax evaders and professional politicians. It was puerile populism.

Grillo claimed there was 'a generational conflict in which the issue is age, not classes'. Coming from a 64-year-old comedian, that was quite funny. He damned pensioners and civil servants. 'Every month', he wrote, 'the state must pay 19 million pensions and 4 million state salaries. This burden is no longer sustainable' (cited in Wells and Schwarz 2013). Again, this is populist rhetoric. Were frail elderly people to be denied benefits? Were the police, nurses and doctors, firefighters and garbage collectors to be denied salaries? Grillo was advocating a populist strategy to cut rather than restructure the social protection system. This is unlikely to appeal to the precariat, once it realizes what is at stake.

However, the M5S also advocated an unconditional basic income of €1,000 a month. Some critics said that was intended to replace existing pensions and state salaries. Whether or not this was Grillo's aim, the M5S helped to legitimize the idea of a basic income, which must be part of a renewed progressive strategy that emerges from the demise of the social democratic model. Henceforth, egalitarians in Italy could not say that it was unrealistic politically.

Finally, Grillo's stance was personally contradictory, since he was part of the Italian plutocracy with an income in 2005 of over €4 million. The M5S co-founder was the wealthy Gianroberto Casaleggio, an IT entrepreneur, with support from Enrico Sassoon, head of the American Chamber of Commerce in Italy. Supporters of the movement included billionaire steel entrepreneur Francesco Biasion, who said he voted for Grillo because 'companies today are in the grip of the bureaucracy and the unions.'

The M5S is a form of populism that stems from a feeling of being under siege. It is not democratic: Grillo and Casaleggio run the movement as a private firm, as Wells and Schwarz (2013) show. However, progressive critics must not lose sight of two aspects of M5S's success. It was probably the only way old political structures could be disrupted. Antonio Gramsci's famous aphorism about the old dying but the new not yet born applies. And it helped advance the transformation by moving from the struggle for recognition, won in 2011, to an initial burst of representation, even though it was not the form of representation that progressives would want. It is fraught with dangerous overtones, which may lead to a split into neo-fascist and egalitarian movements.

Grillo said before the election: 'Italy has turned its back on its political class, and a new language of community, identity and honesty is filling the gap' (Kington 2013). At a rally, he hurled abuse at the political establishment, 'It's finished! Give up! You are surrounded.' Fans waved a banner stating, 'We want to get out of the darkness.' Perhaps a rhetoric of extremism was the only way to sweep aside the sterile bastions of twentieth-century politics.

Other countries await a similar moment. But it is still the primitive rebel stage of the Global Transformation. Grillo has nothing in common with Roosevelt or Attlee, or Gösta Rehn and Rudolf Meidner who forged the Swedish model of social democracy. But in a small way, he is welcome in the pantheon of figures of political change. He may fall off the stage soon, but his disruptive work may have been done. That will take years to clarify. There was a salutary, predictable outcome to the Italian upheaval, however. The social democrats formed a coalition government in alliance with the right-wing party then led by multi-convicted Silvio Berlusconi.

And now....

The global protest movement does not resemble the Communist movement, which declared that the world had to be overturned according to its viewpoint. This is not an ideological revolution. It is driven by an authentic desire to get what you need. From this point of view, the present generation is not asking governments to disappear but to change the way they deal with people's needs.

Stéphane Hessel, 2012, author of *Indignez-Vous!*

Hessel caught the mood in 2010 when he vented his fury at the legacy of his generation's long struggle against tyranny, denial of human rights and inequalities. He died in February 2013, aged 95. But his 32-page pamphlet, *Indignez-Vous!* (2010, translated into English as *Time for Outrage*) was inspirational for the Occupy movement, *los indignados* and many others. It was a call to action. It is the task of others to take that forward, in ways and in places we cannot fully predict.

In thinking of a Precariat Charter, we should adhere to several guidelines. Priorities will vary across countries and over time as the debates unfold. What follows focuses on issues that directly affect the precariat, and thus does not deal, for example, with measures to combat tax evasion and avoidance by the plutocracy. The precariat may support such measures, but we should focus on matters of direct relevance to its lifestyle and aspirations.

What a Charter must do is harness the anger and disillusion with old political agendas. Polish philosopher Jaroslaw Makowski, commenting on *The Precariat* and the four As, and how anomie, anxiety and alienation breed the anger, put the matter nicely:

> The question we are facing today is this: how can we forge courage from this fury? Firstly, let's not forget that courage in thought derives from a courage of vision. Let's therefore say it out loud: 'Let's not be afraid of our hatred'. We have the right to it, our situation being as it is. There is only one condition: anger, revolt, and, ultimately, hatred must not be directed against another (Makowski 2012).

He went on to cite Claus Leggewie's book *Mut statt Wut* [*Courage Instead of Rage*], which argues that great change requires 'constructive imagination and initiative', and what the Czech philosopher Jan Patočka called a 'solidarity of the shocked'. That is precisely what is required.

In the following, policies and institutional changes are proposed that correspond to the need to revive the great trinity of freedom, fraternity and equality from the precariat's perspective. The big question is: Where is the agency to give it strength?

Article 1: Redefine work as productive and reproductive activity

All forms of work should be recognized and valued, not just paid labour. Much valuable work, such as care for relatives and voluntary work, is unpaid and uncounted. So are many labour-related tasks that people are expected to do in their own time. Meanwhile, labourist policies aim to maximize the numbers in jobs, no matter how pointless, demeaning or resource-depleting.

Work must be rescued from labour. We must stop making a fetish of jobs and economic growth as conventionally measured. This is crucial to the development of a progressive strategy.

It cannot be claimed validly that all paid work is productive, all unpaid work is not. For instance, it has been estimated that the average office worker spends 16 hours a week in meetings, of which four hours are 'a waste of time'. But just because they are in a workplace and are paid, those four hours are regarded as work. By contrast, someone chatting with others in a public place would be regarded as not doing work, and might be accused of being idle. The distinction shows that, conventionally, work is measured not by what we do but by whether we are paid for doing it, productive or not. There is no justification in saying that everybody has a duty to work or that being in those time-wasting workplace meetings is doing 'the right thing' or being 'responsible'.

A broader concept of work must be legitimized as a high priority. It is an advance to recognize unpaid care work as work. But that should not divert us from demanding that all forms of work should be recognized as work. Let us consider forms currently not counted.

In the UK and elsewhere, the state has encouraged the growth of charities to fill gaps left by a shrinking welfare state. Vast inequality has also prompted discretionary philanthropy, enabling charities to expand activities favoured by donors. The hardship associated with austerity, and the shrinking help given by governments to those in need, has drawn more people in the salariat to devote time to charitable work. Governments are contracting out services to a mix of commercial firms and voluntary non-profit organizations. So, the amount of voluntary work grows. Unlike their paid counterparts, unpaid volunteers are not counted as working. Yet such voluntary work does have an impact on the labour market. It allows the state to cut jobs in public services and puts downward pressure on the pay and conditions of those doing similar wage labour.

Then there is what should be called work-for-labour, work linked to jobs that is unremunerated and unrecognized statistically or in social policy. This includes unpaid off-the-clock hours, a growing phenomenon that concerns the precariat most. People are doing more work away from formal workplaces, completing tasks that cannot be done in paid hours. And they are doing work in trying to remain 'competitive' and up-to-date, networking, learning new skills, going through lengthy job application processes, and the like.

Work-for-labour also includes activities the state requires people to do if they are claiming benefits, including lengthy form-filling, regular reporting, attending compulsory meetings and training sessions. If people are obliged to do these activities, taking away their time, why are they not called labour or work? People are not choosing to do them. So they cannot be called leisure or play or economic inactivity. As far as the precariat is concerned, those unwanted chores are work.

Then there is work-for-citizenship. The modern state puts heavy demands on the time of its citizens to fill in tax forms, peruse legal documents, apply for services (more forms) and so on. These activities are not leisure. They should be recognized as work, and then taken into account in assessing people's use of time and the extent of their obligations.

Article 2: Reform labour statistics

> Labour statistics should be reformed to count all forms of work. They should reflect the realities of work so as to guide policies that respect non-labourist and ecological values.

Developed in the 1930s and 1940s for industrial economies, standard official labour statistics are misleading. As Chapter 3 indicated, they underestimate labour slack in a flexible labour market. They overestimate employment and, in an era of benefit sanctions and efforts to push more of the unemployed into unpaid 'work experience' or out of the labour market, they underestimate unemployment. However, the main criticism is that they do not show us the extent of work that people do and have to do. For instance, official statistics should measure the amount of work that the state requires people to do to be a full citizen. Regular public statistics should be presented on the full range of work people do.

One indirect objective of reform should be to relate 'work' to entitlement to state benefits in the same way as 'labour'. Social democrats want a revival of contributory social security. This raises an old dilemma. If somebody is not in employment due to illness or maternity, should that count as a period in which a contribution is paid? The standard answer is that it should. But what else should count in that regard? If a person becomes unemployed through no fault of their own (to make the example easy), should the subsequent period of jobseeking be treated as covered by contributions? What about somebody who stops employment in order to look after a frail or sick relative? Add that case, and move to the next. Ultimately, the choice of activities covered by contributory schemes is arbitrary and unfair. Statistics that measured all forms of work would make this evident.

It is also particularly important for the precariat that official statistics reveal whether the labour being performed yields enough for a subsistence standard of living. Many jobs exist only because they are subsidized. In 2012, the UK government set out to develop a 'multidimensional indicator' of child poverty that would shift attention from income to an alternative headline statistic. One element for inclusion was 'family worklessness'. Having a parent in a job was to be regarded as automatically reducing a child's poverty. But many parents are in jobs that do not pay a family income. Depending on the weight given to having a job, the indicator could define children as out of poverty just because a parent had a job, irrespective of how much it paid. The consultation was also told to ensure that the measure should resonate with the public, opening the way for the indicator to be shaped by negative perceptions created by prejudiced media stories about feckless families. Labour statistics should not be used in that way.

Measure labour slack

Chapter 3 argued that in a flexible labour market, the official unemployment rate is a low and distorted measure of labour underutilization. It will also be a bad proxy for it, since there is no reason to think that the ratio of labour slack to unemployment will be constant, cyclically or over time.

In some countries, policymakers were flummoxed by the fact that, in the post–2008 recession, employment held up while output plunged. This implied that productivity fell and unit labour costs rose. But perhaps 'the employment content of employment' fell. More of those classified as employed on a full-time basis were in fact doing very little labour. The main response of employers was to lower wages and cut paid hours. Zero-hours contracts spread, and more of the nominally employed were effectively unemployed.

Statistical paradigms

In each transformation, a statistical paradigm breaks down and pressure builds to replace it with one that can display current realities and yield answers to questions policymakers and analysts are asking.

In nineteenth-century censuses, people were classified by their usual occupation, providing data that could not show the extent of unemployment. In the 1930s, after much experimentation, that was replaced by what became known as the labour-force approach, by which adults were arbitrarily defined as economically active or inactive. This yielded a measure of open unemployment, at the cost of loss of information on people's occupation rather than current job.

In the Global Transformation, a new statistical paradigm is required – a work and occupation framework that could identify people's work patterns, their occupational skills, their social income and patterns of social mobility. It is time to escape from the warped images provided by labour statistics.

Article 3: Make recruitment practices brief encounters

Incentives should be introduced to discourage use of prolonged and complex recruitment procedures that impose high costs on the precariat in terms of money, time and stress. The job application process should be regarded as work. Applicant-screening software should comply with ethical codes, including use of personal information and referee statements.

One activity taking up a growing amount of time of the precariat is searching and applying for jobs. In a flexible labour market, job churning is extensive and labour surplus conditions mean it is a buyer's market. Automatic filters screen out many qualified applicants before a human being enters the scene, and much time and thought is needed to pass through the filters to secure an interview. That is only the first stage. For graduate jobs, it is now common for applicants to have to go through many rounds of time-using, stressful and costly interviews and tests. Even for jobs that are for standard skills or limited skills, employers are turning to prolonged recruitment practices that must make little difference to the selection of individuals to fill the vacancies.

An extreme example of software screening cited by Peter Cappelli, author of *Why Good People Can't Get Jobs* (2012), concerned a company that received 25,000 applications for a standard engineering job, all of whom were rejected as not qualified. In another case, a jobseeker was told he had all the qualifications needed, except that his previous job title did not match the vacancy, a title unique to the prospective employer (Wessel 2012).

Recruitment has become a major industry, nurtured by recruitment agents and 'headhunters', with batteries of tests, assessments, interviews, required demonstrations of behavioural traits and psychometric status, and sundry other make-work exercises. Firms are using sophisticated layered recruitment procedures that include outsourcing to companies specializing in 'talent' assessment and use of 'human resource' consultancies with a vested interest in maximizing their market. One US firm helping to multiply the hoops is the Chemistry Group, a 'talent consultancy' that has designed an online game by which to analyse the credentials and sharpness of candidates. Similar firms in the UK include SHL.

For applicants, the time involved in job applications is growing, but for employers it may be falling, since instead of sifting through application forms and interviewing numerous candidates, they will only interview a small number who have successfully gone through the layers of tests. One recruitment consultant told the BBC: 'Face-to-face interviews, because they are time-consuming and costly for both parties, will increasingly be reserved for the very final stages of hiring' (Millar 2012). For applicants, the reverse is happening. For every interview they obtain, they may make 20 or more job applications, each requiring extensive documentation and tests. To land their first job, the number of applications may be far greater. According to the Trendence Institute, in 2013 new graduates in the UK, Germany, Italy and France sent or expected to send over 30 applications before obtaining a job; in Greece the figure was 64 and in Spain it was 69.

Thus millions in the precariat are being expected to go through a tortuous process, mostly for zero gain and a lot of cost. Firms are taking the time of applicants for granted. Some will claim, perhaps truthfully, that hiring qualified people is expensive and important, due to the potential cost of making errors. But for most the difference made by having a complex process is probably small. As it is, even with sophisticated selection schemes, major corporations still often make the wrong choices – in about a third of new US managerial hires, for instance (Fernández-Aráoz, Groysberg and Nohria 2009).

The answer is to equalize the costs to the two sides, the final employer and the job applicant. The application process should be regarded as work. Companies that insist on having multi-round recruitment practices should agree to pay for the applicant's time and supplementary costs for every round after the first. Making applicants bear the cost of the first round would deter frivolous applications. Some might object that paying applicants for their time in subsequent rounds would still encourage some to apply without intending to take the job if offered. If paid, those desperate for income might see that as a way of obtaining some money. But it is a risk worth taking, in that it would put pressure on firms to make the process less time-consuming and more direct.

Much attention is paid to personal résumés, or CVs, and the precariat surely regards them as a curse. To be without an up-to-date, well-formatted CV to whip out of the computer at a moment's notice has become a sin. It sits waiting for use, silently mocking our pretensions and our past. There are short versions, long versions and comprehensive versions. There are coaches for CV writing, including use of correct keywords ('passionate' is one favourite) that may get applicants past the automatic screening stage.

Gaming a silly system is legitimate. However, the challenge is to reduce the costs of job applications and jobseeking. Some governments have introduced a new condition for welfare claimants, that they must prepare CVs. This is unfair, paternalistic and insulting. Benefit recipients are also being required to keep diaries of their jobseeking, which they must show to the employment services. This too is insulting and stigmatizing. Moreover, an application involving a multi-round recruitment process may result in a double penalty for benefit recipients; they may face all the costs of applying for a job, with what may be a very low probability of success, and in addition they may be threatened with removal of benefit for not actively seeking other jobs in the period covered by the multiple rounds.

It would also help if job applicants were given an estimate of the probability of being selected after the first round. They would then have some information to help decide whether they should continue to use up time in what could be a demoralizing process. Having people waiting in false hope is not a good way to run a society.

Finally, the software being created for processing job applications should be subject to ethical rules. These should include guarantees that information on applicants will not be divulged to third parties, and that references containing potentially defamatory material should be divulged to candidates so they have an opportunity to refute the claims. While this should not apply to opinions about a person's capabilities or personality, it should be divulged if it pertains to specific acts, such as a crime or misdemeanour. Anecdotal evidence suggests that references often do not meet fair or objective criteria in this respect.

In sum, given the flexibility, job churning and importance of efficient job-matching procedures, the precariat needs ethical codes of conduct and procedures that do not impose unsupportable costs.

Article 4: Regulate flexible labour

Flexible forms of labour should be regulated, mainly by Voice mechanisms. The precariat should not oppose flexible labour in principle, but should oppose the loss of rights and other consequences in a system lacking appropriate forms of social protection and regulation.

Labour market flexibility has produced a bewildering variety of labour contracts and more indirect labour; third parties have come to the fore, notably employment agencies, some of which have become huge multinationals. A buzzword among labour lawyers is 'triangulation'. Temporary employment agencies are modern labour brokers. New are their global reach, size and sophisticated use of electronic technology. With numerical and functional flexibility, combined with the new information and communication technologies, has come a proliferation of types of labour relation, bringing distinctive challenges and insecurities. Many of the old forms of labour regulation are inadequate or counterproductive.

In support of demands for Voice-based regulation and countervailing sources of security, we may highlight labour relationships that are growing globally – internships, zero-hours contracts, labour broking via employment agencies, 'crowd-work' ('crowd-labour'), and forms of unpaid work-for-labour integral to the emerging flexible labour process.

Interns

For most who do them, internships are an introduction to life in the precariat, though for a tiny minority, they may be a stepping stone to a stable job. Not everything about them is bad. But overall they are among the most exploitative forms of flexible labour, particularly when unpaid, and are a ruse to deny social rights. They should be regulated internationally by an ILO Convention. But that would merely set a framework for decency.

A report in *Dissent* (Schwartz 2013) noted that a key skill of interns is not to cause a fuss. They must learn to be docile, to accept that they should be tractable, flexible and a supplicant. One blog advised, 'Be a chameleon!' and 'Use constant apology' as devices of ingratiation. The internship is a modern method of habituating workers to uncertainty and unstable labour. To obtain approval, interns must accept almost any task, as a test of suitability. The mantra must be, 'Thank you so much for this opportunity.' This is labour 'feminization' (sic) – showing flexibility, submissiveness and gratitude.

Internships have become a means of obtaining cheap, disposable labour, mostly to undertake low-level tasks. Firms benefit from this labour directly and from displacement and substitution effects. By taking on routine tasks, interns can free higher-paid employees to concentrate on high-productivity activities. Often, interns displace employees at the lower-skill end, or remove a need to recruit them. And while it is hard to measure the effects of internships on the wages and benefits of the precariat in general, they must be negative, since firms acquire low-wage labour that weakens the bargaining position of others doing such labour.

Internships are also being used as a form of modern apprenticeship, to create a low-level, low-paid labour force that does not receive enterprise benefits or entitlement to regular state benefits. These interns are misnamed. They are indentured labourers. A similar characterization applies to unpaid work, offered with a hint that it might lead to paid labour or have spin-off benefits, such as a byline for aspiring journalists (Kendzior 2013).

Internships have also become a stratifying device that hinders social mobility. In effect, they are lottery tickets paid for by the interns themselves (or more usually their parents). For a tiny minority, the ticket proves to be a winner, with an offer of a longer-term job afterwards. But most buy a ticket of little value, which may even be negative if people are deluded into taking dead-end jobs imagining they offer an avenue into a career. In addition, being able to buy the lottery ticket is not random. Most parents who can afford to support their offspring through an internship are in the salariat or elite. They are also more likely to have 'connections' with firms and organizations offering internships. Few from precariat family backgrounds will be able to obtain an internship, even supposing they can support themselves, and even fewer will find one with a high probability of leading anywhere.

Internships thus perpetuate a new form of dependency. While politicians pour scorn on alleged benefit dependency, they have kept quiet about parental dependency, perhaps because they or their friends have children they intend to steer through internships into the salariat.

The precariat must campaign against internships by recognizing them for what they are for the majority. Exceptions will always be cited. But only when enough people come to appreciate the need to apply a 'veil of ignorance' test (not knowing where one would be in the distribution of outcomes), will a credible opposition to them emerge.

The extensive use of interns by Foxconn and others in emerging market economies, noted in Chapter 3, may give the global precariat leverage. Foxconn is linked to the American plutocracy; 40 per cent of its revenue comes from Apple. So just as pressure has been put on multinationals to respect labour standards and avoid child labour in their supply chains, all firms should be required to avoid contracts with suppliers misusing internships.

Interns themselves are mobilizing, with groups such as Intern Aware in the UK, *Génération Précaire* in France and *La Repubblica degli Stagisti* in Italy. While collective opposition builds, remedial action is needed, along the lines of the 2012 European Charter for Quality Internships and Apprenticeships.

First, interns should be paid, even when they are doing the work as part of their university degree. Several court cases have been brought successfully in the USA for payment, based on the fact that interns had done productive labour. In the UK, the tax authorities are investigating a number of companies employing unpaid interns and have already taken action against a few held to be breaching minimum wage laws.

Second, internships should be short and non-extendable. This would limit the substitution and displacement effects since it would be more difficult for employers to use interns as cheap substitutes for regular employees.

Third, nobody should be able to buy internship positions – let alone bid for them at auction. In 2013, an internship (initially billed as with the UN but later changed to make clear it was with a UN-related NGO) was auctioned for over $20,000. The online auction site concerned, CharityBuzz, offers other internships for sale on its website. The sale of internships should be banned as discriminatory.

Finally, interns should be informed of their rights and entitlements on being signed up, with a written description of the tasks they will be expected to perform, and assignment of a designated supervisor (not a 'boss'). In sum, the relationship should be transparent and established in advance.

Zero-hours contracts

A growing number of people are trapped in zero-hours contracts. Once a feature of just a few sectors, they are now pervasive. While they have spread up the professional spectrum, a development linked to the privatization of social services and the contracting out of public services to commercial providers, they have mostly hit low-paid, financially stressed people, often young or migrants. It is symptomatic of the class-based labour market in the UK that 100,000 or so interns have received much more public attention than a million direct care workers, most on zero-hours contracts, whose plight is far worse.

A feature of the so-called standard employment contract is 'mutuality of obligation' – the worker turns up for labour and in return is remunerated. Each side obtains agreed security. This seems absent in zero-hours contracts, although the UK's Employment Tribunal has ruled that if an employer agrees to make labour available whenever possible and if a worker agrees to be available at all times, there is a mutual obligation that gives the employee 'rights'. This should be clarified by law.

There are several reasons for the growth of zero-hours contracts. For employers they offer cover for fluctuations in demand and increased flexibility; they also enable employers to pass on labour-cost risk to workers and avoid the non-wage obligations owed to 'employees'. Some firms have attempted to call people on zero-hours contracts 'workers' or independent contractors of services, rather than 'employees', to avoid the need to provide benefits such as maternity or medical leave, or to give notice of redundancy or respect rules on unfair dismissal.

Zero-hours contracts lead to minimal occupational development and intensify uncertainty. The amount of 'work' relative to paid labour is often considerable, including the waiting around, unable to do other work. Most on such contracts must be constantly on standby, preventing them from travelling in search of other jobs, or attending training courses, or even gaining the 'work experience' that politicians claim is so desirable. They are subjected to induced inertia, an impediment to social mobility, and in most cases degrading labour. In some cases, people are obliged to purchase their own uniforms and equipment, even company badges, just to be on standby. The employer is under no pressure to train workers or make good use of them and, as with any free commodity, need not fret about labour inefficiency. And zero-hours contracts can create a form of 'unemployment trap', since being under contract blocks workers from doing paid labour elsewhere.

The worker is nominally employed but unemployed, in a twilight zone of not earning and not receiving benefits. Unfortunately, the growth of the practice suits governments, as having large numbers on such contracts massages the unemployment statistics downwards. The UK government has encouraged the growth of zero-hours contracts through its contract commission system, whereby umbrella contracts are given to private firms without any specified amount of service being agreed in advance. This has led firms to mirror such contracts by making similar arrangements with workers. The government could, if it wished, stipulate that zero-hours contracts should not be used, or used only sparingly. Or it could make their use a factor to be taken into account when awarding contracts.

The widespread use of zero-hours contracts is reminiscent of what happened after the collapse of the Soviet Union in 1991, when millions of workers were kept on enterprise rolls without pay or benefits. Some foreign economists said the low official unemployment figures at the time meant the labour market was flexible. The reality was that millions on 'unpaid leave' died prematurely, starving, committing suicide or dying from social illnesses (Standing 1996). The use of zero-hours contracts in countries such as the UK and USA is not in the same league. But it is a feature of the insecure underbelly of society in which the precariat is scrambling. In denying social and economic rights, zero-hours contracts turn more people into denizens.

The denial of non-wage benefits lowers social income. In addition, wages are lower than for people with other forms of contract, and zero-hours contracts are more common in firms that pay low wages in general. They are also associated with lack of collective Voice, and with job, employment and work insecurity (explained in *The Precariat*). And since zero-hours contracts are often disguised unemployment, their expansion means that if the economy picks up, unemployment will not fall by as much as in the past.

A ban on such contracts would not succeed, and may not be desirable, since some people may want highly flexible arrangements. But they need regulation. The presumption must be that, for the most part, they stem from an unequal power relationship in the labour market. That means there is a need to raise the costs to employers of using zero-hours contracts and a need to tackle the forms of insecurity that drive people to accept them, primarily inadequate and tenuous state benefits and lack of alternative sources of support.

As an interim measure, nobody who is unemployed should be

required to accept a job with a zero-hours contract or indeed any contract that could mean big week-to-week fluctuations in the amount of labour and income. Many countries require people claiming unemployment benefit (jobseeker's allowance in the UK) to accept job offers, but it would be unfair to impose sanctions for refusal to accept a zero-hours contract with all its uncertainties. For similar reasons, those on zero-hours contracts should be able to quit their job without losing entitlement to benefits. It would be ridiculous to describe the act of leaving such a job as voluntary or one of 'choice'.

Regulation of zero-hours contracts should aim to provide a fair balance of interests, now heavily weighted in favour of employers. This could be done in several ways. *First,* firms offering zero-hours contracts could be required to provide a bonus payment as compensation for the inconvenience and insecurity, a policy already implemented in Germany. This might be called a 'standby bonus', which could be varied according to the degree of flexitime in the contract, set higher for lower guaranteed hours and vice versa.

Second, employees on standby should be given minimum notice of, say, 24 hours when being called in and no one called in with less notice should be penalized or discriminated against if they decline. Some people on zero-hours contracts can have as little as two hours' notice of available work, making it impossible to plan a day or arrange childcare. And some firms use their pool of people on zero-hours contracts as a labour reserve, to instil disciplinary fear in others and to act as a mechanism to allocate labour to those who labour hardest, with favourites being given more work or better shifts.

Third, those on zero-hours contracts should be paid at least the minimum wage for all their hours of labour, properly calculated to include travel time where travel is part of the job. In the UK, the majority of domiciliary care workers, who visit people at home, are on zero-hours contracts with private firms and most are not paid for their travel time between visits. A 2011 study estimated that if travel and other unpaid hours of labour were taken into account, over 150,000 care workers were being paid less than the minimum wage (Hussein 2011).

Reform should go further. Firms are developing devices to close the pores of the labouring day in ways that hit workers on zero-hours contracts particularly hard. Care workers are being tagged with tracking devices to ensure they are where they are supposed to be and for the time for which they will be paid. If a care provider stays for less than the time stipulated, she may receive no wage at all. One care worker put the predicament well:

> For a 30-minute visit you need to be there at least 23 minutes and arrive within seven minutes of the scheduled time. Even if you finish up early and you are late for the next appointment, you can't leave. You won't get paid. It's Big Brother, except it's no joke. The owner knows what she's doing. What's not in your pay packet is in the owner's. There are 200 women here. If you bring it up you will suddenly have your number of hours cut. One girl went down to eight hours a week when she asked about it. You cannot live on that. So we all keep quiet (Ramesh 2013).

Requiring firms to pay for all the labour time, including travel and waiting around, would help curb such surveillance tactics. Care is a personal relationship, and the time spent on it should ebb and flow free from commercial dictates.

One policy that has gained popularity is for local councils to offer care-work contracts only to firms that pay the designated 'living wage'. This might shame some firms into paying more. But it would not stop them using zero-hours contracts or paying only for time 'on the job'.

Fourth, zero-hours contracts should be fully transparent. The worker when recruited should be informed exactly what is involved, in writing. *Fifth,* there should be curbs on the ability of employers to change the contracts of existing employees into zero-hours contracts, a practice that has been reported. The aim of regulation should be to give workers the same flexibility as employers, free to do other forms of labour (and work) while waiting, free to decline the labour offered without penalty, and with sufficient advance notice of labour needed to adjust other schedules.

Labour broking and employment agencies

Most people employed by employment agencies are effectively on long-term zero-hours contracts. They can be hired out for hours, days or longer. Often they have no idea in advance; they could go without labour for months. Long banned or severely curtailed in many countries, private employment agencies have become important labour intermediaries and large suppliers of temporary labour. As commercial concerns, they will naturally serve their own interests first in trying to maximize profits. But as labour intermediaries, they can be expected to allocate costs to the respective parties according to their bargaining power and to their prospective benefits and costs for the agency.

Someone with rare skills should gain from an intermediary, since it should create an implicit auction for talent. It will also pay the talented to use an intermediary and pay a high fee. By contrast, the precariat is mostly operating in a buyer's market. An intermediary may be useful, since it should be efficient in identifying opportunities. But a broker will also be able to charge the precariat a high price, for the same reason. Indeed, intermediaries will tend to become local monopsonists, sole buyers of labour services. This is a market failure that should be met by a regulatory response by any government concerned with equity.

Some activists and trade unions have lobbied to ban 'labour brokers'. This might make sense if brokers played no valued economic or social function. But however hostile one might feel towards the exploitative and oppressive tendencies associated with labour brokers over the ages, they do potentially serve functions for workers as well as employers or 'labour demanders'. Seeking jobs is time-consuming, costly, inefficient and often degrading. For most of the twentieth century, hostility to brokers resulted in the state taking over labour-market matching through public employment agencies. Whatever one feels about the erosion of that system, there is no realistic prospect of its return.

It is however vital to confront the limitations of the commercialization of the labour intermediary function. These include the imposition of hiring costs on insecure jobseekers, cherry-picking discrimination, profiling and statistical discrimination (selection based on arbitrary indicators such as age or length of unemployment spell). Above all, as argued in Article 5, the governance structure of this public essential service should be overhauled.

Crowd-labour

As noted in Chapter 3, one new form of labour – now involving many millions of people around the world and growing fast – has no parallels in history. It goes under the misleading name of 'crowd-work'. Crowd-work is the type of flexible labour that most needs regulation, because it preys on vulnerabilities at a distance. Contracts are for piece-rated tasks. A worker in Boston who objects to non-payment can be blacklisted and bypassed by the next contracts given to crowd-workers in Dhaka. Yet crowd-work is the hardest labour to cover by protective regulations. Governments – and unions – have yet to be engaged.

There should be proper contracts signed and co-signed before tasks are undertaken. International codes of good practice are needed. There should be a legal requirement that any 'requester' rejecting labour by any crowd-worker should provide a written reason, which in principle the worker could challenge. And due process is needed as in any other of the precariat's transactions with employers or the state. Yet in the longer term, the only way to overcome the extreme exploitation that crowd-labour involves is a combination of collective Voice and basic economic security. Desperately insecure members of the precariat cannot hold out atomistically.

Interim managers

As managers themselves become subject to flexibility and more become contracted interim managers, as described in Chapter 3, the class differentiation inside the emerging profession opens the way for opportunistic and unethical practices. Given the social externalities of their activities, which necessarily affect the lives of the workers they judge, there is a need for a statutory code of ethics to ensure they respect the interests of all parties, not just those of shareholders or the company appointing them. Ideally, such a code should be developed by a body representing interim managers, but it must be accountable and transparent.

* * *

In sum, all forms of flexibility, including casual labour, temporaries, 'permanent temporaries', standby labour, crowd-labour and interim managers, make work and labour more insecure. There are measures that could reduce that insecurity and make labour relations less stressful. However, vulnerability to abuse and exploitation will persist unless there is a fundamental restructuring of social protection and unless there is a more coherent revival of fraternity and associational freedom. Without collective Voice or agency, is it realistic to think the insecurities and strains of modern flexible labour will fade? A fear must be that neo-liberals and utilitarians do not want them to do so.

Article 5: Promote associational freedom

> The precariat needs independent Voice to give it agency, the capacity to defend and further its interests, individually and collectively. This requires institutional mechanisms based on the idea of 'republican freedom', that it is only through associational freedom that we can identify and defend our interests effectively. Labour unions can play a role but more important to most in the precariat will be community and occupational associations.

To overcome its insecurities and supplicant status, the precariat needs independent Voice. The use of a capital letter is a bow to the late Albert Hirschman, whose famous book (1971) contrasted the use of Voice and Exit options (as well as Loyalty). In most economic transactions, in the face of disappointment, the main options are exit from the relationship or action to request or demand change.

The neo-liberal Chicago school emphasized Exit as the market principle. Hirschman realized that the existence of exit options only would entrench the status quo and permit the persistent oppression of the weak or vulnerable. The triumph of neo-liberalism allowed the state to make exit increasingly painful, as in quitting a job, which now results in disentitlement to unemployment benefits. And governments have weakened Voice mechanisms via tighter regulation over what unions and civil society groups can do.

The precariat needs both individual and collective Voice, the latter being essential for the former. Institutional mechanisms are required for 'agency', a capacity to act without fear of retribution or excessive dissipation of energy and loss of time. The insecure, and those categorized as abnormal or non-conformist who are deemed to forfeit rights, must have the capacity to speak up, to have their interests represented and to bargain with more powerful interests in society.

The precariat is far from where it needs to be in all these respects. The challenge is to construct associations that can bargain with diverse interests, including some irrelevant to the proletariat. In thinking what this implies, we should recall the essence of republican freedom, originally developed by Aristotle and refined by Hannah Arendt (1958), which is that freedom can be sustained only through collective action, through acting in concert. It contrasts with the liberal view of freedom as individualistic, or as the liberties emphasized by Isaiah Berlin – negative liberty (absence of constraints) and positive liberty (the opportunity to pursue one's own interests).

The republican view is that we can defend our interests only through associational freedom. Indeed, we only come to realize fully what our interests are through collective action. We cannot see clearly what we want or need in the absence of actual involvement. And freedom is only real if we have the capacity to act collectively. Supplicants have no freedom. This perspective is alien to the neo-liberal paradigm.

In the neo-liberal scheme, the precariat is not expected to have agency. Its members are structurally unfree, treated by the state as people to be assessed, reformed, sanctioned, nudged, made more 'employable', trained, re-trained, taught to be 'more socially responsible' and so on. Without collective Voice to resist, the state can turn more of the precariat into denizens, without rights, supplicants for conditional entitlements for which they are expected to be grateful. In spite of – or revealed by – the protests of 2011, the precariat has existed so far as the Voiceless, at best to be pitied for its insecurities and absence of occupational identity, or criticized for its floundering and alleged shortcomings. Days of rage are no substitute for institutionalized Voice.

To fill this vacuum, several types of association are needed, not just one. For republican freedom, society has always required an array of 'congregational' bodies in which counter-narratives can be forged. Historically, these have included the churches, unions and political parties.

For the precariat, labour unions cannot easily play a central role, since they properly side with the values of labour and defend their members' interests. That does not mean society no longer needs them. They are needed to focus on workplace issues, to bargain on behalf of employees with employers and with the state. But the precariat must be able to represent itself and to bargain with representatives of labour as well as other interests.

The precariat needs a synthesis of the occupational guilds and craft and labour unions. It needs associations that can enable those in it to become more like proficians, more able to be project-oriented in work and more able to build on secure competencies in ways they wish, to construct an occupational life in basic security. An objective should be to reduce a pervasive sense of uncertainty.

If we could accept the radical claim that the essence of the precariat is detachment from labour in a positive sense – as non-habituation to stable subordinated labour – then we could envisage the type of Voice organization that is needed. Most in the precariat have dreams of what they wish to do by way of work and labour. They just cannot realize anything like those dreams, and do not have the institutions to do so. The radical transformative character of 'civil society' was hijacked by the commodifying instincts of neo-liberalism. Too many took the silver shilling and produced entrepreneurial rent-seeking bodies that depend on a diversified vulnerable society.

Associations of common interests, grounded in principles of reciprocity, empathy and solidarity, could change that, enabling those in the precariat to work on their enthusiasms, to be creative and to be reproductive in the sense of reproducing life and its various communities – family, local neighbourhood, artistic, sportive, musical and so on. These activities all involve work, even if they are not labour.

The precariat can accept jobs and labour as instrumental (to gain income), not as what defines or gives meaning to life. That is so hard for labourists to understand. They think of the precariat as deprived of labour and wanting labour security. This may apply to some, but not the progressive part. The desire to work, in the broadest sense, is the human condition; a desire to labour is a contrived condition.

The guilds

For hundreds of years in much of the world, professional and craft guilds set standards of occupational practice for their members and potential members, for carpenters and masons and for weavers and dyers as much as for lawyers and doctors (Standing 2009). They set terms and conditions under which their members were expected to work and to labour. They set and enforced codes of ethics and principles of social protection. They stood against market opportunism. They had drawbacks, such as rent-seeking and 'grand-fathering' (giving undue income and status to senior members). But they gave structure to working lives and the communities around them.

From the 1980s, the neo-liberal and social democratic onslaught on the guilds was remorseless, and their dismantling went unopposed by labour unions. A new version of the guilds is needed that can spread the right to practise while providing social protection for its members and offering good prospects for those wishing to develop an occupational life.

Will such associations spring up without external stimulus and despite existing restrictions? As nature abhors a vacuum, they will probably evolve without state help. But they would be more vibrant if the state, through actions by governments and supranational agencies, promoted them and created space for them to thrive. That may need special legislation, like Canada's seminal Status of the Artist Act, 1992, which broke the stranglehold of labour law preventing associations of freelance artists.

Efforts to revive guild traditions have been impeded by state regulation of occupational practices through licensing by boards and government agencies (see Article 7). New associations must recapture the territory currently occupied by the licensing regulators. This is the most important arena for precariat representation.

Twilight of labour unions

The demise of labour unions is regrettable. They were a progressive force. Then, trapped in their history, they became defensive. Once an institution mainly wants to reproduce its yesterday, it is doomed. Unions must be restructured, renamed and re-legitimized, before they fade beyond repair.

In 2012, union membership in the USA fell to 11.3 per cent (and just 6.6 per cent in the private sector), its lowest level for nearly 100 years. In the OECD overall, unionization of wage workers was only 17.3 per cent in 2011. In the countries most exposed to globalization – the USA, UK, France, Germany and Japan – the numbers in unions in 2011 were only half what they had been in 1980.

The neo-liberal goal of neutering collective Voice has been largely achieved. Regulation was used to help, nowhere more so than in the 24 'right-to-work' states in the USA, which prohibit unions from requiring workers in unionized plants to pay union dues. President Barack Obama described 'right-to-work' laws as strengthening 'the right to work for less money', but did nothing to oppose them.

Every country following the Washington Consensus has been pressured to weaken unions and roll back labour securities. As labour flexibility spread, the defensive labourist strategy of labour unions became a source of distrust for the precariat. Unions gave Voice to their members in core jobs and in the public sector salariat. While understandable, it meant that for much of the precariat there was no counterpart for collective bargaining.

Unions have four possible positions on representation of non-regular workers (Heery 2009): they can exclude 'atypical' workers altogether, subordinate their interests to those of standard employees, include their interests in an overall agenda, or actively engage in defending their interests. While there has been a trend towards the fourth option, some national unions, such as those in Spain, have shown little interest in organizing the precariat.

One difficulty is the changing ratio of membership costs to benefits. With a shrinking pool of employee contributors, union dues must rise to cover fixed costs and growing demands for services. For example, an employee eligible to join the US Teamsters Union who earns $12 an hour must pay $360 in annual fees to the union. That is a lot, particularly for someone in and out of insecure jobs, unsure whether he or she will be in the same industry next year.

In an ideal economy in which all interests were provided with the same incentives and assistance, unions would be subsidized by the state by as much – no more, no less – as corporations and financial capital. As they are not, they are at a disadvantage in bargaining and representation of worker interests. Even the right to strike has been eroded. For instance, as noted in Chapter 4, the UK government proposes to take away tax credits from employees who strike. No comparable threat exists with regard to subsidies to firms. Subsidies are justifiable if externalities prevent something socially beneficial taking place. Equalizing bargaining strength between negotiating parties must be socially beneficial, a matter of equity as well as equality.

The other side of the cost-benefit ratio also works against unions. Voice bodies gain legitimacy by a commitment to strengthen or enforce 'rights'. Labour unions offered to improve wages, benefits and working conditions of employees. They rarely went beyond that group and could not do so effectively because they were institutionally oriented to defending their members.

Throughout the Faustian bargain era, unions made concession bargains with employers. They ended up enfeebled. In the UK, for instance, between 1995 and 2012, the wage premium gained by unionized workers dropped from 26 per cent to 18 per cent. From the 1980s onwards, there were similar falls in union wage premiums in Germany and the USA, attributed to foreign direct investment and outsourcing.

Rising overhead costs, falling wage premiums and casualization are causes and effects of union decline, as is their political marginalization. And the precariat and others baulk at paying union dues that help fund labourist political parties.

The precariat must organize outside and alongside them. There are encouraging signs that this is beginning to happen. In the USA, there has been an attempt to revive the historical Industrial Workers of the World (IWW). Known as 'the Wobblies' in the early twentieth century, the IWW claimed to 'organize the workers, not the job'. Its modern variant is being led by 'workers' rights advocates' who take precariat jobs and sign up fellow workers, not to gain government certification as a union, or employer recognition, but to organize sit-ins, walk-outs and other sporadic actions, often meeting in a public place to make decisions. Demonstrations and actions to raise the wages of fast-food workers, which in 2013 spread to cities across the USA, have been led by workers and community groups, not unions.

Elsewhere, new associational bodies have adhered to labourist agendas. These include the Athens Labour Centre, which has opposed austerity and the partnership between the Hellenic Federation of Enterprises and the General Confederation of Greek Workers, because the established unions had failed to defend social goods. The Athens Labour Centre claims to fight for the Greek precariat. But in Greece as elsewhere, several models of representation are competing for supremacy and relevance.

Where unions failed: Spain

Just as the guilds were trapped by their history when industrial capitalism flourished, so labour unions have struggled with their labourist history, and have usually failed to touch the consciousness of the precariat. What has happened in Spain shows this rather tragically.

Spain's labour market was shaped by Franco's 1938 labour laws, which in turn were inspired by Mussolini's 1927 *Carta del Lavoro* (Charter of Labour). Franco's laws offered loyal employees employment security and collective bargaining rights, so as to promote social harmony in the absence of democracy. It was a perverted form of labourism. But after the Franco regime ended, the political left opposed changes, prompting growth of a parallel labour market outside the ambit of labour protections.

As the unions defended the *Estatuto de los Trabajadores* (Workers' Statute) of 1980 and fought to preserve labour-based entitlements, they privileged a shrinking share of the labour force. In 1984, they agreed to allow more temporary contracts. But by adhering rigidly to centralized and sectoral collective bargaining, they gave employers greater incentive to bypass union agreements by hiring more workers on temporary or short-term contracts. Excluded from the bargaining table, the precariat was unable to entice the social democrats into more enlightened action.

In short, as elsewhere, the Spanish unions made an historic error when resisting the flexibilization of labour relations that came with globalization. They should have accepted flexible labour practices in return for basic economic security as a right, for all. The unions and the Spanish Socialist Workers' Party (PSOE) failed to move in that direction when they had the power to do so in the 1990s.

Instead, they opted for concession bargaining, giving ground to employers and the government in a desperate effort to save jobs. In 1997, they accepted less stringent dismissal conditions in permanent contracts. But dualism was preserved. Between 1985 and 1993, 73 per cent of all new contracts were temporary and transition into permanent contracts was minimal. Fewer than one in ten of those with temporary contracts moved on to regular contracts. The precariat was enlarged by the shift to temporary contracts in the public sector – rising from 8 per cent of public employment in 1987 to 25 per cent in 2005.

Spanish unions dealt with the precariat as a political issue – trying to limit the number of temporaries, opposing private employment agencies, making temporaries more like regular employees – rather than re-orienting bargaining or organizational tactics, or developing appropriate services for the precariat. They gave priority to a struggle for stable employment. This was a defence of labourism. No effort was made to harmonize working conditions for standard and temporary employees. The unions simply defended permanent contracts for an aging workforce.

Other reactions gathered strength. Although the youthful protests of the M15 (*indignado*) movement may be the actions of primitive rebels, these are necessary steps in a countermovement. In early 2012, *los indignados* organized what they called an 'invisible' strike by the precariat of students, temps, the unpaid, immigrants and old-agers. It was part of a struggle against cuts by the state in the precariat's living standards. And setting an example for the rest of Europe were the *iaiaflautas* (a play on *perroflautas* – crusty), pensioners and grandparents who occupied banks to protest against bank bailouts, buses to protest against price rises, and health departments to protest against health care cuts. Had the elderly ever before taken such a lead in a social struggle?

The stance of the labour unions also prompted the emergence of independent youth associations, such as the *Associació de Joves de Gracia* (Youth Association of Gracia) in Barcelona, which offers services to individual workers. This is an example of a form of representation required by the precariat. However, the old unions have resisted their attempts to bargain with employers or represent their members. This must change or collective bodies will self-destruct. Occupational bodies built on union lines – bargaining with the state as well as with employers and other occupations – are an essential part of the solution. But they must be based on the values of work, not labour.

In 2012, the Spanish government set out to curb unions' bargaining power and weaken labour security. The unions organized a general strike, bringing out hundreds of thousands of protesters. But they failed to offer a vision of work and security going beyond an atavistic yearning for a labourist past. Intuitively, the precariat understood the contradiction. Although they mobilized against neo-liberalism alongside the unions, *los indignados* were not trapped by the past. They stood for a future, however uncertainly.

Where unions are failing: Sweden

Sweden has been regarded as the nirvana of social democracy. Unions remain numerically strong, accounting for two-thirds of the labour force in 2011, the same as in 1970, albeit down from a peak of over 80 per cent in the 1990s. But this reflects two special factors: they still administer unemployment insurance, and they have bent with the globalization wind, becoming management-friendly, favouring free trade and accepting downsizing by firms with minimal protest.

The main expanding union, Unionen, has bolstered the salariat by enabling members to gain protection and benefits, marketing its services with TV advertisements. It offers insurance and retraining courses for members. And it stays out of party politics. The employer organizations approve because, as one representative put it, Unionen 'stands alongside its members, it doesn't interpose itself between them and their employers' (Economist 2013c). This begs the question whether Unionen is a union at all, since the purpose of unions is to interpose between employers and employees. And it is inherently regressive, disadvantaging the precariat by gaining privileges for salaried white-collar members, who are financially in a good position to pay for a collective service.

Such bodies are a harbinger of the future everywhere. Unionen has made concession bargains with employers, including introduction of 'time banking' of unworked hours that can be paid back when demand picks up. Other unions have sought to become indispensable by becoming agents of increased productivity. And the LO (Swedish Trade Union Confederation), the blue-collar labour federation and bastion of adversarial labour bargaining, helps government and employers to run training places for unemployed youths, who are paid lower wages. Mixing roles may, however, lead to loss of autonomy and identity as representatives of workers, with unions seen as part of management rather than agents for reducing inequalities.

Association for precariat services

While labour unions try to steer between capital and labour, one new type of Voice organization is actually a variant of an old proto-industrial type, namely a body providing services and benefits to workers who are not stable employees. The aim is to fill the gap left by the erosion of enterprise benefits, such as pensions and medical insurance, and by the fragmentation of state benefits. An example is the New York-based Freelancers Union, which provides insurance plans, a client-rating system, discount offers and networking oppor-tunities. By 2012, it had 200,000 members.

While valuable, such bodies suffer from several hazards. They can be sidelined by commercial competition that attracts the least risky members, pushing up premiums for the remainder. And their innovators and leaders can be enticed to defect by higher offers. A related risk is that the leaders can become too entrepreneurial and end up serving the same system that disadvantages their members.

Sara Horowitz, founder of the Freelancers Union, has become an entrepreneur for freelancing, receiving a MacArthur Foundation 'Genius' grant and publishing a book with the seductive title *The Freelancer's Bible* (2012). She sees the upside of freelancing – freedom from authoritarian workplaces, autonomy to set one's own work schedule, freedom to make alliances with like-minded people (horizontal networks with friends) and to share resources and outsource work in boom times. She also sees the commercial opportunity offered by the third of American adults who are freelancers, very broadly defined, and by the loss of enterprise benefits for others. Thus the Freelancers Union model is one of adaptation, not structural change to redistribute income and bargaining power in favour of the precariat. It looks like becoming a commercial venture. But it could also be a harbinger of worker-controlled service bodies.

Voice for precariat bargaining

Other quasi-unions are emerging, some in unlikely places. One challenge is that most collective bargaining on behalf of the precariat must be done indirectly. It may be done with government, to establish codes of conduct or minimal standards that employment contracts must respect. Or it may involve creation of an umbrella organization for certain labour relationships, as has happened with temporary employment agencies. The situation is complicated by 'triangular' relationships involving contractors and sub-contractors.

Around the world, new Voice bodies are trying to deal with the challenge. Associational freedom is emerging through 'workers' centres', 'domestic workers' cooperatives', 'cab-driver groups' and so on. They can be undercut, since they cannot control ports of entry. Desperate individuals will work for less than they demand. However, incentive structures and occupational practices could limit that tendency.

In Jamaica, a domestic workers' union does not negotiate with individual employers, but has been bargaining on guidelines with the Jamaican Employers' Federation, a form of centralized bargaining. These negotiations include demands that 'employers' must pay wages in full and on time, and should give domestics a day off each week. The union concentrates on education, advocacy, gender mobilization and training, including in telephonic labour, and research and data collection. In 2011, an ILO Convention (C189) was passed on domestic labour. By September 2013, only nine countries had ratified it (not including Jamaica). A union like the Jamaican one cannot expect much from C189, but it has used the Convention to increase moral pressure on employers and government to improve working conditions.

Perhaps the most celebrated body of this type is SEWA, the Self-Employed Women's Association of India. With nearly two million members, it combines: bargaining on behalf of occupational groups, with cells for different types of precarious work; financial services through its bank and micro-credit activities; bargaining with firms, middlemen and the state; and lobbying at all levels of government. It gives high priority to education, with an emphasis on competencies needed for survival and comprehension of society. The struggle is constant and hard. However, SEWA has achieved a great deal, perhaps most of all by giving dignity and pride to very poor women, and it has forced political parties, trade unions, moneylenders, local bureaucracies and other civil society groups to give higher priority to their concerns. In 2010, it embarked on a basic income experiment, as discussed in Article 25. It is a classic precariat body.

Voice as networking

Voice does not mean learning to sell oneself. It should mean constructing a capacity to overcome commodifying forces. Social media and internet networking have the potential to mobilize people for mass events. However, they are a passive, reactive mode of articulating opinions. They have yet to show their force as a progressive Voice system, although they are emerging as a valuable way of opposing illiberal and regressive reforms, as with the 38 Degrees network. Elsewhere, ominously, networking is under siege by commodifying agendas. We come to this in Article 23 on education.

Voice, mutualism and the precariat

In June 2013, the UK Labour Party announced support for a shift to contributory benefits. One of its leading MPs, Frank Field, said it was essential to mutualize contributory funds to avoid politicians 'getting their hands on them'. Presumably, a mutual fund would be run by its 'stakeholders'. But if elected politicians are not representatives of the stakeholders, who are? The risk is that the precariat would be excluded. The fund would be for the salariat and old core proletarians. Only if the Voice of the precariat were in the governance, setting and implementing the rules, would there be any hope of a progressive outcome.

* * *

In sum, with unions in transition if not decay, new Voice mechanisms are struggling to emerge. All those in the precariat or who think they may be should join or help to form the new bodies. Without them, their supplicant status will persist and the inequalities will grow.

In constructing alternatives, the governance structures must reflect the justice principles outlined in Chapter 4. Unless the security of the most insecure is improved by their actions, and improved by more than for others, these bodies will lack progressive legitimacy. Unless they strengthen rights and lessen the scope for discretionary benevolence, they will be co-opted. And unless they respect reproductive work, they will fail to promote dignified work or ecological priorities. Ultimately, their task is to abolish the precariat. But that is a long way down the road.

Articles 6–10: Reconstruct occupational communities

The dismantling of occupational guilds, started by neo-liberals and pursued by social democrats, must be overcome by the re-construction of occupational communities. The precariat would gain from reform of occupational licensing. It should be reduced and its governance overhauled, so that the precariat has Voice inside the boards regulating occupational practices. And collaborative bargaining must be actively promoted.

For hundreds of years, professional and craft guilds made occupations into communities, with standards of quality of work, codes of ethics, mechanisms for social protection and systems of education and promotion. Their faults lay in their strengths. They easily became bastions of privilege and rent-seeking closed communities, in which elites took and held onto power. However, they gave their members security and pride.

The neo-liberals highlighted their negative side and disliked their positive side, oriented to social solidarity and resistance to market forces. Governments under their influence proceeded to take away guild powers and constructed strict systems of licensing designed primarily to serve consumer and market interests rather than the workers inside those communities. As a result, power has been transferred to commercial interests and administrative bureaucracies.

They have overseen the disruption of internal modes of social mobility and promotion. In the process, they have introduced systems of class fragmentation, so that numerous occupations, including the great professions such as teaching, law, accountancy, engineering, medicine and architecture, have been restructured with elites, salariats, proficians, core workers and a precariat, with a proliferation of auxiliaries, adjuncts and assistant titles that symbolize inferiority and stunted mobility. Intra-occupational inequalities have grown, as have inter-occupational inequalities, with benefits and privileges for elites and salariats, and low insecure wages for precariat tracks.

Several reforms are needed.

Article 6: Set up an international occupational accreditation system

The right to practise one's skills and use one's qualifications is a precious economic right. It is probably weaker today than at any time in history. There is no international body charged with occupational regulation. The ILO has always been labourist, and has not allowed occupational bodies to be part of its governance. None of its 189 Conventions have dealt with occupational regulation. The World Bank and the World Trade Organization have dealt with occupational licensing without the mandate or expertise to do so.

An international body should be set up with the specific task of establishing general standards for occupations and harmonizing qualifications and accreditation systems, so that people can practise more easily in countries where they did not obtain their qualifications. Even within the European Union, whose member states are supposed to recognize each other's qualifications, recognition was automatic for only seven of the more than 800 professions identified by the European Commission and the rest required compliance with often complex local rules (Economist 2012b).

Article 7: Roll back licensing

Commodification of services has accelerated the shift from self-regulation by professions or crafts to state licensing (Standing 2009).

There were grounds for reforming the guilds, which tended to give monopoly rent to elites of the professions and crafts. But state regulation in the interests of consumers and commerce has accelerated de-professionalization and helped to create a class structure inside and across related occupational communities that resembles the globalization class structure.

Licensing blocks people from practising designated occupations, either because they do not have officially approved qualifications or because of some action they have done or not done. This leads to neglect of due process and to arbitrary decisions taken by those put in control over such matters as acceptance of qualifications, suspensions and 'excommunication' of individual practitioners. Entrenched insiders, in the elite or salariat of the occupation, can give their interests advantages and impose conditions on others, pushing them closer to the precariat. One example is a 'recency of practice' condition, as with nurses.

In the USA, nearly a third of workers require licences to practise their occupation, compared with one in 20 in the 1950s. Occupations requiring licences in some US states include florists, handymen, wrestlers, tour guides, frozen-dessert sellers, firework operatives, second-hand booksellers and interior designers. For comparison, the proportion of US workers who belong to a trade union was just 11 per cent in 2012. In the UK, 13 per cent of workers require licences, double the proportion in the late 1990s.

Licensing is justifiable if there are potential externalities, as when malpractice could have health or safety repercussions. But for most occupations it is unnecessary and is designed to boost the incomes of the licensed by restricting entry, or to force up prices, or to allow commercial firms to set standards from which they can profit. For many occupations licensing should be turned into voluntary accreditation. Then if you wish to risk obtaining the services of an unaccredited painter or plumber, for example, that would be your free choice.

Article 8: Mutualize occupational regulation

Occupations should not be regulated by boards consisting entirely of inside experts, because that leads to moral and immoral hazards (Summers 2007). Nor should they consist entirely of outsiders. Governments have tended to favour boards headed by outsiders to protect consumers and commercial interests. This is likely to lead to neglect of issues of concern to lower echelons of the occupation.

All interests should be represented on occupational boards. Occupational regulation is linked to the need for precariat Voice. For instance, privatizing public services easily allows an elite within professions to seize positional advantages. The UK government created National Health Service (NHS) clinical commissioning groups that can award contracts to private providers. Group members can bid for contracts themselves or via firms in which they have an interest. This is elite governance, licensed corruption and an outcome of state regulation for elite interests. Although board members must absent themselves from discussions of contracts from which they might benefit, they are in an advantageous position to draw up a successful bid. And colleagues on boards must work together after such decisions, making it likely they will do each other favours. There should be a rule that no board member can be a bidder. And the precariat, not just the elite of a profession, should be independently represented on such boards and be able to appoint its own representatives. Without democratic governance, immoral hazards will too often prevail.

Many youths cannot obtain basic economic rights because of domination of occupational governance by elites and the salariat. For example, in Italy, young lawyers must practise with an authorized law firm for two years before they can obtain a licence. In that period, a law firm can decide whether or not to pay them. Many work unpaid, living at home, disguising their employment and working long days. One told the *Nordic Labour Journal*:

> Don't mention my name, and don't take my picture. If the bar association gets wind of this I will never get my licence. This is a system built on recommendations, so it is important to do a good job and be willing to serve. I know of several people who got good grades in written exams but fail to get their licence because someone's delaying approving it, and those responsible claim they have failed their oral exams. It's no good going abroad. There are people with good exams from Harvard and other well-known universities who can't get their licence to practice law in Italy. The bar association is corrupt (Kvam 2010).

Such situations arise from having junior and insecure groups excluded from the governance structure. That should be changed. If there is an association or board with governance claims over a profession or craft, it should be a legal requirement that all levels of the occupation, including those on temporary contracts and trainees, should be represented on the boards. Ideally, they should have representation equal to their share of the occupation.

Article 9: Promote collaborative bargaining

In flexible labour systems, especially in services, some of the most vital bargaining should be between different occupations. Such bargaining should be formalized, with occupational associations encouraged to reach bargained agreements with complementary occupations (for example, doctors' associations might bargain with associations of nurses, paramedical and auxiliary staff). Too many occupational arrangements are made without the involvement of more vulnerable groups within the occupations or within the broader range of related occupational families. This has contributed to the stratification of occupations, with more pronounced precariat groups denied access to wage supplements, bonuses, benefits and avenues of mobility.

Article 10: Promote occupational social protection

Throughout history, occupations, notably the great professions, have operated their own systems of social protection for current and past members. In the labourist era, they were dismantled or converted into cosy arrangements for elites and long-serving salariats within professions. Now that the state has converted social protection into a more residual mode, based on means-testing and narrow conditional entitlement, it is vital that a multilayered social protection system is regenerated, one in which occupational social protection could play a subsidiary but useful role. This would also be a useful supplement to a universal basic income (see Article 25). To do so, occupational funds should be strengthened and made internally democratic, again with the precariat part of the occupation fully represented to ensure the system provides some protection for it, and that it is not yet another source of social-income inequality.

Articles 11–15: Stop class-based migration policy

As far as possible, migrants should have the same rights as everybody else. Demonization of migrants should be stopped. The class bias of migration policy should be reduced. Labour export regimes should be curbed and penalized.

We live in a migratory world. In 2013, 232 million people, 3.2 per cent of the global population, were living outside their country of origin, compared with 154 million in 1990. Many of us will be migrants at some stage or have relatives and friends who are. So most have an interest in ensuring that migration policy satisfies the five justice principles outlined earlier and passes the 'veil of ignorance' test. A country that applies inequitable measures against migrants may find that others will retaliate against its citizens. Sadly, utilitarian politicians have increased the denizen status of migrants. They are an easy target, especially those who have no vote.

Migrants comprise a high proportion of the global precariat. Depicted variously as villains (causing others' insecurity), victims (persecuted by local people and governments) and heroes (remitting money and goods to impoverished families and returning with skills and money to invest), they are the light infantry of global capitalism (Standing 2011).

In recognizing the migratory aspects of the global market system, it is necessary to retain a sense of proportion. In most countries, foreign-born residents are a significant but still small minority. The 2011 average for OECD countries was about 13 per cent. And a high share of migrants in the population is correlated with economic success, not low growth and high unemployment (Boubtane, Coulibaly and Rault 2013; Burke 2013). Claims that migration is linked to high unemployment are based simply on prejudice. France, Italy, the UK and the Netherlands, where populist politicians have fanned anti-migrant sentiment, have a below-average proportion of foreign-born residents. And a growing number of rich countries need migrants. In Italy, for example, women on average have 1.4 children, which is why the population has been shrinking and ageing for decades. Without migrants, its economy would have collapsed.

Anti-migrant rhetoric and imagery have nevertheless been successful. According to YouGov polls in 2012, 80 per cent of UK adults backed the government's cap on migrants; nearly 70 per cent wanted zero net immigration. They should be reminded that there are more Britons living or working in other countries than there are foreign migrants in the UK. And, since many are students who leave after their studies are completed, 70 per cent of immigrants stay less than five years (Goodhart 2013).

Growth of migration is associated with more people not having rights anywhere. Some lose them in their own country, but do not gain them where they stay or labour. This may even apply to those working in their own country for foreign firms, as they may not gain the social rights of workers in the firm's country while lacking those of workers in their own. And they lack agency or Voice in their dealings with employers and the state.

The Precariat Charter must deal with the most crucial aspects of migration, beginning with one sphere that is a long-term threat to the precariat everywhere.

Article 11: Curb labour export regimes

Labour export regimes are a new phenomenon integral to the global labour process. Some countries have allowed them to evolve. The classic case is The Philippines, which has long organized or facilitated the export of workers, notably Filipina maids, many lured into bonded labour via labour brokers. But China, Vietnam and some other countries have been doing something rather different, which is to transport thousands of workers *en masse* to labour on projects around the world (Standing 2011).

The practice of organizing mass labour export is linked to convict labour and quasi-slave labour. Governments should be persuaded to desist, and countries where this occurs should ban companies that transport workers in this fashion. So far, too many countries have allowed projects that bring in foreign capital, even when they know that the mass labour brought with them is unfree. This practice creates a wedge that lowers wages and working conditions of local workers, especially in the lower rungs of the labour market.

Article 12: Stop making migrants denizens

As long as nations exist, there will be differences in national citizenship and residency requirements. This does not justify treating people more unequally in terms of the five types of rights. The trend to reducing migrants' rights must be reversed.

While migrants commonly lack specific rights presumed to exist for citizens, they also face situations of double jeopardy and denial of due process. Thus, with respect to civil rights, migrants are often treated as 'guilty until proven innocent', subject to discretionary and discriminatory treatment and unable to demand due process before legal institutions. Among barriers being erected in the UK and Australia is denial of legal aid to challenge migration decisions. In the USA, the right to take the US Citizenship and Immigration Services to court was scrapped in 1996. Migrants are also often subject to prolonged periods of 'the law's delay'. The worst cases concern the world's asylum seekers, many of whom wait years in limbo awaiting determination of their status.

Migrants often lack economic rights, notably in being denied the right to practise their occupation. They lack cultural rights, including restrictions on religious practice and on membership of occupational communities. They are losing social rights, as governments make discriminatory changes to benefits and services. And they lack political rights, rarely having the right to vote or the right to stand for political office. Lack of political rights makes it easier for governments to remove other rights, gaining popularity with locals with little risk of electoral retribution. Gaining political rights for migrants should be a high priority.

Demonization of migrants, noted in Chapter 4, has gone with double standards and distorted imagery. One reason for demonization is that migration tends to be highly concentrated, including in capital cities where the political classes and media are also concentrated, making it easy for them to depict migration and superficially related problems as greater than the reality. For instance, migration to London has boomed. By 2012, more than one-third of Londoners were born abroad, compared with 18 per cent in 1987. But migration into London is far greater than into the rest of the UK. Two-fifths of all migrants live in London; in the rest of the country only 8 per cent of the population is foreign-born.

The focus on London gives migration a distorted image. The city is a magnet, helped by its history, English language, tradition of political liberalism, access to private schools, and the 'time zone'. The financial services sector largely consists of migrants. London is the sixth biggest 'French' city, with 400,000 French residents.

Similar pictures could be drawn for New York and other capital cities. The challenge is to mix and blend cultures. Sadly, some current social policies are intensifying ghetto-type trends. The consequences of increasing the number of denizens in these ways are worrying.

As migrants lose rights, some groups are particularly vulnerable to denization. In Europe, the persecution of Roma is widespread. In

2012, the new French socialist government arranged for dawn raids on Roma encampments on the outskirts of French cities, such as Lille, Lyon, Marseilles and Paris. Many Roma were deported. The interior minister claimed the camps were unsanitary and dangerous. When Nicolas Sarkozy was president, the left had protested against such actions, but then did the same. In 2011, thousands of Roma received *aide du retour*, averaging €300 each. This changed little, since it was an incentive to re-enter France. The Roma population has stayed stable, at below 20,000. But their civil rights have been weakened.

In Sweden, Roma are expelled just for begging, although begging per se is not banned. Elsewhere, more countries are introducing laws that prohibit vagrancy and begging, or penalize behaviour associated with homelessness such as sleeping, drinking or bathing in public places.

Migrants are losing civil rights by changes in legal treatment. In the UK, the former Labour government tightened the rules on foreign national prisoners (FNPs), making deportation automatic for any adult given a jail sentence of a year or more. The charity Bail for Immigration Detainees estimates that a quarter of their clients facing deportation came to the UK as children and know no other country. Until 2013, FNPs could obtain legal aid to appeal against deportation and one-third of appeals were successful. But from April 2013, FNPs have been denied legal aid. Few have the resources to take their own cases or hire lawyers.

Asylum seekers are the worst affected. In the UK, they come under the jurisdiction of the UK Border Authority (UKBA), which has been criticized for lengthy delays in processing asylum claims, leaving people in legal limbo for years on end. In the meantime, responsibility for housing them has been contracted out to three multinational companies – G4S, Serco and Clearel – that also provide immigration, detention and 'removal' (deportation) services to UKBA. They are notorious for their heavy-handed approach. One woman was evicted on the day she was due to give birth; this was known by the subcontractor, who claimed to be following orders of the contractor (G4S), which in turn said that evictions require UKBA's prior approval. The UKBA claimed not to know of individual cases. Once again, there is no due process. The contractors have power over asylum seekers and no accountability.

The control is suffocating and coercive. If someone stays away from their hostel for more than 14 nights in a six-month period, they are deemed not to be in need of support and have benefits withdrawn. They have no money, no space in which to live decently, no friendships, no right to work for income, no civil life.

The politics of deterrence means that more asylum seekers are criminalized. Private security firms make huge profits from contracts to run immigrant removal centres, where detainees have fewer rights than people held in ordinary prisons. And private security escorts gain contracts to enforce deportation policy.

Another group that has suffered denization is the army of 100 million migrant domestics around the world. Wages go unpaid, physical and sexual abuse is common and goes unpunished, long hours of work are required, minimum wage laws are ignored, and so on. They are denizens in distress, often without any rights. In 2011, 92 years after its founding and following years of tortuous negotiation between employer organizations, trade unions and governments, the ILO adopted a Convention Concerning Decent Work for Domestic

Workers. It merely encourages governments and employers to limit domestics' working hours and guarantees a weekly day off, a minimum wage and protection from violent employers, all basic civil rights. But some employer bodies, including the Confederation of British Industry, voted against it. Worse, the British government abstained, claiming that regulating domestics' working hours and health and safety would be too 'onerous' for employers and governments. Yet ILO Conventions, while they have moral force, only bind countries whose governments ratify them. The UK posturing was ideological.

Foreign students are another group whose denizen status is growing. In the UK, a contradiction arose between a commitment to cut migration and the desire to use the higher education system to earn foreign exchange. One proposal was to declare students as 'temporary visitors', not migrants. But as the globalization of education advances, pressure for harmonization of rights should grow.

Finally, internal migration has also generated more denizens. In 2012, there were over 250 million migrant workers inside China. Of these, 160 million had no rights in the urban areas where they were employed because they lacked the *hukou*, the household registration document granting residency rights. Without a *hukou*, they have no entitlement to health care or other benefits available to legal residents, nor can they send their children to local schools. So, many leave their children behind, a breach of the human right to be with their family.

Article 13: Stop class-based migration policy

One under-appreciated aspect of globalization is the intensification of class-based migration policy that gives preference and preferential treatment to people with money. Migration has become more explicitly part of commercial policy. People are welcomed or rejected depending on whether they seem good commercial prospects. This is regressive and utilitarian. There is no ethical justification.

Class-based policy even extends to tourism. Governments have been tightening checks on visitors who might overstay. Entering many countries has become more difficult and unpleasant. Australia demands that local sponsors put up as much as AU$15,000 (£9,000) as security that family visitors from 'high-risk' countries will leave. This is collective punishment. It is also part of class-based migration policy.

The UK has increased fees for visa applications, doubling the charge for short-term student visas and raising the cost of applications for indefinite leave to remain on behalf of a dependent family member (often a frail elderly parent) to well over £2,000. Meanwhile, prospective investors and entrepreneurs pay lower fees. The immigration minister said the fee structure was designed so as 'to continue to attract those businesses, migrants and visitors who most benefit the UK'.

Permitted residency in many countries is now determined on class lines. Several EU countries, including Spain, Portugal, Greece and Ireland, grant non-EU citizens residency visas (and so the right to live and travel within the EU) if they invest or buy property to the tune of €500,000 or more. Apart from raising the cost of applications, the UK has tightened its already restrictive rules on family reunification, which accounted for 18 per cent of non-EU in-migrants in 2010. Until 2012, someone wishing to bring a spouse into the country for settlement had to show earnings of over £5,500 plus housing costs. This has now been raised to £18,600, more if the couple has children. Oxford University's Migration Observatory estimated that 47 per cent of British jobholders would not qualify to bring in a family member, nor would 58 per cent of those aged 20 to 30 or 61 per cent of women. The class bias was clear. The move is also likely to be tested in court as infringing Article 8 of the European Convention on Human Rights, which deals with the right to a family life.

A number of countries are making it easier for migrant 'entrepreneurs'. Chile's Start-Up Chile programme, introduced in 2010, gives foreigners start-up grants of $40,000, without taking equity in return; this has led to an influx of hundreds of firms to what has been dubbed Chilecon Valley. Canada launched a Start-Up visa in 2013, available to any foreigner with CA$75,000 to invest in a new business. The USA also offers special visas for investors, but only for the elite, since they must guarantee an initial investment of $1 million, or half that if investing in a depressed neighbourhood. The annual quota of 10,000 visas is seldom filled. Britain offers visas to people with promising commercial ideas who attract £50,000 of venture capital to back them. Singapore requires $40,000. New Zealand does not demand a given sum, but grants permanent residency after two years if the business is 'beneficial to New Zealand'.

Australia, New Zealand, Canada and the UK use point systems to give priority to skilled migrants, increasing inequality of opportunity. Others, such as the USA, have special visas for skilled workers. China offers skilled returnees free homes and cash to buy furniture.

The UK coalition government entered office promising to cut migration to 'tens of thousands' a year. But as most migrants come from other EU countries and have a right to enter freely, the government was obliged to focus on non-EU students, an important source of university funding. It tried to limit their 'right to work' on graduation, restricting their economic rights. This was particularly unfair on poorer students, facing study costs averaging £11,800 a year. Many wished to stay simply to earn enough to pay off debts. Given the negative effect on student numbers, the government hastily changed course, not for principled reasons but for commercial reasons. After giving up on students, it turned to restricting economic and social rights of migrants already in the country.

Internal migration policy can also be class-based and regressive. Again China leads the way, with its class-based migration regulations. When deciding to grant selected *hukou* permits, some cities such as Guangzhou and Shenzhen now give applicants points for investing and owning property in the city.

Class-based migration policy offends the Rights-not-Charity Principle and the Security Difference Principle. It is utilitarian, rationalized as part of commercial policy. But it is neither ethical nor consistent with a global market system. Why should elites be given subsidies and rights that others are denied?

Empathize, don't demonize

In 2013, the new Pope Francis visited the Italian island of Lampedusa, the landing place for tens of thousands of migrants making the hazardous sea crossing from Tunisia and Libya. Thousands more, crowded into flimsy craft, have died at sea. Two years before, Silvio Berlusconi, then Italy's Prime Minister, went to Lampedusa and played the populist card, saying he would expel the migrants (and build a holiday home on the island). The Pope played on empathy instead, calling the migrants 'brothers and sisters of ours trying to escape difficult situations to find some serenity and peace' and praising the coastguard for saving lives: 'You offered an example of solidarity' (Squires 2013). (In response, one hard-line member of the anti-immigrant Northern League was reported as saying: 'I'd be happy if one of the boats sank.')

The islanders had reacted to the migrants' plight with generosity and tolerance, reserving their protests for the authorities. They welcomed the Pope with a banner emblazoned 'Welcome among the *ultimi*', a word implying both furthest and least. The Lampedusans had shown empathy; they understood the migrants' suffering.

End phoney citizenship tests

Citizenship requires rites of passage. Becoming a citizen means gaining the same rights as others. The route to that status should be transparent and fair; any test or set of procedures should surely be such that the average, normal existing citizen could pass. In reality, citizenship tests are increasingly a discriminatory obstacle course. In the USA a survey by Xavier University suggested that over one-third of Americans would fail their country's naturalization test (Kuper 2012). The German equivalent poses constitutional questions that few Germans could answer unless they had studied law at university. The UK requires people to know all about the Magna Carta and in

2012 was considering adding questions on Robert Browning, a great poet now little read. The French test asks about Brigitte Bardot, though her glory days are long past. In the Netherlands, aspiring citizens must watch an *integratiefilm* featuring a gay wedding and bare-breasted women, inspiring the far-right Danish People's Party to propose topless women in the Danish equivalent.

Article 14: Treat migrants as labour market equals

Although migrants in some countries have above-average unemployment rates, they have been obtaining an increasing share of employment. One UK commentator said the only difference between the Conservative and Labour parties was that the former blamed high benefits for making Britons unwilling to take low-paying jobs, whereas Labour thought that the 'nasty, brutish and short-term' jobs induced firms to prefer migrants.

In 2012, Ed Miliband, the Labour leader, proposed that firms employing more than 25 per cent migrants should be required to inform the local Jobcentre Plus, as a way of putting pressure on companies to cut the number of migrant employees. Miliband also said employment agencies should be banned from favouring foreigners. It was part of an effort to rebrand Labour as the party of nationalism, to appeal to the core working class and salariat. Labour's former Home Office minister added that recruitment agencies should be blocked from supplying only workers from particular countries.

Why should this be illegal? Provided recruitment complies with non-discrimination legislation, it is for the firm demanding labour to decide whether to accept the workers supplied. What principle is respected by banning agencies from supplying Chinese chefs to Chinese restaurants? No doubt policymakers would make exceptions. But it highlights a problem with utilitarian policymaking. Arbitrary unfair decisions pile up. Would Labour penalize agencies that supplied only British workers? Soon, there would be subsidies for supplying locals, penalties for supplying aliens.

Finally, equality in labour markets requires revision of occupational licensing, which gives governments the means of controlling and reshaping migration, since they can refuse to recognize some qualifications and recognize others. As emphasized in Article 7, occupational licensing must be rolled back to give migrants equal economic rights.

Article 15: Stop benefit discrimination

In the austerity era, governments have been chipping away at migrants' social rights, particularly those who cannot vote. A progressive strategy must oppose this and make the principled case for equal treatment. If a benefit or entitlement to a service is cut for one group, it will soon be cut for others.

The Spanish government has led the way in eroding migrants' social rights. Under a health care law of 2012, 'illegal' immigrants lost the right to public health care beyond emergencies, pregnancies and births. Those suffering from chronic illnesses, without a Spanish health card, must pay high prices for medicines and treatments. In 2013, the UK government made a similar move, announcing a registration and tracking system for the National Health Service (NHS) to check on migrant status. Non-EU migrants with visas for less than five years will have to pay an upfront levy of £200 to qualify for free NHS treatment, in addition to higher visa charges, while short-term visitors from outside the EU will be charged for most treatment, including emergency care. What if all countries applied restrictions and imposed higher costs on migrants? Rather than a world of mobility, cost barriers could turn millions into weaker denizens. These moves are regressive, penalizing low-earning migrants; the rich would pay for private health care anyhow.

The UK Labour Party has also called for a review of immigrants' access to benefits and the 'local connection' rules for social housing waiting lists, further reducing the social rights of migrants. Yet although 370,000 foreign nationals are claiming benefits, proportionately fewer migrants claim them than Britons. When in government, New Labour offered unemployed migrants one-way tickets to their country of origin, using a crime service firm. Spain, Japan and Denmark offer migrants cash to return to their countries. In 2011, in violation of EU agreements, the Dutch Liberal Party announced plans to deport Eastern Europeans who had been unemployed for more than three months, and to require them to have been in the Netherlands for at least five years before being eligible to claim unemployment benefits. Such laws are bound to prompt anti-migrant sentiment. Policies of unequal treatment always do.

Avoid social apartheid

One outcome of utilitarian social policy is that the deprived are steered into ghettos of cumulative disadvantage. Targeted and punitive social policy intensifies this, making migrants easy scapegoats. It has affected some unlikely countries. Sweden has allowed its migrants and refugees to crowd into urban ghettos where unemployment is concentrated. In Rosengård, Malmö, once a beacon of the Social Democrats' housebuilding programme, only 38 per cent of residents have a job. Chronic insecurity and deprivation led to riots and the torching of sheds and cars, an anomic reaction to hopelessness.

In Sweden overall, only half non-European migrants have a job, compared with 84 per cent of natives; migrants make up nearly half the unemployed, a quarter of all prisoners and half those serving over five years. In sum, Swedish policies have created a social apartheid and the strains are showing. Ghettos, not migrants, breed social dysfunction. France with its *banlieues* and the UK with its new housing and benefit policies are moving in a similar direction.

* * *

A progressive countermovement to overcome the demonization of migrants and class-based migration policy must be based on values and respect for the justice principles. One priority must be to support and build migrant Voice organizations. One pioneer is Building and Wood Workers' International (BWI) in Malaysia, which has developed a Migrant Workers' Rights Passport and opened an SMS helpline to enable migrants to solicit advice.

Article 16: Ensure due process for all

Due process is a fundamental human right, recognized down the millennia. It is needed to protect citizens from the arbitrary power of the state or its proxies and ensure that other rights can be protected and enforced. Due process rights, as enshrined in the Universal Declaration of Human Rights, require citizens to have access to courts, tribunals and other independent institutions that resolve disputes according to fair procedures, and to be granted effective remedies if their rights are violated.

The subject who is truly loyal to the Chief Magistrate, will neither advise nor submit to arbitrary measures.

Junius (1812)

Access to justice has always been a class issue. But a feature of the neo-liberal hegemony has been the deliberate shrinking of access to justice and due process for the precariat, in legal proceedings, in the labour market and in the benefits system.

Nobody should be required or expected to submit to arbitrary decisions made by unaccountable bureaucrats. It is the discretionary power given to officials dealing with the precariat that is so infuriating, so infantilizing and so stressful. It is the source of more petty injustice than any other aspect of the modern state. And it is the source of inequality.

Recall T. H. Marshall's opening paragraph of his celebrated essay on *Citizenship and Social Class* (1950), referring to what he called the first element of citizenship:

> The civil element is composed of the rights necessary for individual freedom – liberty of the person, freedom of speech, thought and faith, the right to own property and to conclude valid contracts, and the right to justice. The last is of a different order from the others, because it is the right to defend and assert all one's rights on terms of equality with others and by due process of law.

Due process means that nobody should have rights suspended or confiscated, or taken by other means, without a legal process that is the same for all. Unfortunately, even when claimed as a constitutional principle of equality, this robust principle can be abused *de facto*: nominally a group such as the precariat could be said to have the same rights as others – and equal rights to defend them – but in practice be denied them because the process is too complex, too opaque, too costly or too stigmatizing to be feasible.

Due process has a proud history. The judicial principle that a person is innocent until proven guilty goes back to ancient times. The Magna Carta of 1215 asserted that all free men were entitled to be judged by their peers – their equals – and that even a sovereign was not above the law. The assertion of the right of due process was at the heart of that great document. The unifying factor behind the insurrection that led to the Magna Carta had been the difficulty of obtaining redress for the king's abuses of power and abuses by royal officials, that is, the government. Eight hundred years later, Magna Carta's clause 20 still resonates:

For a trivial offence, a free man shall be fined only in proportion to the degree of his offence, and for a serious offence correspondingly, but not so heavily as to deprive him of his livelihood... None of these fines shall be imposed except by the assessment on oath of reputable men of the neighbourhood.

Witnesses and assessments made under oath, no condemnation without due process and nothing disproportional – all this was strengthened by later clauses, with the 'we' referring to the king:

38. In future no official shall place a man on trial upon his own unsupported statement, without producing credible witnesses to the truth of it.

39. No free man shall be seized or imprisoned, or stripped of his rights or possessions, or outlawed or exiled, or deprived of his standing in any other way, nor will we proceed with force against him, or send others to do so, except by the lawful judgement of his equals or by the law of the land.

40. To no one will we sell, to no one deny or delay right or justice.

Read clause 38 as saying that no official or bureaucrat should be allowed to declare someone guilty of something without witnesses or proof beyond reasonable doubt. Read clause 39 as saying that nobody should be declared guilty of something without a lawful process before equals and by reference to specific laws. Read clause 40 as saying that nobody should be subject to delayed justice, reflecting the time-honoured principle that 'justice delayed is justice denied'. Sadly, all those clauses have been wilfully abused by governments in the period in which the precariat has become a global force.

Winston Churchill described the Charter of Liberties – the Magna Carta – as 'the charter of every self-respecting man at any time in any land'. His political heirs should revisit it. On due process, matters went forward in the 1688–9 English Bill of Rights – and its Scottish equivalent, the Claim of Right Act – that became part of the UK's informal constitution, when it declared that all 'grants and promises of fines or forfeitures' were null and void without prior conviction.

This commitment to respect due process was further encapsulated in the French Declaration of the Rights of Man and of the Citizen in 1789, the US Constitution and Bill of Rights, and the UN's Universal Declaration of Human Rights and its progeny. Fundamental to all those great constitutional documents was the principle that there must be a legal process before individuals or groups can be sanctioned; this must entail a pre-determined legitimized procedure, by which an accused person must first know the charges, then have the resources necessary to contest them, and then have a decision on guilt or innocence determined by independent persons. Yet respect for due process has been systematically eroded, with virtual impunity. This is not just a rich-country concern. A study by Martin Whyte (2010) showed that China's farmers were most angered by 'procedural injustices' and lack of legal channels to obtain redress.

The failure of due process can reflect measures that block people from obtaining rights, measures to suspend their rights, measures to weaken access to such rights, or measures to deny rights to those who previously had them. Policies and institutional practices also need to respect the Rights-not-Charity and the Paternalism Test

Principles, outlined in Chapter 4. The former states that practices are unjust if they strengthen the unaccountable authority of government officials, or their privatized surrogates, thereby weakening the rights of recipients. The latter states that controls applied to some groups that are not applied to the most free in society are also unjust. When actual practices appear to go against those principles, there should be an absolute rule that they at least respect due process.

In the neo-liberal era, the erosion of due process has happened piecemeal, with often small changes barely noticed at the time adding up to an edifice of unaccountable decisions and actions. Many of those actions also hit other groups. But they matter most to the precariat, and only this group will have the critical mass of affected people to constitute a social force for change.

Due process is relevant to all five forms of rights. Lack of legal aid denies people the civil right to a fair trial. The denial of social rights has become so extensive that most benefits have ceased to become rights at all. Benefits can be suspended without due process, and people can be criminalized in trying to avoid precarity traps. The spread of occupational licensing, and the proliferation of associated tests and criteria, can block people from practising the occupation for which they are qualified, denying them an economic right. Respect for due process in this sphere is now the exception rather than the rule.

Political rights are increasingly being lost or weakened without due process. For example, many more acts are today regarded as criminal than used to be the case and, in some countries, including the UK and India, prisoners lose the right to vote as well. In some parts of the USA they lose the right to vote for ever, even after they have served their term in jail. That affects lower-income groups more than members of the salariat and core workers, and as such tilts the political process in a conservative direction. *De facto* too, being criminalized through a conviction for even a minor misdemeanour may have long-lasting adverse effects, for example, ruling out any prospect of a political career or public office.

Due process in legal proceedings

It is a fundamental principle of any justice system that all should have equal and good opportunity to defend themselves against any charges or to obtain redress for a violation of their legal rights. Obtaining legal representation is expensive. So in industrialized countries the welfare state has traditionally provided subsidized legal aid for those on low incomes. The neo-liberal project has not looked kindly on this particular subsidy; it goes to the most insecure.

Indeed, inequality before the law has intensified. In the UK, the coalition government has tightened means-testing for legal aid in civil cases, including cases involving employment and family law, and, with few exceptions, legal aid has been withdrawn altogether for people with housing, benefits, debt and immigration problems.

Under government proposals published in 2013, those facing criminal charges were to be denied the right to choose their own lawyer and legal aid fees were to be cut, with legal aid services put out to tender. Moreover, a planned disproportionate reduction in fees for defendants who plead not guilty and opt for a jury trial would create a financial incentive for those appointed lawyers to put pressure on clients to plead guilty even when they were not. More innocent people would be put at risk of a miscarriage of justice.

The rationale cited by the UK Justice Secretary, Chris Grayling, revealed the utilitarian bias and lack of respect for his fellow citizens and denizens:

> I don't believe that most people who find themselves in our criminal justice system are great connoisseurs of legal skills. We know the people in our prisons and who come into our courts often come from the most difficult and challenged backgrounds (Bowcott 2013).

He was saying that 'They' were not competent to make choices for themselves, and could not consult somebody they trusted to recommend legal counsel. It revealed a lack of compassion and empathy.

Protests by the legal profession subsequently forced the minister into an about-turn on the free choice of solicitor, but political opposition was muted as the former Labour government was also responsible for chipping away at the legal aid system. The outcome of the envisaged reforms will be cut-price low-quality services for the precariat, provided by a legal-aid precariat of low-paid paralegals. Sure enough, among those planning to tender for criminal legal aid were a road haulage company, a private security firm, and Tesco, the supermarket chain. The reforms mark a further advance in the commodification of legal services started by the Labour government with its Legal Services Act, nicknamed the 'Tesco Law' because it allows legal services to be offered in supermarkets. The whittling away of due process is accelerating, along with the de-professionalization of a major profession.

The UK is not alone in depriving the precariat of due process. Cutting legal aid for disadvantaged groups is a global trend of the neo-liberal utilitarian state. As the UN's Special Rapporteur on the Independence of Judges and Lawyers, in giving vent to the sense of alarm, remarked in May 2013:

> Legal aid is both a right in itself and an essential precondition for the exercise and enjoyment of a number of human rights… Beneficiaries of legal aid should include any person who comes into contact with the law and does not have the means to pay for counsel… it is of paramount importance that legal aid schemes be autonomous, independent, effective, sustainable and easily available in order to ensure that they serve the interests of those who need financial support to have access to justice on an equal basis with others (Office of the UN High Commissioner for Human Rights 2013).

Due process in labour market policies

During the twentieth century, a stream of legislative measures increased labour security, giving employees so-called rights, notably employment security. The neo-liberal agenda of flexibility has rolled back the laws and institutions giving such security. Many of these reforms have increased the scope for discretionary decisions that disadvantage the vulnerable, depriving them of their right to due process.

For example, respect for the employment contract means that a 'permanent' employee should not be dismissed without due cause and only after agreed procedures have been followed. Anybody who believes their employment contract has been unfairly broken should have a feasible, timely and affordable opportunity to contest the action. If one party can afford the protracted process and the other cannot, or would face a greater risk of unsustainable costs, this surely offends the Security Difference Principle.

However, in 2013, the British government introduced legislation requiring employees claiming unfair dismissal to pay fees to take their case to a tribunal, which up to then had been a free service. The ostensible argument was that it would deter frivolous claims that waste scarce public funds and cost employers time and money. But there is little doubt that the primary objectives were to strengthen the bargaining position of employers *vis-à-vis* employees and to reduce public spending. Whatever the reasons, a precious civil right was weakened – all the more so given the earlier increase from one to two years in the length of time people must be employed by a firm before they can bring an unfair dismissal claim at all.

Due process in state benefits

The precariat is most exposed to denial of due process in trying to obtain and retain access to state benefits. In many countries, governments have made that harder and harder, with more severe penalties for minor deviations from arbitrary rules. In doing so, they have turned the system of social protection into a stressful, humiliating and stigmatizing process. And it is not just the supplicants who are affected. Those required to operate the procedures are often victims in their daily grind, dealing with the precariat and being part of it themselves.

Many governments, including nominally progressive social democratic governments, have required the unemployed and others to behave in certain ways in order to have entitlement to state benefits. Lawrence Mead, called in to advise the UK's coalition government, has stated openly that one motive has been to make unemployment an unpleasant experience that individuals would not wish to prolong or repeat (Mead 1986). The traditional idea of 'unemployment insurance benefits' has been discarded step by step. The elements of solidarity and compassion have been jettisoned.

In the UK, the renaming of unemployment benefit as 'jobseeker's allowance' signalled how a social right was being turned into an instrument of state charity. With insurance, you pay to cover a risk, and receive a payment if the risk occurs. You do not have to report weekly or daily to an insurance office, or constantly prove you have done this or that action with no relevance to the prior mishap. But when policymakers change the name to an allowance, they turn the meaning from a right into an object of bureaucratic discretion. In doing so, respect for due process is eroded.

One aspect is the requirement that the unemployed must not only constantly look for jobs (irrespective of whether there are any feasible jobs on offer) but prove they are looking in ways that satisfy the bureaucrats, even if informal methods through community networks, for example, would be more effective. In Australia, the UK and other countries, welfare claimants must keep a diary of where they have looked for work and must produce the diary for regular inspection. They have to attend interviews with job centres on request, at any time. Not complying can result in termination of benefits.

In the UK, even tougher sanctions against benefit claimants were introduced in 2012. Under the new rules, not looking for a job intensively enough leads to loss of benefit for one month for the first 'offence', three months for the second. A higher-level sanction for someone who refuses a job or is deemed to have left one without good reason is three months for the first 'offence', six months for the second, and three years subsequently. Who will decide, and on what grounds? It will be a government-appointed agency with a mandate, explicit or implicit, to find ways of reducing the number receiving benefits.

The Social Security Advisory Committee, an official body responsible for monitoring welfare reforms, worried that such severe penalties could result in 'claimants turning to the black economy, crime or prostitution' and 'would not incentivise someone to enter employment and would almost certainly damage children in a family where income is severely reduced for a prolonged period' (Social Security Advisory Committee 2012). American research was cited as evidence that

> severe conditionality can result in families becoming disconnected from society: they are neither in work nor receiving state support. Given the government focus on supporting families with children in their early years, respondents urged this level of sanction should be used with extreme caution (p. 96).

The committee did not challenge the legitimacy of punishment, even though it noted that those on the receiving end could be disorganized or have lost confidence or skills. Such sanctions tend to be meted out to the most vulnerable, intensifying their vulnerability. And pushing people into jobs they neither want nor feel capable of performing may result in deeper depression and incapacity later. Responding to the committee's report, a spokesperson for the Department for Work and Pensions (DWP) said:

> Under universal credit, all jobseekers will sign up to a personal claimant commitment and receive individual help and support so that they can look for and take up work – as they are required to do now. We expect most claimants to meet that commitment, and only those who fail to engage with us or play by the rules will be sanctioned (Boffey 2012).

This represents a further infringement of civil and social rights. Without doubt, such commitments will be onerous and enforced on people at a desperate time of their lives. And free legal help is no longer available to challenge either commitments or sanctions.

In early 2013, I received an email from someone who had become unemployed. Part of it reads as follows (reproduced with permission):

> I am part of the academic flexibilised labour market. I applied to claim Jobseekers Allowance in January and have had four meetings to get the application started and to keep this entitlement... The utter loss of soul for those working in the Jobcentre as well for those attending is palpable to me... My 'advisor' is shackled to a bureaucracy that dehumanises him and me. He sits across from me populating fields in a computer. He has no interest or incentive to see me as a person...

Last week he informed me that in three months I would be asked to attend a two-day workshop on how to use Twitter, LinkedIn and Facebook to look for jobs. My jaw dropped. Two days? Today I explained to him that I am considering retraining. He said, 'Don't you have enough qualifications?' He asked for my job-seeking workbook in which I am to log all the steps I am taking to find employment. I had written three. Even after explaining all that I am doing to find employment and improve my CV he said, 'You need six things.' He then fixed my next appointment. It is in two weeks. I will be with my two young children visiting their grand-parents. He told me I am not allowed to travel while claiming jobseekers allowance. I asked why. His response, 'It's not allowed.'

This email conveys all too vividly the supplicant nature of the system that the politicians have created. It also shows how both sides are dehumanized in being forced to adjust to unwelcome insecurity, demeaning both their humanity and their citizenship status.

If, as we should, we see unemployment as a mishap that is not the fault of individuals, we would wish to make the experience of unemployment as painless as possible, and neither stigmatizing nor humiliating. We would wish to provide a benefit to make dignified survival possible and provide services that people could use or not according to their perceived needs and aspirations. The trend away from that perspective must be reversed.

Nudging undermining due process

Use of 'nudging' has become integral to the utilitarian state. It threatens due process as well. Thus in 2012, the UK's DWP piloted a scheme requiring the unemployed to complete a detailed questionnaire drawn up by the government's Behavioural Insight Team ('Nudge Unit'), which was based on a longer one devised by the Ohio-based VIA Institute on Character. The questionnaire came to public attention because at least one person – a single mother of two with low literacy skills – was threatened with loss of her jobseeker's benefits unless she completed the online test within three days. Among the questions she and others were required to answer was one asking for graded answers to the statement: 'I have not created anything of beauty in the last year.'

VIA promptly claimed that the Nudge Unit had used a flawed shortened version of their questionnaire, which the DWP had told jobseekers was 'scientifically shown to find people's strengths', a dubious claim even in the best of circumstances. But it is irrelevant that the questionnaire was 'scientifically' poor. It was the lack of due process that was improper.

Where is the law authorizing withdrawal of benefits from an unemployed woman if she does not complete an intrusive questionnaire on her strengths and weaknesses? What moral reasoning gives bureaucrats this discretionary power over people struggling with the indignity of unemployment in a hostile environment? Those in trying personal circumstances, embarrassed by failure, desperate for an income to sustain themselves, should not be exposed to further humiliations by such treatment. The practices derive from a utilitarian, moralistic perspective.

Community service as social punishment

A different aspect of social benefits concerns the treatment of people convicted of petty offences. Following Germany, in 1973 Britain introduced community service orders as an alternative to custodial sentences, initially on a pilot basis. The practice has since been adopted in much of Europe, Australasia, the USA and parts of Asia. Community service was conceived as mild punishment for someone convicted of a misdemeanour, the objective being to rehabilitate. Studies showed that by comparison with a prison sentence, it reduced the probability of reoffending.

At the outset, community service orders were determined by the courts. They required someone to be charged with an offence, tried before properly constituted authorities, and convicted by a court with constituted powers to make such a decision. When a local bureaucrat or commercial company makes such a decision these days, none of those conditions apply. As the first probation officer to implement a community service order in the UK lamented, the utilitarian bent of modern policymakers has turned community service into community punishment, community payback and a new zone of unpaid labour, fostering simmering resentment among those punished (Harding 2013).

The stigma associated with this moralistic policy is reminiscent of the excesses of the nineteenth century. 'Today's offenders wear fluorescent tabards over their clothes to indicate they are offenders, easily recognisable by members of the public,' said John Harding, that saddened pioneer of community service. And the 'service' has been privatized, contracted out to a profit-making firm (Serco), which has been given the discretionary power to direct those who have been convicted in ways it can choose, without being subject to any legal process.

In 2013, the UK government put out half its probation services to private tender. A measure to ensure that every community service order contained a punitive element was also introduced. By giving profit-making private firms discretionary powers in the administration of justice, the state deprives citizens of their civil rights.

Due process in social protests

The right to protest is another area where due process is being circumvented so as to allow the state to penalize the precariat. After the riots of August 2011, the British Prime Minister justified drawing up plans to intervene more in family life, saying 'We've got to be less sensitive to the charge that this is about interfering or nannying.' He went on to support evicting people from social housing, while the Work and Pensions Secretary of State advocated cutting the benefits of those participating in anti-social activity.

The courts are the proper place to decide on penalties, as long as they are constituted so as to be impartial. This was clearly not the case following the riots. Sentences were absurdly out of proportion to the severity of the crimes supposedly committed – for example, six months in jail for taking a £3.50 bottle of water – and summary justice was administered through hastily convened courts reminiscent of the shameful treatment of protesters in the eighteenth and nineteenth centuries.

It is not just in Britain where these trends are growing, so far largely unopposed. In Spain, the government has moved to make unions liable for damage that may occur in public protests, as if unions are social police. No legal process is used to determine guilt in such circumstances. And a report by the International Network of Civil Liberties Organizations (2013) documents how democracies around the world are moving to suppress even peaceful protests by force and/or criminalize dissent, providing examples from the UK, USA, Canada, Israel, Egypt, Argentina, South Africa, Kenya and Hungary.

* * *

The widespread and growing abuse of due process makes it one of the most important challenges for the precariat. One way to give due process more respect by all concerned would be to impose equivalent penalties on those private profit-making agencies or public bureaucrats who take away benefits from supplicants, if it is subsequently proven that they did so incorrectly. They should be penalized to the same extent as they penalize the supplicants.

Would recourse to the law help the precariat gain due process? Most analysis suggests the law courts favour the rich. But there are three types of legal case, all of which are needed to strengthen the egalitarian right to due process (Brinks and Gauri 2012). 'Regulation' cases force governments to change the rules to improve access to a basic right. This type of case offers most hope for the precariat, simply because the benefits are universal. 'Obligation' cases change the behaviour of those obliged to provide a rights-based service. An example is a judge spelling out what rights to information patients have in medical treatment. 'Provision' cases demand some new good or service for supplicants to enable them to realize a right. The value of provision cases depends on how broad in scope the ruling is.

In the end, respect for due process is vital if we are to reverse the *de facto* erosion of all forms of rights and to check the tendency for many to become denizens without realizing it. Using legal means to assert due process is only one way of reversing the trend. Demanding political action is the most important.

Article 17: Remove poverty traps and precarity traps

Poverty traps and precarity traps should be removed, failing which people should be allowed to adapt their behaviour accordingly without penalty or sanction. Those penalized by precarity traps linked to the implementation of the social assistance system should be compensated financially.

Governments have created disincentives to labour for those in the precariat and then depicted them as lazy and 'scrounging'. They reduced average and marginal tax rates for high- and middle-income earners, claiming these groups needed more incentives to labour, to save, to invest, and to 'remain in the country'. Meanwhile, social benefits were converted into a predominantly means-tested system. This inevitably led to a plethora of behaviour tests (as well as means tests) to determine eligibility because, in the process, the precariat was confronted with marginal tax rates of 80 per cent, 90 per cent or even more, removing the incentive to labour deemed so important for others.

When in opposition, Iain Duncan Smith, who became the UK minister in charge of welfare reform after 2010, produced a report that concluded it was 'rational' for people not to take jobs in these circumstances. In government, he promptly condemned them and introduced penalties for not taking jobs. People are being punished for being rational.

The UK is not alone in drifting into this situation. What is happening can be seen as a combination of poverty traps and precarity traps. The precariat suffers from both to an extraordinary degree. They should be abolished, along with the abuse of people caught in them who are merely trying to function in dysfunctional situations.

Poverty traps

At the height of the welfare state era, before globalization took off, the mainstay of all European social security systems was social or national insurance, the so-called Bismarck and Beveridge variants. Everybody in employment supposedly contributed, or had contributions paid for them, into a fund from which benefits were paid to those who experienced what Beveridge in the 1940s called 'interruption or loss of earning power'.

Under these systems, those with a low risk of adverse outcomes (unemployment, sickness, accidents, etc.) subsidized those who faced high risks. That was the essence of the contributory principle, and why the systems were called solidaristic. Although never very progressive in terms of reducing inequality, they worked reasonably well provided a majority of people were contributing, or were benefiting from contributions paid by or for a 'breadwinner' partner. For their legitimacy they required a broad social consensus in which a majority felt they might need support from the system at some time.

Once labour markets became more flexible, fewer people gained entitlement to full benefits because of gaps in their contribution record. And once those in the salariat realized that they were unlikely to need support, and that their incomes enabled them to opt out of the system, the social insurance mechanisms ran into trouble.

Thus began the road to means-testing, which the national insurance system had been created to avoid as stigmatizing and inefficient. Means tests rest on the simple idea that benefits should be targeted to those in financial need, 'the poor'. While that sounds reasonable to the ordinary person, targeting raises awkward issues. Besides the difficulty of measuring poverty and identifying the poor, how does the system deal with someone who 'chooses' to be poor? And means-testing creates a poverty trap. Suppose an unemployed person receives £100 a week in unemployment and housing benefit. She then takes a low-paid part-time job at £100 a week. If her benefits are lost as a result, the net gain is zero. She would be labouring for nothing.

Governments have tried to respond by tapering benefit withdrawals and introducing so-called 'in-work' benefits. But they have failed to overcome the poverty trap. In 2010 in the UK, many people were facing income deduction rates of over 80 per cent; the government claimed that its planned 'universal credit' (bundling benefits) would reduce the average deduction rate to 65 per cent. In Germany, the average income deduction rate for people moving from benefits to jobs was over 80 per cent, as it was in Denmark and in various other countries (Gautie and Schmitt 2010). In the USA some low-income families can face a marginal tax rate of 95 per cent (Kearney et al. 2013).

A reason for the poverty trap becoming so pervasive is that the precariat's wages have been falling, and at a faster rate since 2008. If wages fall, and benefits stay the same, the poverty trap worsens and the incentive to do low-wage labour becomes even weaker.

More people also find themselves in a 'pay-neutral' trap, where the income from jobs does not cover the costs of taking them, since they not only lose benefits but must also pay for childcare, transport, suitable clothes and so on. Of the 40,000 parents who sought help in 2011 from the British debt charity CCCS (Consumer Credit Counselling Service, now renamed StepChange Debt Charity), those earning under £10,000 had a monthly budget deficit of £54. Those earning between £10,000 and £20,000 had just £16 left over after paying living expenses. Many in the pay-neutral trap, particularly women, nevertheless persisted in their job in the hope that it would lead eventually to something better, while they feared that giving it up would be too risky.

The reconstruction of the labour market and benefit systems has denied economic rights to millions of women, in that it does not pay to take the jobs available and it does not pay to leave them. One single mother with two young children told *The Observer* that as a part-time accounts manager her net monthly income was £920, while childcare costs were £1,400, of which she could claim 70 per cent for the first daughter and 80 per cent for her second in tax credits. She said stoically:

> I'd be better off if I claimed benefits, as I'd get my housing costs paid. But I won't do that. Even though I hardly earn anything, my work gives our lives a structure, and my children benefit from the social interaction of nursery. We get by, but if the fridge breaks down I have no money to pay for a new one (O'Connell 2012).

In the absence of monetary incentives to enter low-wage jobs, governments are forcing people to take them. And they have rationalized further cuts to benefits and tighter conditions for entitlement as 'making work pay', arguing that those receiving benefits should not receive more than those in jobs. This opens up a vicious circle of declining income and benefits.

Poverty traps create moral and immoral hazards. In both cases, we should ask if it is fair to blame people who seek to escape from a trap that is not of their making. Moral hazards arise where incentive structures and institutional barriers discourage people from doing what would otherwise be in their interest to do. If there is no financial incentive to take low-paying jobs, people can scarcely be blamed for not seeking or taking such jobs. For many, the moral hazard translates into loss of jobseeking zeal and energy, since the cost of looking for work in terms of money, time and self-esteem will quickly exceed the probable income gain, especially where unemployment is high and vacancies few and far between.

Another moral hazard arises from a variant of the poverty trap, a savings trap. People find that after years of prudent saving, they lose their job or their earnings drop. Means-testing rules deny them entitlement to various benefits solely because their savings put them above the bureaucratically determined poverty threshold. They must see their savings dribble away until they are minimal or gone, before they can receive benefits. Why save if there is a high risk of being in that situation?

These moral hazards were exemplified by the case of one British woman who lost her job as a forensic scientist. Her savings were initially too high for her to qualify for benefits. She told *The Guardian*: 'I couldn't claim until I was down to the minimum £5,000. Then it took six months to get any money, by which time I was down to my last few pounds' (Robinson-Tillett and Menon 2013). She could find only part-time jobs paying very little, adding: 'There's no possibility of going full time and, even if I could, I'd lose my housing benefit. On such a low wage I wouldn't be able to pay the rent.' She appealed for help from her union, Prospect, which provided her with some training and gave her four days of paid labour as a trainee. As a result, she lost her jobseeker's allowance (unemployment benefit) because she was employed!

Now consider what should be called immoral hazards. Someone facing an 80 per cent income deduction would probably wish to avoid declaring a little bit of extra income. Inevitably, many enter the shadow economy, concealing income-earning activities. The plutocracy cheats, so why shouldn't I? The moral economy of society is degraded. If the law is an ass, why should it be respected? Governments are left trying to make people fear the law instead.

The corresponding immoral hazard with regard to the savings trap is to conceal savings or dissipate them in some way one would not otherwise wish to do. Many people will be tempted to conceal savings in an attempt to preserve some security. However, they are at risk of being criminalized. To prevent people taking that rational course of action, governments have tightened the rules and used public resources to pursue 'benefit cheats'. Moralistic posturing replaces equitable and rational policy.

Precarity traps

The situation is even worse than the discussion of the poverty trap has suggested. The flexible labour market and social assistance system combine to produce a series of precarity traps. Perhaps the most common precarity trap runs as follows. A person loses a low-wage casual job and has to apply for benefits. It can take weeks or even months before she gains entitlement to benefits, during which time she must queue, fill in complex forms, respond to intrusive questions about her home life and finances, and return again because she has not brought the right documents the first time or filled in the forms correctly. By the time she starts to receive benefits, she may have used up savings, exhausted help from friends or relatives, lost her apartment or fallen into high-interest debt.

Then an official at the jobcentre, or a privatized alternative, tells her there is a job opportunity on the other side of town. It is a short-term job, paying the minimum wage, without benefits. She faces a poverty trap, as she will earn only about 20 per cent more than her meagre hard-won benefits. And there are commuting costs to consider, and the extra costs of 'working', including better clothes, a new pair of shoes, and so on. There is also a high probability that she will lose the job in a few weeks. Then she would face the prospect of starting the claim process all over again. This time she might have to prove she had not lost the job through her own fault or left it 'voluntarily', which would disqualify her from benefits altogether. She does not know all the rules. She is in fear. It would be irrational for the woman to take that low-wage job. She would risk impoverishing herself. Yet, if she declines, she will be branded a lazy scrounger.

Another precarity trap arises from a modern phenomenon linked to how flexible labour markets work in practice. Unemployed people with skills and qualifications are being pressured to take low-level jobs, even though there is powerful statistical and anecdotal evidence to show that this can lower the probability of subsequently obtaining a job requiring and using those qualifications. Taking a short-term low-level job can significantly reduce expected life-time earnings.

Temporary jobs are rarely stepping stones into 'permanent' jobs. This is a global trend. In Australia, for instance, studies have shown that casual jobs do not generally lead to permanent jobs (Burgess and Campbell 1998; Mitchell and Welters 2008). Casual jobs lock workers into a cycle of them. One more recent study found that while men were slightly better off accepting casual jobs rather than remaining unemployed, for women it was better to stay unemployed in terms of enhancing the probability of being in a permanent job later (Buddelmeyer and Wooden 2011).

Studies in other countries have also shown that only a minority of casuals make it into regular jobs later (Gauttie and Schmitt 2010).

And education has only limited value in helping people escape casual jobs, suggesting that the conventional advice to go further with schooling is wrong once one is in the precariat, a finding also reproduced in Japan (Inui, Higuchi and Hiratsuka 2013). Moreover, taking a casual job in prime-age years turns age into a greater liability, as the transition probability declines, trapping people in casualized labour. In Italy, there are numerous reports testifying to the potential long-term cost of taking the wrong job out of short-term expediency (e.g. Fumagalli and Morini 2012; Fumagalli 2013).

Consider two letters to the 'Money' section of *The Guardian* (20 April 2013):

Letter 1: Part [of the human cost of recession] is that benefits are so low and the hassle and humiliation of getting them so high. It's easier to sign off and get by somehow on bits and pieces of low-paid work. I signed on briefly recently. I had 20+ years of work behind me and no previous claims. Immediately, I was treated like a scrounger and bullied by young 'advisers' who knew nothing about my line of work or how best to get a job in my field.

For those with a solid work history there should be a short period – before Jobcentre Plus starts the strong-arm tactics – to allow them to try to get a job that uses their skills. Otherwise those skills might be lost to the economy forever.

Letter 2: Made redundant in December after 25 years in the public sector. Signed on for the first time in my life to receive £71 per week JSA [jobseeker's allowance]. Received no help or useful advice with finding work, just fortnightly interrogations about my job-seeking activities and threats about how my payment would be stopped if I didn't accept what they deemed to be appropriate. After 10 weeks, I was glad to get a 20-hours-per-week job as a receptionist in a vet's surgery for £7 an hour. As I don't have children, I receive no additional state help – my outgoings, including mortgage and utilities, are almost £1,000 per month. Thankfully, I have some redundancy money but wonder what will happen when this runs out. The longer I am out of my specialist field, the harder it will be to return, and my qualifications and experience will be wasted.

Another precarity trap is linked to fluctuating incomes typical of the precariat. One woman had taken out a loan of £15,000 on her home in 2006, when she was in a relatively well-paying job, and her debt had grown to £24,000 by early 2013. She said:

My mortgage is £251 a month and £223 on the loan. At best, I am only earning £775 a month, and because my working hours fluctuate, I can't claim tax credits when they drop below 30 hours a week.

She had sold her car, cut back on food and could not afford a computer. As the tax credit regime was being made meaner, her predicament was about to become worse.

A new precarity trap is in the making. In the UK, the Child Support Agency (CSA) has been wound up and replaced by the Child Maintenance Service. The CSA took payments directly from the absent parent's account if the father failed to pay. There were 1.2 million parents receiving money through the CSA. But from 2014 they must pay £20 to apply for the money if it is not paid by the absent parent. Each party will have to pay if there is a dispute on payment or charges for the collection of the maintenance, a service that was previously free. In many cases, a father will be able to avoid payment by working off-the-books and declaring that he has no money. This flows from the flexible labour market. So, in the name of saving public money and imposing a tax on claimants (£20), and by making it harder to obtain payments, a new form of indebtedness has been created.

Another type of precarity trap affects ex-prisoners. In the UK, someone coming out of prison can receive £46 for expenses until they become eligible for state benefits or start earning. But they must apply for jobs at a jobcentre. Many do not have a national insurance (social security) number (or have lost it), which leads to a long process of paperwork. One ex-prisoner, pointing out that after six weeks he had not succeeded in obtaining any benefits because he had no national insurance number, added bitterly, 'And without that, no bank account, no place on the myriad databases that comprise a modern existence, I do not exist – except on a police national computer' (Gunn 2012). This is a case of double jeopardy, being punished twice for the same offence. What chance of re-offending?

* * *

The existence of poverty traps and precarity traps has been used by utilitarian policymakers as the pretext for coercion. That is their only way to overcome the disincentives to take low-wage casual jobs. Poverty traps will not go away as long as means-testing and low wages persist. The UK's much touted welfare reform will not remove the poverty trap. Universal credit, combined with raising the amount a person can earn without paying tax, will mean that for every £1 of extra income benefits will be cut by 65 pence. The £1,000 increase in the personal tax allowance in 2013 will give £200 per year to every basic-rate taxpayer except those on universal credit, who will gain only £70.

Poverty traps and precarity traps must be removed. Until they are, nobody should be penalized if they act rationally in the circumstances they face. If, say, 30 per cent is the standard rate of income tax, nobody should be penalized if they refuse a job that would involve an effective tax rate above that. The same principle should be applied to all forms of precarity trap, and the process of applying for benefits needs to be overhauled. In addition, penalties should be imposed on agencies for undue delays in processing applications, and applicants should be compensated with that money.

Article 18: Make a bonfire of benefit assessment tests

> Governments should restrict the use of assessment tests to the minimum necessary, and should subject any tests to independent evaluation as to their objectivity before they are implemented and used to determine entitlement to benefits or services. In the longer term they should be phased out as conditionality is rolled back.

Means-testing, conditionality and selective benefits require personalized assessment tests. Those are invariably intrusive and probing.

But they veer from their ostensible purpose into being instruments for monitoring, directing and punishing. The nudging and surveillance state is increasingly using elaborate tests to monitor, sift and control people, obliging them to adapt to rules implicit in the tests they are required to take and pass.

The precariat has most to lose from the unchecked extension of this mode of regulation. The plethora of tests must be rolled back. They are an infringement of freedom and a regressive divisive device, with objectives that include humiliation and habituation to deference to authority. Many of these tests offend the justice principles laid out earlier, making people subject to them more insecure, applying paternalistic controls over the most unfree people in society, and taking away rights while allowing bureaucrats more discretionary power.

Some of the strains are borne by those required to operate the tests; often they are part of the precariat themselves, and in their insecurity take care to err on the side of what government wants, rather than on the side of those they are supposed to serve. Some resist and act as 'streetside' bureaucrats, quietly trying to use their discretion on behalf of claimants (Grant 2013). But increasingly their supervisors are using panopticon techniques to stop that happening, setting targets with accompanying threats to job contracts.

The official rationale for testing applicants for state benefits is that 'taxpayers' must be protected against 'fraud' and that 'scroungers' must be made 'independent'. Yet official statistics show that fraud is minimal. A more worrying reason for the tests is to make it more unpleasant to apply for and to continue to receive benefits.

Jobseekers' tests

Consider the tests to receive jobseeker's allowance (unemployment benefit) in the UK, remembering that most applicants will already be humiliated, stressed, financially worried and ashamed. To be unemployed and seeking help is not a status that is chosen. As part of the process, the claimant may be required to supply and prove the accuracy of all sorts of private information, including educational qualifications, vocational training, employment history, aspirations for future jobs, description of skills that might be relevant for jobs, work-related abilities, childcare and other care responsibilities, paid and unpaid work being done at the time. If the information was to be used solely to assist the claimant obtain a job, such intrusive questions might be understandable. But that is not their primary purpose; their primary purpose is to find a reason for not giving a benefit or to identify further work the applicant must do in order to receive it. Whistleblowers revealed that jobcentre staff were being set targets for imposing sanctions, while the Department for Work and Pensions (DWP) acknowledged that action was taken against jobcentres that did not sanction enough people.

The current procedure starts with a set of questions online, which requires access to the internet. Phone calls are no longer accepted. After the online test, applicants for jobseeker's allowance (JSA) must fix a first appointment with Jobcentre Plus, which is supposed to test the claim's validity. Another appointment is made to establish what the claimant was doing before making the claim, and to ask how he or she can be 'helped' into a job.

At this stage, most claimants are required to draw up a jobseeker's 'agreement' – a contract the supplicant is forced to make with the state. In law, contracts signed under duress can be regarded as null and void. But for most claimants the cost of not signing – withdrawal of benefits – is too great to bear. While some do withdraw, we cannot presume this is because their claims were 'fraudulent'. Many of us would baulk at signing a contract obliging us to do a host of unwanted activities that would be potentially endless and reward-less. Nor does the process stop there. The claimant must have regular appointments with a 'personal adviser' at the Jobcentre Plus or Work Programme offices, depending on prior assessments. And the adviser may oblige the claimant to come in for other appointments and do designated activities, as the adviser sees fit.

The unemployed in the UK used to have social rights; now they are denizens. It is not as if the tests serve any useful purpose. The Work Programme, which is based on those assessments, has a dismal record. Set up in June 2011 and estimated to cost £3–£5 billion, early results showed the private providers were no more successful in finding jobs for the long-term unemployed than if the programme did not exist. It is a waste of 'taxpayers' money'.

Family needs tests

Because means-tested benefits in the UK take into account household income, people's status must be checked. So, the state requires suppli-cants to prove they are not in a couple. They must show they have their own bank account and that a suspicious 'other person' also has an independent bank account. The same goes for utility bills, council tax payments, and tenancy agreements. If two people live under the same roof, are they sharing a room? Do they share food stores, cooking arrangements and shopping expeditions? When they go out socially, do they present themselves as single or as a couple?

There are no fixed criteria. The bureaucrats, charged with trying to reduce benefit costs by proving coupledom, build up a body of evidence. But many people share accommodation out of a need to reduce costs. Many ex-couples stay in the marital home because they cannot afford to move to separate accommodation. They are then faced with further humiliation and deprivation. This applies to tax credits and to all Jobcentre Plus benefits, including JSA and the employment and support allowance (ESA) for disabled people.

In answering intrusive questions, some people will give wrong answers, perhaps out of confusion, sometimes out of fear. Most of us in such circumstances, knowing our financial survival depends on passing the tests, would be nervous, however 'innocent' we were.

In the UK, housing benefit claims have been moved in the same direction. Applicants are required to complete online questionnaires for entitlement, penalizing those without internet access or proximity to a public library. In 2013, the housing claim assessment process was compounded by the vindictive 'bedroom tax' measure that deducts benefit for any bedroom deemed to be surplus to requirements (including separate bedrooms for two children of the same sex and rooms occupied by an occasional carer). To claim housing benefit and council tax reduction, claimants must prove they are paying rent. That is all right if there is a written tenancy agreement and an up-to-date rent book. But in the nether reaches of all societies, those conditions do not apply. Some landlords do not provide them, some refuse even when asked, some do not provide receipts.

Then there are tests to obtain child tax credit. It may be difficult for some, including migrants, to prove children are theirs. A claimant may just receive a terse letter saying that Her Majesty's Revenue and Customs does not accept the evidence provided, be it a passport, birth certificate or something else. There may be mistakes, but there is no due process (Article 16). Undoubtedly, there is organized crime in this area, forging evidence and trafficking women and children. But the collective punishment is unfair.

Disability tests

One egregious set of tests harasses people with disabilities. The 'work capability assessment' test imposed on claimants for ESA and personal independence payment (PIP) is discussed further under Article 19. It involves a computerized 'tick-box' medical question-naire read out to the claimant, sometimes coupled with a brief physical examination, conducted by an assessor from a division of the multinational company Atos, which has been contracted by the DWP to carry out the test. The score on this test supposedly indicates whether or not a person is 'fit to work', and therefore liable to benefit sanctions if not in a job or deemed to be not looking for one assidu-ously enough.

The test is repeated as often as the Jobcentre Plus chooses, every few months. The initial humiliations are followed by 'work-focused inter-views' with the Work Programme provider. Although some may escape these interviews if they are put into the so-called support group, later there will be a further work capability test, with more work-focused interviews to follow. This will go on for six months. Disabled people become denizens, losing rights and being reduced to supplicants.

The indignity is conveyed by people demonstrating with placards on their wheelchairs stating: 'We are not robots. Atos computers decide our futures in 15 minutes.' Inevitably, such tests involve many Type 1 errors (classifying someone as fit to work when they are not) and few Type 2 errors (classifying someone as not fit when they are). As a commercial firm in business to make profits, Atos will prefer to make Type 1 errors. A public agency or one run in the interests of claimants would set up procedures that worked the other way round.

A commercial firm works to the terms of its contract. If, as is the case, Atos is paid according to the number of people it tests, it will want to maximize that number and therefore make the tests as quick as possible, never mind the mistakes. But if payment was reduced according to the number of Type 1 errors identified by an independent body, Atos would tend to make more Type 2 errors and fewer Type 1 errors. In addition, until an appeal against denial of benefit has been heard, people should continue to receive the benefits, or some interim amount if the process is scheduled to take some time. That would at least shift the pressure back onto the government agencies to make both the initial and the appeals process efficient and equitable. However, the government would probably only alter the nature of these contracts if there were strong social protest and pressure. That must come.

In 2013, a tribunal ruled that the DWP had not made reasonable adjustments to ensure people with mental health problems were treated fairly, resulting in many losing benefits. With characteristic insolence of office, the DWP immediately said it would appeal while continuing with the tests. The judicial review related to the case of two individuals required to take the test, who were incapable of understanding it or explaining their condition. Paul Jenkins, CEO of Rethink Mental Illness, summed up the situation nicely:

> The judges have independently confirmed what our members have been saying for years – the system is discriminating against some of the most ill and vulnerable people in our society, the very people it is meant to support. The work capability assessment process is deeply unfair for people with a mental illness – it's like asking someone in a wheelchair to walk to the assessment centre.

Pensioner tests

In another example of turning migrants into denizens by removing social rights, in 2013 the UK government announced plans to deny pensioners living abroad entitlement to winter fuel payments, worth £100–£300 a year, after a European Court of Justice ruling that expatriates – about 440,000 – were entitled to them. The traditional justification for such payments, part of national insurance benefits, was that recipients paid contributions and UK taxes over decades. Now, the government has introduced a 'temperature test'. People living in Cyprus, France, Gibraltar, Greece, Malta, Portugal and Spain, where average winter temperatures are higher than in the warmest part of the UK, will lose winter fuel payments. Apparently, the 'average' winter temperature measurement for France includes its tropical overseas departments in the Caribbean and Indian Ocean, which explains why France is rated as a 'hot' country and Italy is not. This is absurd.

Charity qualification tests

In the UK and elsewhere a new layer of interrogation has emerged, for state-funded charity. Charity hand-outs have replaced crisis loans and community care grants that previously helped people in emergencies. Local authorities now have no ring-fenced funding from central government to help in these circumstances; spending is entirely discretionary, at a time when local authority budgets have been slashed.

To receive hand-outs, claimants must be quizzed by Citizens Advice or other designated charities on the reasons for the emergency. What benefits do they receive? Why are they not managing? Do they have other sources of money? They may then receive vouchers for food and utility bills, topped up with a small amount if needed for second-hand furniture and domestic appliances. When they request the goods, they are questioned again by the voluntary agencies administering the services, to ensure they really are in need. If the firm supplying the furniture decides the claimant does not *need* them, it takes them away. It is all about rationing and avoiding fraud, so ordinary people, once again, face inquisitorial treatment designed to deal with villains.

* * *

The 'test regime' should worry everyone, since a test for one group can easily lead to tests for others, as the state moves from one perceived minority to another. Governments and their privatized agencies should roll back tests the precariat is required to take. They should be limited to a minimum. No tests should be demanded or questions asked unless they are required for objective judgements to be made, and unless they have been agreed by independent boards on which those subject to the tests are represented. Any test should be required to satisfy the 'veil of ignorance' principle, and thus overcome the utilitarian trap. Unless you yourself would be content to take the test in the same circumstances, surely you should oppose it.

One interim policy would be to compensate financially those required to take the myriad tests devised to determine entitlement to a benefit or service. After all, taking the tests is onerous, particularly if one is stressed or has a disability. And the state or its profit-making agent is doing the test for its benefit, not for the benefit of the person required to take it. If the agency had to compensate the test-taker for the time involved, it would have an incentive to make the test as simple and as undemanding as possible. That would be fairer than treating claimants' time and supplicant position as unimportant.

The state is constructing an assessment regime driven by utilitarianism, with conditionality applied to the precariat that is not applied to the salariat and elite. Not only should those subject to tests be compensated for the humiliation and time used. There should also be penalties imposed on those who apply the tests if their testing is proved wrong or punitive. If there are sanctions for the precariat, there should certainly be sanctions for the profiteers. It is not good enough for Atos or some other agency to say its tests are being refined when it comes to light that it has erred on many occasions. Whenever errors are made, it should be penalized financially and those unfairly assessed should be compensated, not just in having backdated benefits but also for the stress and discomfort.

Besides social justice, there is also a fiscal matter. The assessment regime is expensive, and a cost-benefit analysis would surely show it costs more to operate than any savings made by weeding out a few who should not be receiving benefits. The system is growing more unwieldy and prone to penalize those least able to put up with the pain. If officials were motivated by empathy and compassion, they would not wish to insist on such tests, and would feel ashamed to impose penalties that must cause extreme hardship. Sanctions can lead to debt, homelessness, alcoholism, social illnesses, crime and prostitution. The longer-term social costs are greater than any savings made by identifying a few dubious characters.

The edifice of tests and assessments gives a lie to any claim that governments are committed to a deregulated labour market and a roll-back of 'red tape'. It is a case of less regulation for the elite, more for the precariat. Let us have that bonfire.

Article 19: Stop demonizing
the disabled

Social and economic rights of the disabled must be strengthened.
Benefits should be related to their needs, not to their supposed
work capabilities. Agencies that make Type 1 errors (denying
benefits to those who should receive them) should pay proper
compensation, not just backdated benefits.

People with disabilities comprise a substantial part of the precariat
and are treated increasingly as denizens rather than citizens. Indeed,
'the disabled' is a peculiarly modern category, or one that has
been reshaped in the neo-liberal era. That goes with the emphasis
on competitiveness and 'survival of the fittest', measured by one's
striving and commercial capabilities. It goes too with modern
utilitarianism, individualism and the apparently admirable qualities
of non-dependence. There has been a moralistic reinterpretation of
disability, with differentiation based less on medical or physical needs
than on intrusive quibbling about an individual's 'ability to work'.
Governments have become more judgemental and have widened
the definition of 'ability to work', making tests more 'thorough',
intimidating, humiliating and stigmatizing.

We concentrate here on British policy changes. But the trend
to conditionality and workfare is global. For instance, US Social
Security Disability Insurance provides benefits and, after two
years, access to Medicare. But it requires beneficiaries to have
worked for income for at least five of the previous ten years.

The Supreme Court restricted the definition of what counted as inability to work, thus denying benefits to many who hitherto had disability rights.

Disability policy has also been subject to linguistic manipulation, intended to shift imagery away from rights to moralistic demands. Thus the British government abolished the term 'benefits' in favour of 'allowances'; then 'disability living allowance' became 'personal independence payment' (PIP). Entitlement is not based on a person's condition but on how it is supposed to affect him or her, enabling policymakers to tighten conditions and reduce eligibility.

The disabled as victims of utilitarianism

For two decades the main UK political parties have adopted a similar ideological position towards disabled people. The New Labour government set a ten-year plan to cut one million from the 2.8 million receiving disability benefits, arguing that more people should be pushed into jobs. It replaced the 'sick note' with a 'fit note', making local general practitioners (doctors) part of the social policy apparatus. The Secretary of State for Health said: 'We know that being in work can be good for your wellbeing' (ME Association 2009), a glib generalization epitomizing the labourist prejudice.

The coalition government has moved the goalposts further, tightening conditions, imposing more complex assessments and privatizing the process, while giving incentives to private contractors to limit entitlements. Worst of all, as noted in Chapter 4, it has created an atmosphere in which the public is made suspicious about those with disabilities. Losing social rights accompanied loss of the cultural right to belong to an integrated community.

The disabled have lost economic rights through the spread of occupational licensing and negative licensing, closure of specialist workplaces, and flexible labour relations that give little incentive to provide suitable facilities for disabled employees and push the disabled down firms' employment priority lists. Successive governments closed Remploy factories that employed people with disabilities, and in 2012 plans were announced to close half of the remaining 54. The government said they were loss-making, but they had given work and dignity, often with a rehabilitation goal.

Social rights have been degraded. For years, people qualified for a higher-rate mobility allowance – which covered the cost of using an adapted car – if they could not walk unaided for 50 metres. In 2013, to qualify for the higher mobility rate as part of the new PIP, it was decided to shorten that to 20 metres. The motive was to restrict entitlement. Where was the empathy and compassion? It was estimated that over 50,000 people would lose higher-rate mobility benefits as a result, in effect isolating them at home. And once cut to 20 metres, what is to stop zealous reformers cutting it to 10? Whatever the number, the rule creates a special precarity trap reserved for the disabled. Henceforth, a person with a physical disability will have a financial interest in not struggling to walk.

In another example, in 2012 the government disbanded the Independent Living Fund, which provided support for 19,000 people with severe disabilities to help them live independently. It could be closed without public fuss, since it applied to a quiet minority. On what reasoning were benefits withdrawn to cover the cost of maintaining home adaptations, such as stair-lifts, hoists to lift people out of bed, warden-call systems and other equipment to enable them to live independently? Repairs will not be done; falls and injuries will follow. It could not be on cost grounds: annual expenditure from the fund on all the disabled needing help was less than one or two bankers' bonuses. It could only be attributed to a utilitarian or crude Darwinian rationalization. These people do not matter politically or economically!

Allegedly, the primary purpose – classically utilitarian, in appealing to a perceived majority of 'hard-working families' – has been to cut spending of 'taxpayers' money'. In chasing that mirage, a complex array of procedures set up to weed out the undeserving from the deserving disabled has used a great deal of taxpayers' money. The government's own estimate of fraud is less than the value of the contracts awarded to the private company charged with identifying scroungers, those having the temerity to claim they are disabled when they are not. Any 'savings' have been made at the expense of the disabled, making the lives of already disadvantaged and vulnerable people more miserable and difficult.

The new portrait of the disabled should be challenged more robustly. Otherwise, those with impairments will continue to lose social, economic and cultural rights, drift into even more vulnerable denizen statuses, and be relegated to the lower echelons of the precariat.

Benefit assessment tests

Article 18 addresses benefit assessment tests in general. There are two types of assessment for claiming disability benefits, one medical-physical and the other labour conditionality. The second is more objectionable. A rights-based approach would compensate those with disabilities for their ill luck, enabling them to live a more dignified life. They may aspire to do much more. But benefit conditionality punishes, stigmatizes and is inevitably subject to errors that can lead to people being wrongly deprived of essential support. It is far better to make Type 2 errors – compensating a person with disabilities because they are wrongly deemed unable to work – than Type 1 errors – failing to compensate someone with disabilities because they are wrongly deemed 'fit to work'.

To compound the unfairness, in 2013 the UK government more than doubled the fine for sick and disabled people categorized as 'fit to work' who fail or refuse to take part in mandatory work-related activities. They will lose £71 a week – 70 per cent of their weekly employment and support allowance (ESA) – against £28.15 previously. The sanctions policy is implemented by bureaucrats and involves no due process. Yet in taking a right away from someone for whom all of us should feel compassion and empathy, that basic principle of justice has been ignored.

Those with disabilities should be encouraged to play as active a role in society as possible. But imposing conditionality is not the same as encouragement. And we should not allow the utilitarians to pretend this is what they are trying to do in imposing conditionalities. It would cost less to have just a medical assessment, and err on the side of generosity, rather than multiply sanctions and denial of rights and dignity.

Austerity's unfairness

As far as the disabled were concerned, respect for the justice principles was jettisoned in the policy responses in the austerity era. Almost by definition they are among the most insecure people in society and they lost more than anybody. In the UK, social benefits were cut across the board. The benefit system has become so complex that the disabled rely on an array of benefits, each with different rules. They face cuts in all of them. Demos, a think-tank, estimated that 3.7 million disabled people would lose a total of £28 billion by 2018, and over 200,000 would face cuts in three or more benefits simultaneously. This will drive more disabled into debt and reliance on charity, particularly as care services are being cut and local councils are introducing charges or higher co-payments for care. This means deep erosion of disabled people's social income.

The government also tightened rules on entitlement to benefits. Thus ESA is harder to obtain than the disability allowance it replaced. Only the sick who have no spouse or whose spouse is unemployed will pass the means test for cash payments. Someone married to a low-income earner cannot receive a benefit. And people claiming ESA are now subjected to stressful 'fitness-to-work' tests designed to reduce the numbers receiving benefits.

In all these reforms, the Rights-not-Charity Principle has been disregarded. The disabled can be denied benefits at the discretion of bureaucrats, without due process. And they can be reclassified as available for jobs and obliged to participate in a workfare scheme, the Work Programme, even though the programme appears to have had no effect on their probability of employment.

Privatization of social services

The UK government has given profit-making firms the discretionary power to determine whether or not someone should have entitlement to a state benefit. At huge public cost, the government has effectively privatized conditionality.

In its zeal to privatize services, the New Labour government contracted out medical examinations of claimants for incapacity benefits to a French information technology company, Atos Origin. It rapidly declared that three-quarters of claimants were actually fit for labour. Huge numbers lost benefits due to Atos assessments. Most could not afford to appeal; many were too ill or incapacitated to do so. But in some areas lawyers voluntarily took up appeals, with a success rate of about 80 per cent. Atos and the government had denied many disabled people the benefits to which they were entitled.

Despite its dismal record, Atos has continued to be the government's preferred contractor. It is now being paid £110 million a year to conduct 'work capability assessment' (WCA) tests to determine eligibility for ESA, the new sickness and disability benefit. Those who fail the test are told to apply for jobseeker's allowance instead (which requires them to show they are seeking work and takes weeks to process). They can appeal, but this may take months. Some have committed suicide when denied ESA. Some have been so ill that they have died before their appeal could be heard.

Atos tests about 11,000 claimants a week. Between October 2008, when WCA tests were launched, and February 2012, the Department for Work and Pensions made more than 1.36 million decisions on new ESA claims following a WCA, finding 794,000 people 'fit for work'. In 2012–13, there were 465,000 appeals against ESA decisions and the success rate was around 39 per cent. Of the successful appeals, 60 per cent had scored zero in the Atos test – that is, deemed fully fit. Meanwhile, the cost to the taxpayer of running the appeal tribunals rose to £66 million in 2012–13. But from April 2013, legal aid was ended for claims for welfare payments. This will hit the disabled particularly hard. It amounts to a further chipping away at their civil and social rights.

Labour MPs said they favoured the aims but not the implementation. They should have criticized the aims. It was disingenuous to claim, as one did, that the tests were intended to 'help more people back into work'. The primary aim was to cut spending; a secondary aim was to force more into jobseeking. It is the move from facilitating and encouraging to persuading and enforcing that is wrong. To offer a service of 'work-related activity' sessions is not the same as requiring people to attend them on pain of losing benefits if they do not.

Perversely, Atos tests penalize those who make an effort to overcome impairments or who stoically claim they can do things that on most days they cannot. For example, the Atos test asks, 'Do you shop and cook for yourself?' A yes answer would reduce the probability of obtaining an ESA. But yes could mean you have to shop and cook because there is no one to help, or that you resolutely do so, even though it exhausts you.

Atos is paid for each assessment but loses nothing if decisions are overturned on appeal. This is a licence to profit at the expense of the disabled. The company can make mistakes with impunity, knowing the government will pick up the bill. Meanwhile, Atos is taking government money to force poor people with impairments to seek low-paying jobs in fear and insecurity.

In 2012, the government gave Atos Healthcare another contract worth over £400 million to test eligibility for the so-called personal independence payment (PIP) that replaced the disability living allowance (DLA) from 2013. The DLA paid up to £130 a week to help people look after themselves, notably to help with mobility, while the PIP is supposed to 'help people into work'. The government's stated aim is to cut spending on the PIP (and by implication the number receiving the benefits) by 20 per cent between 2013 and 2016. This followed a 30 per cent rise in the number claiming DLA between 2002 and 2011, to 3.2 million.

The chief executive of disability charity Scope, Richard Hawkes, reacted in exasperation:

> The government and Atos… have come under a great deal of criticism about how this assessment is being delivered to disabled people. Yet in less than a year from now, disabled people could have to go through two deeply flawed assessments in the same month to get the essential financial support they need to live their lives (Ramesh 2012).

After complaints about the Atos tests, improvements were made. The number of new claimants receiving the ESA rose considerably. But the methodology was still unfair, and was described as 'deeply flawed' by the head of Mind, Paul Farmer, for not properly recognizing the impact of mental health on the ability to work. As he told *The Guardian*:

> The system is based on assumptions that claimants need to be forced back to work, rather than supported on their own terms; and that those not well enough to go back to work are somehow perceived as scroungers. These attitudes only serve to further damage individuals' mental health and increase the time until they may be ready to return to work (Gentleman 2012).

In 2012, Citizens Advice dealt with over 450,000 problems with the ESA, 54 per cent more than in 2011, showing that the shortcomings were chronic. The disabled will continue to suffer from Type 1 errors. This could and must be corrected.

* * *

The counter-demands should be clear. Any firm contracted by government to deliver services for the disabled should be required to have a treble commitment, to the disabled first, the government second and to society, since everybody has an interest in how the disabled are treated. We could be next. If the firm fails to provide services for the real clients, the disabled, it should be penalized. That is the nature of a market-driven contract. If the firm uses tests that are shown to be erroneous – misclassifying someone as 'able to work' – not only should there be penalty clauses in the contract but the firm should be required to compensate the disabled person directly. That compensation should be substantially more than the value of the benefits lost.

For utilitarians, the disabled are a minority, so there is likely to be less public objection – and fewer lost votes – to cuts in benefits and social services for them. In the austerity era, benefits for the disabled were cut by more than for others, while taxes for those with median and high incomes were reduced and subsidies increased. The policy mix profoundly fails the Security Difference, Rights-not-Charity and Paternalism Test Principles. Those with disabilities must have rights restored.

Article 20: Stop workfare now!

Workfare – compulsory labour as a condition for receiving benefits – punishes the precariat and should be stopped. It is unfair; it increases inequality; it increases social and economic insecurity; it costs more than it saves in terms of public spending; it undermines the right to work; it is stigmatizing at the time and long after; it is politically and socially divisive; and it worsens the labour market and economic situation of others. Privatized workfare is an unproductive scam.

Workfare essentially means obliging people to perform state-chosen labour as a condition for receiving state benefits. It can also mean requiring benefit recipients to do labour-related activities – jobseeking, preparation of CVs, training – or lose entitlement. Often, it is dressed up as a 'job guarantee'.

Workfare in its various guises has a long unpleasant history. It can be traced to the English Poor Law of 1536, dealing with 'sturdy vagabonds', and the French *Ordonnance de Moulins* of 1556. But its most infamous precedent was the English Poor Law Amendment Act of 1834, by which assistance was targeted on those deemed to be the 'deserving' and desperate poor. Under its rules, anyone wanting support had to agree to labour in a parish-run workhouse, which according to the Poor Law Commissioners had to be 'the hardest taskmaster and the worst paymaster'. The labour had to be worse than that done by independent labourers so as not to compete with them. To make it even more unpleasant, partly because the workhouses were overloaded, the authorities also operated an 'outdoor labour test' as a deterrent to potential claimants.

The 1834 measures were modified by the Unemployed Workmen Act of 1905, by which unemployed men were directed into labour. Winston Churchill was among those in favour of obliging the poor to be 'under control', as he put it, on the grounds that they should not be allowed to be 'idle'. Of course, nothing was ever said about the idle rich.

Why workfare became mainstream policy

For much of the twentieth century, the practice of forcing people to labour was pushed into the background, although it remained part of the ideology of Christian democracy, social democracy and communism. All emphasized, for different reasons, that the poor had a 'duty to labour'. The early labourists were characteristically illiberal. Beatrice Webb advocated sending the long-term unemployed to detention camps.

However, the re-emergence of workfare as mainstream policy was a predictable consequence of the neo-liberal strategy in the globalization era (Standing 1990). As labour market flexibility drove down wages and eroded non-wage forms of remuneration for the precariat, state benefits tended to rise as a percentage of wages, implying a rising income-replacement rate.

As shown in Article 17, with the shift to means-testing, the precariat's incentive to labour fell to close to zero. In response, urged on by agencies such as the IMF and OECD, governments reduced benefits and made them harder to obtain or retain. In euphemisms that were to become standard refrains, cuts were rationalized as 'making work pay' with 'less generous' benefits. But wages kept falling. So, on the logic used, benefits had to be cut yet further and made even harder to obtain. The outcome was deeper poverty traps and the maze of precarity traps. For policymakers with this mindset, the only option left was to force the unemployed and precariat to do very low-paid or even unpaid labour. Workfare was the end of the road for the neo-liberal model.

However, there had to be a rationalization to legitimize forcing people to do something against their will. Enter the quasi-religious or moralistic tradition of political thinking, which emphasizes social duties and takes the class structure as it is. The poor have a duty to labour to justify the rich providing them with sustenance, in charity. The Soviet Union was the most religious, putting into its constitution the idea that someone who does not labour shall not be allowed to eat. But Catholic and some other religious traditions have been scarcely less judgemental.

The utilitarian consensus

After three decades of re-interpretation of unemployment, there is a consensus among social democrats and neo-liberals in favour of workfare. This was epitomized by President Bill Clinton's Personal Responsibility and Work Opportunity Reconciliation Act of 1996, which built on Republican welfare reforms in Wisconsin. Clinton said he wished to 'end welfare as we know it'. So, single-parent recipients of social assistance were obliged to take low-paying jobs after two years, and nobody was allowed to receive welfare assistance for more than five years in a lifetime.

In the UK, New Labour also moved towards workfare. And David Cameron, on becoming Conservative leader, expressed admiration for the Wisconsin model. In 2007, he told the Conservative Party conference: 'We will say to people that if you are offered a job and it's a fair job and one that you can do and you refuse it, you shouldn't get any welfare.'

After 2010, the coalition government moved further, with mandatory 'work experience' measures and more circumstances in which benefit recipients can be obliged to take jobs. The planned universal credit scheme rolls most benefits into one payment alongside tougher demands on jobseekers and sanctions for up to three years if they fail to carry out jobcentre demands. In 2012, Boris Johnson, London's mayor, announced he would use European Social Fund money to force 18–24-year-olds to do 13 weeks of unpaid labour.

Not to be outdone, Labour has called for a 'compulsory jobs guarantee' that would oblige young people unemployed for a year or more, and the long-term unemployed out of work for over two years, to take a government-subsidized minimum-wage job for six months or lose benefits. The then Shadow Secretary for Work and Pensions, Liam Byrne, wrote:

> Labour would ensure that no adult will be able to live on the dole for over two years and no young person for over a year. They will be offered a real job with real training, real prospects and real responsibility… People would have to take this opportunity or lose benefits (Byrne 2013).

Ed Balls, the Shadow Chancellor, added:

> A One Nation approach to welfare reform means government has a responsibility to help people into work and support for those who cannot. But those who can work must be required to take up jobs or lose benefits as a result – no ifs or buts (Balls 2013).

While politicians have competed with each other on 'toughness', increasing numbers of people are facing the reality or threat of workfare. Since more stringent rules were introduced in 2012, nearly half a million unemployed have faced sanctions for breaching benefit conditions (including missing jobcentre appointments) or have abandoned their claims. Many unemployed have been put on four weeks of unpaid placements under the mandatory work activity (MWA) scheme.

Workfare has been extended to the disabled, with more being reclassified as available for jobs. Some, put in the work-related activity group, can now be required to do unpaid work for 'experience', or face losing up to 70 per cent of their benefits. The uncertainty makes people fearful. One man with cerebral palsy, put in the work-related activity group, said:

> They could call me in on Monday and say, 'Right, you've got to do this, this and this.' And if I don't, they can sanction me and that scares me... It makes me so nervous, it makes me physically sick (Malik 2012).

This is the sort of society being created, based on fear. Ironically, the Department for Work and Pensions (DWP) had found that MWA had no effect on people's chances of obtaining a job. So, driving that man and thousands like him into MWA is a waste of time and 'taxpayers' money'. The policy is not based on economics but on dogma.

The next group to be targeted are those in low-income part-time jobs, or with zero-hours contracts, threatened with loss of benefits and tax credits if they cannot prove they are looking for more hours of labour. Already, in 2013, the government had made it harder for people to claim tax credits by raising the working-hour threshold (below which tax credits cannot be claimed) from 16 to 24 hours a week for couples with children. The ratcheting up of workfare prompts the question: Who next? The salariat and elite may shrug with indifference, but should think through the ethics of what is happening.

So, let us consider the rationale of workfare. Anybody supporting it should subscribe to one or more of the following claims.

A duty to labour?

Workfare advocates usually say that everybody has a duty to 'work' and that those who receive benefits must match rights with responsibilities. They add words like 'reciprocity'. If there is such a duty, it should surely apply to all who benefit from the state and should be an equal duty, with the same costs imposed on all obliged to do it. Those who use the infrastructure and services most are the elite and salariat. So, they should have a greater duty to reciprocate. But the state does not demand they perform the sort of labour being imposed on the precariat.

Unless it is a generalized duty to do social work, is there a duty to labour at all? Why should anybody be forced to labour for a profit-making company for little or nothing? This would either increase its profits, and thus boost the income of wealthy individuals, or result in labour of no economic value. If it has no value, then surely there cannot be a duty to do it. If it has value, then the firm should pay the market rate.

Claiming that people have a duty to labour implies they have an obligation to devote their time to serve the interest of others. It is not society that benefits if you work for a supermarket chain, for little or no pay; the benefit goes to the supermarket's shareholders. The claim also implies that a low-income person has a duty to labour in a subservient position, under conventional labour laws known as 'master-servant' regulations. This is a distortion of the idea of duty. It is sophistry.

Meanwhile, other forms of work, for oneself, family or friends, do not count in the state's economic calculus. Once labour for a profit-making company is accepted as a duty of the unemployed citizen, it leads to the conclusion that if you are a failure in the labour market, you have a duty to labour for nothing. This way of looking at society is alienating and regressive. Labour may be needed, for economic growth or for some other reason. But it should not be a duty.

Coercion to labour

Saying there is a duty to labour is not the same as saying there should be coercion. But most workfare advocates do take that next step. Thus, Liam Byrne justified his support for workfare by noting that some of the Labour Party's iconic figures had supported coercion:

> If you go back to the Webb report, they were proposing detention colonies for people refusing to take work... All the way through our history there has been an insistence on the responsibility to work if you can. Labour shouldn't be any different now. We have always been the party of the right to work, but we have always been the party of the responsibility to work as well (Boffey and Urquhart 2013).

Yet coercion is divisive and undermines commitment to work, by forcing people to do labour they do not wish to do and may not be in their interests to do. Coercion also creates an amoral society, since it removes the freedom to be moral, to choose 'the disinterested performance of self-imposed duties'. And of course it is never imposed on the idle rich, on the friends and relatives of affluent politicians pushing it on others.

Inter-generational state dependency

Another claim is that 'the poor' are trapped in an inter-generational transmission of poverty and state dependency and that a spell in workfare would break that link. But there is no evidence that inter-generational dependency is widespread. Shildrick and colleagues (2012) tried to find two-generation 'workless' families in areas of the country where they should exist if they do at all. They found less than 1 per cent fitted that description. And official efforts to find such families have failed to identify any significant number. But even if there were some instances, that cannot justify collective punishment through workfare.

Social integration

Another claim is that workfare would help in social integration, on the grounds that people not in jobs are socially marginalized or 'excluded'. Yet most of the jobs concocted for workfare schemes have been humiliating, often deliberately so, since the primary objective has been to induce people to leave the benefit system. As mentioned earlier, a study by the UK's DWP showed that the MWA had no effect on people's chances of obtaining a job afterwards, while an earlier report for the DWP concluded that 'there is little evidence that workfare increases the likelihood of finding work' (Crisp and Fletcher 2008). In short, to be put in a mind-numbing job that stigmatizes and exhausts is no moral way to induce social integration.

Breaking the habit of 'worklessness'

A common claim is that large numbers of people have been unemployed or dependent on benefits for so long that they have lost a habit of working. This demonizing tactic has been exposed by many researchers, who have found very few such people. But we should also ask how a spell doing forced labour in unattractive conditions could do much if anything to produce a habit or commitment to labour. It seems at least as likely to do the opposite.

Developing skills

Advocates claim that spells in workfare increase skills. For example, following reports of poor treatment of unemployed people required to do unpaid security duties during the Queen's Diamond Jubilee celebrations in 2012, a government spokesman announced: 'The work programme is about giving people who have often been out of the workplace for quite some time the chance to develop skills that they need to get a job that is sustainable' (Watt, Mulholland and Malik 2012). Sweeping streets or stacking shelves hardly constitutes skills. Indeed, making someone with qualifications do menial labour for months could de-skill them.

Saving public money

Another claim is that putting the unemployed into workfare reduces welfare spending. Those who have studied such schemes have found the opposite. Workfare schemes are costly. They usually involve subsidies paid to employers, heavy administrative costs and little output or taxable income. In 2013, Liam Byrne claimed, 'The best way to save money is to get people back into work' (Byrne 2013). That is not true, as he knew, since most people relying on benefits were 'in work'. Participating in workfare would involve a continuation or an increase in benefits, such as tax credits. Workfare adds to social spending, in a way that provides neither social protection nor security.

Workfare and 'real jobs'

When the coalition government's workfare plans were announced in 2010, Labour's response was to say it favoured 'conditional welfare' but, in contrast to the government, it would offer 'real jobs' with 'real sanctions' if the offer was not taken up (Wintour 2010). In trying to make it harder for others to say that Labour favours idleness, the party surrendered the ethical ground.

If workfare jobs were real jobs, they would presumably have economic value. Then surely the market economy would generate them. Real jobs pay real wages. If they require a subsidy, either they cannot be worth very much, or the state is paying to substitute one worker for another. In reality, politicians and their advisers know that most workfare jobs are low-paying, low-productivity and insecure. Indeed, the government specified litter clearing and graffiti cleaning.

If people do not want to take up insecure low-paying jobs, something should be done to improve the nature of those jobs and the wages on offer, not force people to take them. This goes back to the reasoning by Adam Smith, father of modern economics, who believed wages would adjust to compensate for the unpleasantness of jobs. It has never worked like that. But a progressive should want to move towards that model. Let the labour market act like a market is supposed to act.

Let there be commodified labour (the activity) where the wage adjusts to match supply and demand. But move towards decommodifying people as workers by providing them with enough economic security to refuse jobs they regard as undignified, dangerous or damaging to their development. We should start from the presumption that the human condition is to want to work, to want to better ourselves. If a few individuals want to dissipate their lives, we may wish to encourage them to think differently, but not with sanctions. Trying to identify the 'undeserving' is arbitrary and undignifying for all concerned.

The claim that workfare is justified as long as the unemployed are put into 'real jobs' runs into the problem of defining such jobs in a way that could be defended ethically or economically. Suppose a 'real job' is defined as one paying the minimum wage, justified by its productivity. Putting the unemployed into such jobs would put downward pressure on the wages and conditions of others, dragging them into poverty. On what ethical principle would this be justified? Or suppose the jobs were of a kind that others did not want to do, being dirty, dangerous, stigmatizing or undignified. They would have the opposite effect to what workfare advocates claim to want.

Why the precariat should oppose workfare

Jobs in workfare schemes are done under duress, in desperation. Progressives cannot support this. Egalitarians should want the labour market to operate so that wages in unpleasant jobs rise until labour supply emerges freely. This would benefit the precariat above all, which is why it should oppose workfare.

Principles of justice

Recalling the justice principles in Chapter 4, workfare offends the Paternalism Test Principle, since it imposes controls on the precariat that are not imposed on the most free in society. Indeed, it imposes exploitation that nobody else in society is expected to endure. For instance, in 2011, refining New Labour's Flexible New Deal, the coalition government introduced mandatory labour of up to 30 hours a week spread over 28 days, during which people had to do work 'of benefit to the community' in return for jobseeker's allowance. If they refused to do the labour at what amounted to a rate of £2.50 an hour, or failed to complete it, their benefit was stopped for a minimum of three months, and for six months if the 'transgression' (sic) was repeated. No other group, except convicts in prison, was expected to work for less than the national minimum wage. That was socially unjust.

Workfare also offends the Security Difference Principle, since it increases the insecurity of already highly insecure people. And it offends the Rights-not-Charity Principle, since it takes away a time-honoured social right while giving discretionary power to bureaucrats and their profit-making privatized surrogates. And it certainly offends the Dignified Work Principle, since labour done in unfreedom cannot be dignifying and rarely leads anywhere in terms of personal development.

Workfare disrupts job search

Coercion into short-term jobs must disrupt the job-search process. A market economy requires some unemployment. But people must be allowed to take time to look for the jobs they might be able to sustain, while firms must be allowed to take time to select from jobseekers. If jobseekers are put on workfare schemes, they cannot devote that time to seeking jobs. In fact, for this reason, workfare programmes have been shown to *reduce* the probability of future employment (Gregg 2009). It has been suggested that under the proposed universal credit, people would be able to take micro-jobs while continuing jobseeking to make up a 35-hour week of working and searching. However, to the extent that job search is disrupted, the labour market is made more inefficient.

Workfare lowers lifetime income

Far from increasing the probability of obtaining and sustaining career-oriented jobs, a spell in a workfare scheme can lower long-term income by giving people a history of low-level temporary jobs that do not match their qualifications or experience (e.g. Collins 2008). If so, then it is unfair to drive people into situations that are against their longer-term interest. And this applies as much if they believe it to be so, whether or not it is true. In the context in which past jobs and activities have a strong bearing on future options, individuals should be allowed to decide for themselves the best course to take. If the state takes it upon itself to tell people what they must do, it should compensate them if that turns out to have been mistaken.

Workfare depresses wages

Workfare must have a depressive effect on wages in general, although how big will depend on the level of wages paid to those on workfare and on the type and extent of workfare jobs. Forcing some people to take low-wage jobs and holding this out as a threat to induce others to take lower-paying jobs than they might otherwise have done, encourages employers to lower wages in general.

Although the UK Labour Party advocates a 'national living wage' above the minimum wage, it proposes to force the long-term unemployed to take government-funded jobs at the minimum wage. Perhaps the rationale is not to compete with 'real jobs'. The position is contradictory, and would put downward pressure on the wages of others doing similar labour.

If politicians want 'living wages', they should strengthen the bargaining position of the unemployed, not weaken it through workfare. Only if workers' bargaining capacity is strengthened will employers be under effective pressure to pay a living wage, or decide not to employ someone because the job is not needed, because potential productivity is so low. The reality is that the utilitarian mindset does not care about the precariat.

Workfare has unfair substitution effects

If the jobs were meaningful and productive, workfare would be unfair to existing employees and to the short-term unemployed because there would be displacement effects, with subsidized employees displacing existing employees or others who might have been hired. Tesco co-operated with jobcentres to provide 3,000 unpaid four-week placements in 2011. Poundland also announced it would take on unpaid benefit claimants, stating that this 'doesn't replace our recruitment activity but adds to the number of colleagues we have working with us'. Asda and Homebase were also keen to use such unpaid labour. Nobody could really doubt that substitution effects were taking place.

Workfare as state power

The utilitarian consensus on workfare was fully exposed following a legal challenge by a geology graduate forced to do unpaid labour in a profitable firm, Poundland, and a young man who lost his jobseeker's allowance for refusing to do 30 hours a week unpaid for six months on the misnamed Community Action Programme. Both the High Court and Appeal Court ruled that the government had acted illegally, because the relevant law did not stipulate when and how such action could be taken. Iain Duncan Smith, the minister, called the decision 'rubbish', asserting: 'There are a group of people out there who think they are too good for this kind of stuff... People who think it is their right to take benefit and do nothing for it – those days are over' (Malik 2013). This is remarkable coming from someone who has received many benefits in life without having done anything for them, including (via a family farm holding) over a million pounds in European Union subsidies.

In response to the court ruling, the government rushed through 'emergency' legislation in two days, a tactic supposedly only for national emergencies. This made refusal to do unpaid labour a sanctionable offence retrospectively, going against the very foundation of justice. Sadly, the Labour Party abstained, and Shadow Cabinet members were told that if they voted against the legislation, they would be forced to resign. This shameful episode shows how ingrained the workfare agenda had become.

Workfare as welfare-to-work scams

Workfare in the UK has enabled private firms, such as A4e and Ingeus, to make large profits from government contracts to put people in low-wage jobs, made more controversial by links between politicians and those making the money. Another 'charity', Tomorrow's People, run by a Conservative peer, supplied jobseekers as unpaid labour for the Diamond Jubilee celebrations under the government's Work Programme, a case that came to light when the workers involved were left stranded in London in the middle of the night and had to sleep rough under London Bridge.

Welfare-to-work (sic) firms have been paid £13,500 for each person placed in a long-term job, half that if they find them a short-term job. The incentive to 'cherry pick' means there is likely to be discrimination against vulnerable minorities. Revealingly, the Employment Related Services Association, the welfare-to-work industry's own trade body, expressed concern that more of those referred to these companies were people with disabilities who had 'failed' the test for the new employment and support allowance.

Work Programme providers are given wide powers of discretion in allocating people to 'work placements', and are allowed to decide what counts as 'community benefit'. The DWP allows placements in private firms if the jobs are deemed to benefit local communities, but has refused to publish information on private placements. Two of the largest firms contracted to administer the MWA also refused to comment on the suggestion they were forcing unemployed to work for private companies.

* * *

The precariat, and everyone who thinks that they, or relatives or friends, could find themselves in it, have an interest in combating workfare. Except in national emergencies, forcing people to do labour, unpaid or paid, is unacceptable. We must resolutely oppose it under any pretext, such as the claim it would break habits of 'worklessness' or strengthen the 'right to work'.

An experienced Citizens Advice staffer summed up the situation rather well (private communication 2013):

> The boundaries of the acceptable are being pushed further in the direction of unfree labour. We've been here before – breaking stones in return for food during the Irish famine, and similar schemes in 16th & 17th century England, the difference being that technology means people's activity can be monitored more and informal economy lifelines are being pushed further underground. I was talking with a colleague who has picked up growth of prostitution as one means of survival. I don't know what it would take to break us (society, whatever that means) out of apathy to make protests against what we're doing to ourselves.

Workfare is an extreme form of labour regulation. It does not promote growth. It distorts labour markets. (On these grounds, libertarians and neo-liberal economists should be intellectually consistent in opposing it.) Ultimately, workfare takes away rights and converts people into denizens in their own society. It is moralistic policy that should be passionately opposed by every liberal and progressive. If doing so puts political success at risk, so be it. Values matter.

Article 21: Regulate payday loans and student loans

Payday loans should be regulated to the point of making them residual and rare, while public subsidies for education should reduce the role and burden of student loans.

There is the rest of the month left when my wage has gone.

Los indignados, graffito

Payday loans

The payday loan industry is an offspring of financial capital's dominance and the growth of the precariat. It is a rent-seeking device of gross proportions, which austerity governments have allowed to flourish with impunity. The state is responsible for the payday loan phenomenon, with its devastating impact on the lives of millions drawn into its circuit in many countries in Europe, North America, Asia and the Caribbean. That is the inconvenient truth. Governments have diverted attention towards the abuses, such as failure to check creditworthiness due to the competitive nature of the business, and the unsavoury characters in the industry. But the root causes are labour flexibility and the class structure governments have fostered.

Short-term contingency lending has always existed, notably in the form of shabby pawnbrokers in poorer parts of towns and cities.

But the combination of falling wages, fluctuating earnings and lower, means-tested benefits has created the space for a rentier industry of short-term lending. It is the underbelly of neo-liberalism.

With real wages declining, the precariat lives permanently on the edge of unsustainable debt. Any delay in wage or benefit payments, or unanticipated deductions from earnings or benefits, or even a minor increase in necessary expenditure, can plunge someone into a debt cycle from which they cannot escape. In response, the market has generated a parasitic entity, a firm that lends to those in debt and to those unable to pay their bills. It takes advantage of insecurity. Not for nothing was the British government's petty measure in 2013, to make the newly unemployed wait seven days before claiming unemployment benefit, castigated as a prescription for a 'Wonga week', named after the leading payday loan company.

Interest is charged daily on such loans, which can be obtained quickly, with few questions asked. If the loan is not repaid on time, it is rolled over, after which the cost accelerates. For example, a £200 loan from Wonga costs £235 over 15 days, but over 60 days the debt will have increased to £327. As of mid–2013, Wonga's APR (annual percentage rate) stood at 5,853 per cent. A rival, The Money Shop, was charging an APR of over 20,000 per cent. This becomes debt bondage.

'Payday loans' is a euphemistic term to convey the idea that the industry is making quick flexible loans to tide people over until the wage arrives. In reality, the loans are often to cover shocks, unexpected costs or an inadequate income from a job, used to pay for essentials such as food, utility bills or rent. They reflect the economic structure, and reinforce and intensify the inequalities generated by it.

Better regulations are required. But dealing with payday loans effectively cannot be achieved without a progressive strategy to overcome the economic causes of their growth.

In the UK, by 2012, over a million people a month were using payday loans and the industry was lending over £2 billion annually, more than twice its level at the time of the crash. Payday loan debt rose by 300 per cent between 2010 and 2012, according to a debt counselling service, StepChange Debt Charity. The number seeking advice on payday loan difficulties has soared. StepChange helped 31,000 in the first half of 2013, nearly as many as in the whole of 2012. Over a fifth had five or more payday loans outstanding. Citizens Advice reported that one person had contemplated suicide after being contacted 20 times a day by the lender, who also contacted his employer. Others had their accounts drained by lenders, aided by banks.

An investigation by the Office of Fair Trading (OFT) confirmed that payday lenders were using heavy-handed ways of collecting money rather than spending on prior checks that borrowers were in a position to repay. Loans were being given to people with mental frailties, and to minors. Taking advantage of people's vulnerability, lenders were using continuous payment authorities (CPAs) that give them an indefinite mandate to take money from borrowers' credit or debit cards. The OFT issued guidelines saying lenders should not use CPAs without the informed consent of the borrower, should find out why a person is not repaying, and should not take money if the person did not have sufficient funds. But the government and regulators were supine.

Payday loan companies are integrated into the edifice of financial capital. Wonga, which has extended into Canada, Poland and South

Africa, is backed by private equity firms with links to Goldman Sachs, Mitt Romney's Bain Capital and the governing Conservatives (Collinson 2013), as well as other investors, including charities. In one notorious case, Wellcome Trust, a health research charity, invested in a Wonga funding drive; four months later, the key person who negotiated the deal on the charity's behalf moved to work for Wonga.

The industry has flourished in the USA. In 1990, there were fewer than 200 payday lending stores; in 2013 there were over 23,000. Payday lending had become a $50 billion industry, often charging interest rates on loans exceeding 500 per cent annually. According to the Pew Charitable Trusts, 12 million Americans take out payday loans each year, averaging $375, mostly to meet day-to-day expenses. The majority are unable to repay promptly and drift into deeper debt. Pew calculated that the typical borrower ended up paying more than twice the original loan, with bank charges on top.

US banks have played a dubious role in the growth of payday lending. Some have lent money to payday loan companies; some have engaged in it themselves, through 'direct deposit advances'. Mainstream banks such as JP Morgan Chase, Bank of America and Wells Fargo have facilitated recovery of loans and interest from customers' accounts, even in states where the loans are outlawed. More than a quarter of payday loan customers told a Pew survey that the loans had caused them to overdraw their accounts, running up hefty bank charges. Bank customers trying to stop withdrawals from their accounts find they cannot.

In 2012, the New Economy Project brought a federal lawsuit against JP Morgan Chase on behalf of two borrowers in New

York who claimed they had to pay thousands of dollars in bank charges on top of the interest and 'fines' imposed by the lenders. New York prohibits 'usurious' payday loans. Bizarrely, JP Morgan's chief executive described his bank's involvement as terrible, averring that he was unaware of it. Eventually, JP Morgan accepted a court settlement in which it pledged to respect customer requests to stop deductions from their accounts and to monitor and report abusive collection practices.

Payday loans are also part of the precarity trap story. Desperate people obtain easy loans, but are subject to aggressive collection practices, forcing them to sell assets or take on other debts. The payday loan industry makes a profit from its clients failing to pay on time, encouraging the industry knowingly to lend more than borrowers can afford. In the USA the average payday customer takes out 11 loans a year, often to pay off earlier debts. The OFT (2013) found that almost a third of loans in 2011–12 had been rolled over, accounting for almost half lenders' revenues.

After the OFT threatened 50 payday companies with withdrawal of their licences unless they cleaned up their acts, 14 decided to stop payday lending altogether and others were being rechecked for compliance with OFT guidelines. However, although the government planned to give the new Financial Conduct Authority (FCA) power from 2014 to cap loan charges, the payday loan industry should be regulated far more rigorously, with statutory requirements to check the feasibility of repayment, caps on the APR, publication of the costs and longer-term rates of interest, a requirement to guide borrowers in difficulty to debt advisers, a ban on automatic rollover of loans, and substantial penalties for abuse by the firms. Banks should be banned from involvement, either directly or indirectly by investing in payday loan companies.

Credit unions should be encouraged as an alternative source of small loans. But not too much can be expected from them. They require members to have a 'common bond', often related to employment or a local community, and to make savings before being considered for loans. Interest rates are modest, but most credit unions are under-capitalized and cannot carry much bad debt. Indeed, the whole purpose of the 'common bond' is to create an institution based on trust and mutuality. Many in the precariat will not qualify for membership of a credit union, or will be unable to make savings, or will fail credit checks.

The real problem is the rising need for short-term loans. Unless that is addressed, millions of people risk being dragged from the precariat into the lumpenized underclass, homeless, suicidal and lost to society. While there are anarchic means of resistance, brilliantly summarized in *The Debt Resistors' Operations Manual* (Brooklyn Rail 2012), they may end up criminalizing more victims. Removing the causes is the only way forward.

Student loans

Being on the edge between sustainable and unsustainable debt is almost the norm for the educated precariat. More and more people who go to college or university end up in chronic debt that can be truthfully described as debt bondage. They have a low probability of being able to pay off their debts, which drags down their chances of obtaining a home, marrying or having long-term stable relationships. A decade after university, one US graduate described her student debt as 'like carrying a big backpack filled with bricks' (Johannsen 2013).

It is not hyperbole to say that the situation is semi-feudal. The person is exploited both in the labour market and through the debt mechanism; the debt lowers the capacity to bargain for good wages or stand up for social or economic rights. Breaking that cycle of vulnerability is a twenty-first-century challenge.

The US situation is extreme. Students, or their families, now pay nearly half the costs of higher education, the share more than doubling between 1987 and 2013. Public disinvestment has meant that students pay more while the educational institutions receive less with which to educate them. In 2004, the government privatized Sallie Mae (now SLM Corporation), the main provider of federally guaranteed student loans, transferring a profitable almost risk-free business to the private sector. Since then, private student loans issued by Sallie Mae and others have ballooned, which has expanded the rentier character of the economy. Lenders have packaged these private student loans to create a market in student loan asset-backed securities (SLABS), worth $400 billion in early 2013. Investors regard SLABS as low-risk assets that provide a steady income stream from the millions of students with almost lifetime debts to repay. Yet there is already evidence of falling repayments and rising defaults.

Student debt exceeded credit card debt in 2010, and passed the $1 trillion mark in May 2012. Seven million of the 50 million-plus Americans with student debt are in default. Only half of federal student loan debt is being paid back, with nearly a third of loans in deferment, forbearance or default. A terrifying bubble looms. But

SLM Corporation spent several million dollars in lobbying Congress to ensure no political effort was made to regulate the profiteering.

Emulating the USA, the UK coalition government, having hiked tuition fees, is considering proposals to lift the cap on interest rates to promote the sale of the student loan book to private investors. In other countries too, the student loan industry is a rent-seeking device putting millions of young people into chronic debt. As Noam Chomsky put it:

> Students who acquire large debts putting themselves through school are unlikely to think about changing society. When you trap people in a system of debt, they can't afford the time to think. Tuition fee increases are a 'disciplinary technique,' and by the time students graduate, they are not only loaded with debt, but have also internalized the 'disciplinarian culture.' This makes them efficient components of the consumer economy (Weil 2013).

* * *

In sum, a progressive movement must wrest public control of both student loan and payday loan firms. Let them be mutualized, with student bodies being on the boards of any institution making loans to students. The real need is a return to a publicly funded education system, in which fees are moderated by public co-payments that are much greater and more universal than they have been in recent times.

In mid–2013, the Archbishop of Canterbury launched a church-based credit union to 'compete' Wonga out of business. It rightly drew popular praise. But such efforts are band-aid responses that leave the reasons for the growth of short-term loans untouched. The real need is for payday loans to be marginalized by augmenting economic security, by the means proposed in Articles 25 and 26. Without that, band-aid will be useless.

Article 22: Institute a right to financial knowledge and advice

Everybody should have the right to affordable financial advice, and have real opportunity to gain financial knowledge.

Financial knowledge is vital to function well in today's market economy. The precariat lacks affordable access to such knowledge, which increases economic insecurity and inequality. The elite, salariat and proficians can afford to buy expertise, which makes financial knowledge a vehicle for income inequality. Only by universalizing a right to financial advice and knowledge can equity and egalitarian concerns be met. Access to publicly provided financial advice should be a twenty-first-century social right.

Today, most ordinary households must spend a lot of time on financial management – filling in tax returns and social benefit forms, making decisions on savings, mortgages, investments, pensions and insurance, managing debt, choosing energy, phone and internet providers from a bewildering range of packages, and dealing with legal matters such as wills, probate, powers of attorney, divorce settlements, and so on. A sensible way of looking at work would regard this as work. Yet it goes unrecognized and unmeasured.

The UK's tax code is over 11,500 pages long; the US tax code is even longer – 74,000 pages – having tripled in volume over the past decade. One study estimated that Americans spent 7.6 billion hours and $140 billion a year on filing tax returns and four in every five used privately designed software or paid a tax professional (Economist 2013b). Well-paid accountants for the wealthy can minimize what their clients have to pay, using various means legally to avoid tax and some that verge on being illegal. Those in the precariat – who despite their low incomes may have complex financial affairs since they are not regular wage or salary earners – cannot pay for equivalent advice. This is one of inequality's inequalities.

The billionaire investor Warren Buffett had advisers who made sure he paid a lower tax rate than his secretary, as he freely admitted. Former Republican presidential candidate Mitt Romney's advisers ensured he paid less than 13 per cent on his multimillion dollar income. Meanwhile, those in the precariat probably pay more than they should on their meagre incomes.

There should be an economic right to free public advice and knowledge on financial management. And it must be more than a token right. Organizations like Citizens Advice in the UK should be properly funded to enable them to provide such advice to all. Everybody should have access to financial education; in this regard it is good that the UK government has introduced it as a subject on the secondary-school curriculum. And the time needed to learn about and do financial management should be counted as work.

Most people have little reliable knowledge of financial procedures or rules. We may fear breaking the law inadvertently, through not knowing all the rules and regulations. We may make mistakes, which can cost us money and so reduce net income, or worse, inadvertently conceal something and risk being sanctioned or even criminalized. Some may cheat, rationalizing that they have lost something in some other part of the system.

All of these situations cause stress and all are more serious for the precariat. Even if the loss of income is small, it could be a substantial part of the total income for the precariat, intensifying economic insecurity. Demands for recovery of overpayment of UK tax credits, for example, due to a person's fluctuating hours of work and income, can plunge them into financial difficulty.

In another example, UK charities have helped people successfully appeal against demands for hundreds of pounds of back tax from the tax authorities, but many just pay up without checking whether the demand is correct. One charity, Tax Help for Older People (taxvol. org.uk) claims a 97 per cent success rate in appeals against such demands. But most people do not or cannot get free advice and assume they must pay for a professional tax adviser, beyond the means of those on irregular incomes, even if their current income puts them outside the poverty band.

Credit records

A necessary part of someone's financial knowledge is the ability to access and correct the records held by credit reference agencies and others. No company should be allowed to register someone as a high credit risk without that person being informed and given proper opportunity to rectify the cause or contest the claim. Any company found to have marked down somebody's credit rating without their knowledge should be fined, and the person affected should be compensated. A slap on the wrist and an apology would be inadequate. Unless costs are imposed on the companies, they will continue to play safe by risking more Type 1 errors (mistakenly denying good credit ratings) rather than Type 2 errors (granting good credit ratings when there may be reasons for concern). At a time of tougher 'credit scoring' in applying for mortgages and other loans, and with an industry of credit reference agencies, this is increasingly important.

Online tax and debt advice

Many countries are moving towards providing tax-paying citizens with financial advice, usually online. This is desirable and equitable, as long as confidentiality and internet access are assured.

In the UK, the National Debtline is a free telephone helpline, part of the Money Advice Trust, set up in 1991 to provide independent financial advice. With backing from foundations, banks, government departments, charities and corporations, it has aided many desperate people but demand far outstrips resources. Nearly half the 234,000 calls to the Debtline in 2012 were from people with jobs. Citizens Advice is also overburdened. But even if these organizations were properly resourced, they could not function optimally unless the citizenry were educated in basic financial management and had the time and facilities to weigh options and risks.

In Italy, where about a quarter of economic activity is in the shadow economy, the tax authorities can assess income tax on the basis of information they uncover on an individual's spending habits. It is then up to the taxpayer to prove the resultant tax levy is incorrect. In 2012, the *Agenzia delle Entrate* (tax collection agency) introduced Redditest, an online program that enables people to calculate the income they should declare in order to be credible and thus avoid raising the authorities' suspicions. This may be the first time a government has offered assistance for tax avoidance! However, the precariat is least likely to take advantage of it. A third of Italians do not use computers, most of them poor or elderly.

* * *

Some governments have been drawn to the libertarian paternalist route of using financial incentives and opt-out barriers to steer people to make 'the right choice'. This blanket approach is dangerous and contrary to real freedom. The alternative and civilizing way forward is to provide more universal financial education, access to financial expertise and assurance of financial confidentiality. These are not minor matters.

Article 23: Decommodify education

> The education industry must be regulated and restricted, so as to restore public control of education and the practice of teaching. All aspects of education have been commodified, to the detriment of the precariat. Commodification must be reversed, with enlightenment values put at the heart of education.

But a university training is the great ordinary means to a great but ordinary end; it aims at raising the intellectual tone of society... It is the education which gives a man a clear conscious view of his own opinions and judgements, a truth in developing them, an eloquence in expressing them, and a force in urging them.

The Idea of a University, Cardinal Newman ([1852] 1907)

As Chapter 3 reiterated, the claim right to real education is being sacrificed, and the precariat is being ravaged by educational commercialization. All aspects have been commodified – the institutions, degrees and certificates, students, teachers and academics. All have been subject to market pressures, as educational capitalism has advanced.

Education is supposed to provide a road to wisdom and to stimulate curiosity, ethical values and creativity. Instead, as the numbers put through education grow globally, for more and more people it is just about preparing them for jobs and competing for jobs. Education is a public good. That is under threat. Enlightenment values at the heart of education must be revived, giving more scope for healthy non-conformism and the learning of ethics, empathy and morality.

Decommodify educational systems

Education has been commercialized in the globalization era. Profit-making has become the driving force, along with preparing young people to become jobholders. This has led to financialization and to growing dominance by commercial firms building a global 'education industry'.

While making a conventional liberal point that education should not be the preserve of the wealthy, one well-known journalist added: 'Of course graduates should pay fees for their education over 30 years of their subsequent working life... Of course universities should do more to feed business with the lifeblood of scientific and techno-logical knowledge' (Hutton 2013). But why should those criteria be dominant? Society also needs philosophers, poets, archaeologists and historians, for social and cultural reasons, but these and many other occupations (including journalism) do not normally pay well enough to support the huge debts UK and US students are now obliged to incur. Not everyone can get (or wants) a job in the City of London or on Wall Street. Universities must reassert their enlight-enment mission (Collini 2012). Education should prepare people to be citizens, not jobholders. If schooling is driven by financial costs and returns, the wider purposes of education will be shunted into the margins.

Universities have become a global industry, sending representa-tives around the world to recruit fee-paying students and selling packaged courses, with glossy brochures, satellite campuses in China and elsewhere, and academic exchange centres. Despite disquiet, most academics have fallen into line. Academic 'superstars' are recruited and used to generate profits for their universities. They have moved out of a community of professionalism, a guild structure reproducing the ethics and ways of behaving that defined the Enlightenment.

Globalization of education as 'schooling' is accelerating, with universities from the USA, UK and elsewhere competing to sell their brands. It belittles the oral and fraternal traditions associated with the great centres of learning. To go to Cambridge is not the same as going to, say, Manchester or Oxford. Each has something special, steeped in its history, balance of subjects, forms of learning, and so on. The global selling of universities is led by commercial, not cultural or liberalizing considerations (e.g. Seldon 2013). It goes with the conviction that online schooling and teacher-less universities will dominate the future. If they do, there will be erosion of the critical facility to debate, discuss, and reflect.

Standardized curricula lie ahead. Online courses promise to become paradigm-reinforcing, not paradigm-challenging. We should not want the universities of Cambridge, Harvard, the Sorbonne, New Delhi or Cape Town to become 'global brands'. They should be centres for creative critical thinking, and those lucky enough to be there should oppose their conversion into global profit centres.

Commodification has spread to secondary and primary schooling, as well as specialist schooling. Sweden has led the way towards privatization of schooling, allowing competition with state schools and providing vouchers to purchase places in 'free' (commercial) schools. More than a third of Swedish upper secondary schools and a sixth of elementary schools are run by private operators, many now owned by private equity firms. Despite gains in state school achievements, Sweden has slipped down the OECD's PISA (Programme for International Student Assessment) educational performance rankings in recent years, notably in science. It has ploughed on, reorienting schools to job preparation, employability and guidance by employer bodies (Lundahl et al. 2010). In 2013, one of its star educational companies, JB Education, owned by a private equity group, shut down, leaving students stranded, but the biggest, AcadeMedia, also owned by a private equity group, continued to expand.

By contrast, Finland, which has relied on a state system, has consistently outperformed other countries in Europe and North America, according to the standard PISA scores, and moved further ahead of Sweden. Finland has resisted commodification, spending less proportionately than many countries, including the USA, and allowing creative experimentation by its teachers and local schools. As evaluators have testified, the key has been to put trust in professionals, in teachers, not dictate to them with national curricula or performance league tables. Teachers are free to design their curricula and develop their own tests for pupils. The system has remained almost unchanged since the early 1970s.

There is also occupational self-regulation. Teaching in Finland has been preserved as a profession, albeit not well paid, and has not been commodified to the point of class splintering, unlike in the USA, UK and elsewhere where the profession increasingly reflects an elite, salariat and precariat class structure, with little internal mobility.

It is vital that commercialization be rolled back. A properly funded public education system open to everybody and used by all income groups is essential for any Good Society. Commercialization also erodes the desire for education for itself, notably the pursuit of knowledge, culture and morality that the ancient Greeks called *paideia*. We do not have the time! It has no pay-off! The same goes for the commodification of teachers. Authorities are revising remuneration systems to 'reward' productivity. In the USA, states and districts are pushing teachers onto merit pay, in the face of opposition from teacher unions. The objective is to incentivize performance, but it will result in more stress, more competitiveness among teachers and administrators, and more teaching to tests. Other countries have moved in the same direction. It will erode the value of the education process itself.

Decommodify credentials and roll back credentialism

Students go to university or college to search for an education. Most soon realize they have instead bought a lottery ticket. Unless they are very unwise, or take the risk of opting for tough challenging 'options', they soon also realize they can obtain the lottery ticket with little effort, provided they stick the course. Most educational institutions have a commercial reason to maximize the student 'success rate'.

Thus both students and institutions have an interest in gaming the system. But for the precariat, the sham is a scam. Students and their families are paying ever more for the prospective lottery ticket, and incurring ever more debt that could be with them for decades. And the lottery ticket is worth less and less, since the number acquiring tickets is higher than ever and the chance of winning, in terms of access to a high-income job, is lower than ever. There is no easy solution. However, it is essential to recover a sense of education being a social right, an end in itself. The content, governance and objectives must be rescued from market forces.

One campaign would help – to downgrade credentialism, the use of diplomas as recruitment devices when they have no direct relevance. Capital always wants 'more' skilled labour. And manpower planning models always predict shortages, however fast the numbers of educated grow. The McKinsey Global Institute estimated that by 2030 the global labour force would be 3.5 billion; that by 2020 there would be 38–40 million fewer workers with tertiary education than employers would 'need'; that there would be a shortage of 45 million workers with secondary education in developing countries; and that there would be a surplus of over 90 million low-skill workers (defined as without college education in advanced economies or secondary schooling in developing countries). They concluded, predictably, that advanced economies needed to double the growth of college-educated youth, and shift more to engineering and science fields. This is a consequence of interpreting demand as need. Manpower models should be treated with caution. Much of what passes for need is credentialism.

Decommodify teachers and academics

Educational occupations are being converted into mirrors of the global class structure, with an elite, a salariat, proficians, a core of stable workers and a growing precariat. The winners are the elite

– star academics with awards, prizes and consultancies – and the salariat with tenure and non-wage benefits such as pensions, long paid holidays and so on, along with the proficians – niche players selling courses and moving on.

Meanwhile, more people are finding themselves in the precariat. In many countries, new auxiliary categories have been set up, often encouraged by government and commercial interests working with it. There has been a huge growth of 'teaching adjuncts', often on standby, not knowing what and where they will be teaching until the last moment. In Australian universities, more than 85 per cent of teaching staff are casuals. In the USA, half the faculty in public universities are adjuncts, and for community colleges the proportion is over 80 per cent. The University and College Union in the UK says the higher education sector is now the second most casualized after the hospitality industry, with more than a third of the regular academic workforce on temporary contracts, not counting over 80,000 casuals doing jobs such as hourly-paid teaching. Many adjuncts are paid little more than the minimum wage, well below the salaries of tenured teachers and academics doing essentially the same labour.

Another commodifying tactic is the 'ranking' or 'rating' of lecturers, reinforcing the notion that education is a market and students 'consumers' of a product. This is being taken further by the promotion of online courses (MOOCs – massive open online courses) and lectures by academic stars, such as Harvard Professor Michael Sandel, competing with each other in the global market, peddling standardized products and norm-driven conformity.

Education as a liberating process must recreate a community based on ethics. The elite and salariat inside the system must coalesce with the educational precariat to reduce its insecurities and reverse the widening class differentiation. While the elite may gain rental income by preserving a privileged insider category, it will also suffer from the erosion of integrity and educational ethos if the stratification continues.

A truth through the ages is that today's conventional wisdom is tomorrow's repudiated prejudice. Online courses for the millions threaten the spirit of enquiry and non-conformism. Clayton Christensen, of Harvard Business School, claims the traditional university has had its day, noting that Harvard no longer teaches entry-level accounting, because students prefer to use an online course from another university (Friedman 2013). Elite schools run by elite professors for elite people, alongside standardized breadwinner schools for the precariat. This is a future to be resisted.

Decommodify academic research

Governments are manipulating research for commercial and ideological ends through imposed funding and evaluation methods, notably by allocating funds to universities based on rating systems oriented to 'value for money' and 'impact'. This is a global trend. With money dangled in front of them, academics and universities have responded with docile consent. In the UK, the 2014 Research Excellence Framework (REF) will allocate resources and grades to universities according to the perceived impact of their research. How to measure 'impact' is decided by bureaucrats, many appointed by the dominant political establishment, who predictably give high weight to research seen as useful for government and mainstream institutions. Critical or non-orthodox research and thinking will be judged to have little or no impact, and thus will be increasingly under-funded and unrewarded (Colley 2013). Academics will be criticized for not having impact, and will therefore face marginalization. More likely, they will see that the way to salariat security and promotion is to show they are having impact, and will modify their critical ways.

Thus research oriented to helping youth in deprived communities has minimal weight in the assessment of impact, whereas research on issues affecting large corporations or government departments counts for a great deal. Moreover, it is easy for funders, which may be corporations or government departments, to suppress research findings they do not like, and ensure that they are not cited in official reports. By determining what research is given publicity, funders influence measured impact and hence the direction of work. This reproduces and strengthens the positions of the powerful, the elite and the orthodox, who will appoint their own adherents to boards and committees doing the assessments. In return, administrations, fixated with implementing a business model and maximizing university income, will penalize researchers with no perceived or likely 'impact', and will make appointments and promotions accordingly.

Teach empathy, not opportunism

Certain professions, notably medicine, insist that to become a member of the profession a person must take courses in ethics. Given that many more services involve issues of trust and integrity, which may well not be consistent with maximizing income, everyone should be provided with ethical education. In a commercialized world, ethical education is seen as unimportant because it does not help in 'enhancing competitiveness'. A consequence is that the great values of compassion and empathy are in danger of marginalization, leaving people easily swayed by the utilitarian stance of opportunistic politicians, their advisers and the media. There must be a campaign to overcome the business model. Every public and private school should have courses in moral education.

* * *

There must be a campaign to decommodify education and recapture its primary purposes. Too many people in and around the educational systems of the world are bowing to commodifying pressures, in spite of their values and intellects. Instead, they should ridicule the commercial pretensions of standardization and impact assessment tests, oppose their self-commodification, and show solidarity with adjunct professors, auxiliary teachers and precariatized colleagues. This campaign must be led by the elites of the education sphere. They have the least to lose and can take risks from positions of authority and security. However, they should also seek to democratize educational institutions, including funding institutions, in particular by ensuring that the precariat has Voice.

In a global market system, decommodification of education cannot be achieved in its entirety. But for the future of education as a liberating part of life, there must be strong institutions to hold the commercial demons in check. In 2013, Michelle Bachelet, former Chilean president, running for the presidency a second time as the Social Democrat candidate, announced she would end private profit-making in education at all levels. It is a pity she did not do so when she was president. However, she was responding to concerted pressure brought by students in continuous large-scale demonstrations. It was their triumph.

Article 24: Make a bonfire of subsidies

Subsidies are regressive, redistributing income from low-income groups to high-income groups and interests. They distort markets. And they are a source of economic inefficiency. The precariat, which benefits least from subsidies, should campaign for an end to subsidies of all kinds, including most tax breaks.

Subsidies given by governments to corporations, households and special interests account for over 5 per cent of global income. If that were redistributed in the form of money to individuals, income poverty could be wiped out. It will not happen. But this does not justify accepting the subsidy state that has grown up as a corollary of globalization. It is regressive, redistributing income to high-income groups and interests; it distorts markets; and it contributes to economic inefficiency. Subsidies can take the form of direct payments, tax breaks, or provision of below-cost goods and services. They may be promoted as incentives for certain types of behaviour, or they may be conditional on recipients undertaking certain acts.

The precariat is disadvantaged by the system, and has most to gain by its overhaul. It could start by exposing the hypocrisy of politicians who cut benefits for the precariat on grounds of 'state dependency' while taking subsidies that are no less 'state dependency'.

Beggar-my-neighbour competition policy

Subsidies are part of global competition policy. In 2011, Dilma Rousseff, Brazil's new president, went to Taiwan to offer Foxconn tax breaks, subsidized loans and special access through lower tariffs for imported parts if it assembled Apple products in Brazil. The offer worked. Somewhere else lost out. But in providing 'beggar-my-neighbour' subsidies to capital, she was only doing what the rich countries started when they liberalized in the 1980s. Governments have used subsidies to try to make their country or region more competitive for foreign investment.

Within large countries, local governments have used subsidies to attract firms from other parts of the country. According to a database compiled by the *New York Times*, in 2012 the 50 US states provided $80 billion in incentives to corporations to relocate or expand in their states, mainly through tax reliefs. Since many of the firms would have expanded or relocated anyway, this amounted to a gift from the 'little people' who pay taxes. In Texas, 48 companies, including General Motors, all received more than $100 million between 2007 and 2012. In 2011, to try to reduce its budget deficit, the state slashed $31 billion from public spending, including huge reductions in the education budget. So measuring the subsidies' regressive impact should take into account not just the financial transfer to the firms involved, but also the effects of the public spending cuts. There is no evidence that subsidies boost growth or general living standards. If Texas provides subsidies to attract firms, other states will do the same. And there is little to prevent the firm from moving again as soon as it is convenient. The system is a cosy arrangement to transfer income from workers and citizens to corporations and recipients of capital income.

Another form of subsidy is concealed in the term 'quantitative easing' describing the response to the crisis by central banks, principally the Bank of England and the US Federal Reserve, to pump money into the economy by buying government bonds. Rather than helping to 'kick start' economic growth, the trillions of dollars created by the central banks have merely helped struggling banks to recapitalize, others to boost profits and all to line bankers' pockets. Quantitative easing is a subsidy to banks. It has enabled them to borrow from central banks at minimal interest rates and lend that money, via bond purchases, to governments at higher rates. Cheap money covered the hole in bank finances caused by capital flight from Europe's crisis-hit economies. According to Citigroup, €100 billion left Spain in 2011 and €160 billion left Italy, as foreigners withdrew bank deposits or sold bonds. And near-zero interest rates helped boost stock markets and enabled rich investors to pay less for money-making assets. This is state dependency. Moreover, these huge subsidies came without any requirement on borrowers to behave responsibly or to report at an office regularly to account for what they were doing, in sharp contrast to how governments treat the precariat. Why should governments give handouts to the elite while demanding less 'dependency' by others?

Corporate welfare

Rich-country governments have bid down corporation tax rates, so capital is taxed much less than labour. And effective rates are further lowered by subsidies such as the 'patent box' in the UK and the '*innovatiebox*' (innovation box) in the Netherlands that give tax relief on intellectual property. Everywhere one looks, one finds subsidies to capital. Never has capitalism exhibited such state dependency. Never before have governments been so craven before capital.

In 2012, deep in austerity, Portugal cut corporation tax while its people were struggling in economic insecurity. Around the world, there is a beggar-my-neighbour race to lower corporate taxes further. The UK's Treasury Minister, David Gauke, put the matter bluntly, saying, 'We must recognize that we are in a global race' (Houlder 2013). It is a collective action problem, but it also reflects a collaboration within the 'plutonomy': corporations and the plutocracy fund political parties and politicians, who go onto company boards after their spell in politics.

While utilitarians rail against the precariat for being dependent on the state, corporations constantly demand more subsidies. Just before the UK budget of March 2013, financial brokers and businessmen were invited to write proposals in *The Observer* (Goodley 2013). A Deloitte partner argued for 'lower taxes', notably corporation tax, even though the UK corporation tax rate was already one of the world's lowest. The chief executive of Greene King, a brewery and pub chain, called for 'exemption on national insurance for employer and employee for all new jobs created for three years', claiming it 'would not cost the exchequer a penny, would save unemployment expenditure and get young adults into the work habit.' However, a subsidy is always a cost; that approach would also induce deadweight and substitution effects. The head of Linn Products, which makes high-end digital music players, welcomed the 'R & D tax credit scheme', another subsidy, and wanted corporation tax cuts and a national insurance tax holiday for new hires. Meanwhile, a finance broker was given a column to call for 'tax breaks to companies that build factories here' and removal of 'employers' national insurance contributions so that it is more attractive to hire workers' (Wolf 2013). It seems capitalism in OECD countries cannot exist without subsidies. Corporate welfare is state dependency. It is regressive, it distorts markets and it encourages inefficiency.

Personal subsidies

Suzanne Mettler's *The Submerged State* (2011) recounts a 2008 poll in which over half of Americans denied ever using a government programme. But when shown a list of 21 actual programmes, including student loans and tax deductions for home mortgage interest payments, 94 per cent of the deniers turned out to have benefited from them.

Most of these 'personal subsidies' were highly regressive. Almost 70 per cent of mortgage-interest deductions went to those earning over $100,000, as did over half of deductions for employer-provided retirement benefits. Only 16 per cent of workers in the lowest income quintile had employer-sponsored (tax-deductible) health insurance compared to 85 per cent of those in the top quintile. In all, the average subsidy for those earning $200,000–$500,000 was three times that for those earning $10,000–$20,000.

The USA 'spends' $1,200 billion a year on these and other tax breaks, such as deductions for charitable donations, mostly benefiting higher-income groups with access to good accountants. The precariat gains the least. And since most personal subsidies go to the elite and salariat, politicians rarely include them when demanding benefit cuts. But they increase inequality. They also distort markets, since they reduce the costs of certain types of expenditure relative to others.

For instance, one subsidy helping the upper rungs of the salariat is tax relief on pension contributions. As of 2013, the affluent in the UK could put up to £50,000 annually into their pension pot, saving 40 per cent (the top rate of tax) on every pound shifted that way. While proposals to cap tax reliefs would raise considerable revenue, especially in the USA, that could weaken the resolve to do away with them as state dependency. A progressive should wish to see full labour commodification, with a shift from non-wage, less taxable forms of remuneration to money wages.

Government loan guarantees are also a subsidy. The UK government's Help to Buy scheme guarantees up to 15 per cent of mortgages taken out on properties up to £600,000, representing £130 billion of mortgage lending. This is a gift to middle-income earners while the precariat is excluded, not being in a position to buy property. Even the outgoing Governor of the Bank of England, Sir Mervyn King, criticized the scheme, commenting: 'We do not want what the United States have, which is a government-guaranteed mortgage market, and they are desperately trying to find a way out of that position' (Wearden 2013). If young members of the salariat cannot afford to buy homes because there is a shortage, there should be a plan to create more low-cost homes. Subsidies are the wrong answer.

Demographically regressive subsidies

Many in the precariat are 'single'. Policy should treat them as equal citizens. 'Singleism' has boomed. Euromonitor International predicts that globally there will be an extra 48 million solo residences by 2020, a jump of 20 per cent from 2012. In Sweden, by 2020 almost half of households will contain only one person. Half of America's adults are unmarried, up from 22 per cent in 1950. Nearly 15 per cent live alone, up from 4 per cent back then. Among explanations for the growth of singleton living are the incarceration of men, longevity by widows and widowers, and changed attitudes to marriage and child-bearing. Women in particular no longer see marriage as a guarantee of financial security.

Policymakers have neglected singles, whose social rights are restricted. From tax breaks to holiday arrangements, couples and spouses enjoy many benefits that singles do not (DePaulo 2007). This includes subsidies. In the USA, the Healthy Marriage Initiative is a subsidy programme to encourage unmarried parents to marry, at an annual cost of $150 million. Why should singles be social denizens?

Why should couples be subsidized? If being a couple is so favourable, why add privileges?

Labour subsidies and tax credits

Labour subsidies are payments to employers or workers intended to encourage employment or bring wages up to an acceptable or subsistence level. For employers, the most used are marginal employment subsidies that pay firms hiring additional employees, usually from a designated target group such as youth.

Governments have resorted extensively to such subsidies, often under the heading of 'active labour market policies'. The target group may be shown to have benefited. But there are invariably large deadweight effects – providing subsidies to firms that were going to hire people anyway – and large substitution effects – employers hiring someone with the subsidy while displacing someone else not having the subsidy. The primary beneficiary is the firm.

Labour subsidies are a licence to inefficiency. If a firm is only paying a fraction of the wage, productivity need only be equal to that reduced cost. There is no pressure to raise productivity. There are also moral hazards, such as retaining someone who is not really needed, which is inconsistent with dignifying work. And there are likely to be 'auntie effects', hiring friends and relations as shadow workers because they bring a subsidy with them.

In 2013, the new Italian government introduced tax breaks for employers if they hired under-30s on permanent contracts. This will not achieve much, just as the UK's 'flagship' Youth Contract scheme failed to achieve anything. It was found that firms given a large subsidy (£2,275) for recruiting unemployed youth made them redundant after the minimum period of six months and then hired others on the same basis. The stated aim had been to create 'permanent' jobs, but no information was collected on whether jobs were permanent or temporary. The government admitted in mid-2013 that there was 'some evidence to suggest that wage incentives were not always being used as intended' (Mason 2013). This should have been no surprise. Labour subsidies allow politicians to make positive speeches, but are invariably a waste of money.

Tax credits have similar effects. The biggest labour and social security reform of the globalization era, they are a licence to pay lower wages. Their growing use is correlated with the decline of real wages in the precariat's earnings range. One way by which tax credits lower wages is by weakening the incentive for low-wage workers to join unions and other bodies pushing for higher wages and benefits. It is difficult to test this claim empirically, since unionization has fallen at the same time as use of tax credits has grown. But there are strong reasons for thinking that tax credits enable low-paid workers to put up with those low wages.

Evidence against tax credits and labour subsidies does not deter politicians from continuing with them. In 2013, Labour advocated a new subsidy for employers if they paid the living wage. In a speech flagged as defining the party's stand, Ed Miliband said:

> For every young man and woman who has been out of work for more than a year, we would say to every business in the country, we will pay the wages for 25 hours a week, on at least the minimum wage (Miliband 2013).

This would amount to a payment to private firms, which would be regressive. It would have all the classic negatives – deadweight, displacement, labour inefficiency – and would almost certainly have minimal effect on total unemployment, although it would generate more underemployment.

Duncan Smith's state dependency

Iain Duncan Smith, UK Secretary of State for Work and Pensions, has led a robust campaign against benefits for the poor and precariat, saying he is determined to reduce state dependency and end the 'something for nothing' culture. Meanwhile, his own state dependency dwarfs that of any of his targets. A trust run by members of his family has received over £1 million in EU agricultural subsidies in the past decade, in addition to the various tax breaks farmers receive, courtesy of an estate of 1,500 acres inherited by his wife. The EU's Common Agricultural Policy is regressive, since the primary beneficiaries are large landowners. While the UK government was capping benefits for the poor, claiming that nobody should receive more in benefits than the average wage, it vetoed a European Commission plan to cap the amount of money going in farm subsidies to the wealthy.

Charities and subsidies

As welfare states crumble, the role of charity and philanthropy is growing. Donations by the rich to charities in the UK and USA benefit from generous tax breaks. When the UK government tried to scrap tax relief on donations, charities objected and the plan was dropped. In the USA, President Obama tried to limit what could be deducted from taxable income. This proposal also fizzled out.

Charity is discretionary; it can intensify inequality and accelerate privatization. But if charity is a voluntary altruistic act, the state should be neutral. There is no ethical or economic reason to give subsidies to wealthy philanthropists rather than to strugglers in and around the precariat. Such tax relief and subsidies divert money from uses that could reduce the need for charity!

Tax avoidance as implicit subsidy

For years, it has been public knowledge that major corporations, and the plutocracy and elite, have avoided tax on a huge scale. This partly reflected laxer rules by governments keen to attract them to their countries. While governments were lowering state benefits and making it harder for people to obtain them, citing benefit fraud and scroungers, tax avoidance went unchecked, even though it accounted for vastly more lost revenue than any benefit cheating. The European Commission estimates that shifting corporate profits to lower-tax countries is costing governments tens of billions of dollars annually. Only when a few high-profile multi-nationals – among them Apple, Starbucks, Google, Amazon and Dell – were exposed as using tax avoidance devices on a massive scale, paying little or no tax on billions of dollars of earnings, did politicians give the matter attention. The fact that they themselves and their major donors were beneficiaries of tax avoidance may help explain their reticence.

Subsidies and 'small' business

In 2013, the British government extended its Funding for Lending scheme, giving subsidies to banks to induce them to lend more to small businesses. It is commonly claimed that small businesses are more dynamic and generate more jobs than large firms, so should be encouraged with subsidies. Although regressive, this might be justified if the claim were true. However, it is not. A review of evidence by *The Economist* (2012a) noted: 'A bias to small firms is costly. The productivity of European firms with fewer than 20 workers is on average little more than half that of firms with 250 or more workers.' Big firms also tend to pay higher wages.

The link between small businesses and job creation arises mainly from start-ups which by definition create jobs that did not exist before. But many start-ups fail and many small firms stay small. *The Economist* concluded: 'Mature small firms often destroy jobs, as do small start-ups that do not survive.' The array of subsidies given to small firms is part of a regressive, distortionary system.

* * *

Neo-liberals should oppose subsidies as a form of state dependency. However, their utilitarian politics engender a hypocritical stance, since many subsidies go to median voters. The precariat must help them recover a little respect for intellectual consistency, by denouncing all subsidies and by making a nuisance of themselves in doing so.

International regulation would help. The World Trade Organization (WTO) is supposed to curb trade-distorting subsidies. Although it cannot intervene over the use of subsidies within countries, there have been proposals for a domestic counterpart to the WTO dispute settlement system as a way of arresting domestic subsidy competition through tax refunds or reductions, or cash grants, loans or loan guarantees. As an interim measure, firms should be required to pay back subsidies if they subsequently renege on the implicit or explicit obligation made when they obtained them.

A subsidy is a state benefit. If politicians say they wish to end 'the something for nothing' culture, and require the unemployed and precariat to do demeaning time-wasting actions or lose benefits, the same rules should apply to all receiving subsidies. If employers are given a subsidy to take on more workers, they should be required to attend regular interviews to prove they are using the labour wisely and trying to raise productivity. If, as is the case instead, they are presumed to be operating in their own best interest, relying on incentives to motivate them, why not apply the same reasoning when it comes to the unemployed and precariat?

As far as tax avoidance is concerned, the precariat should campaign to boycott goods and services from the worst offenders and from countries known to be using the tactics most aggressively. It should promote an international communication network on such practices, and encourage the construction of indexes of corporate subsidies and national subsidy competition. And it should vote for politicians and parties that commit themselves to legislative reform to reduce and eliminate corporate subsidies.

Article 25: Move towards a universal basic income

Governments should move towards instituting a basic income as a citizenship right. In a global market economy, uncertainty and inequality will only worsen unless new measures are introduced. It is vital to overhaul the social protection system.

The precariat can only face the future with optimism if the state moves towards paying a guaranteed basic income, a monthly amount sufficient to provide every legal resident with basic security. Without such a claim right, insecurity, indebtedness and inequality will continue to grow.

Progressives and libertarians must understand that the context has changed. Every type of economy has a distinctive mode of income distribution. Under industrial capitalism, the two main modes were wages and profits; governments mediated the struggle for shares of total income with regulations, taxes and subsidies. But in a globalized system wages have lost ground, while rental income and financial capital are high and rising. We need to revise our economic imagination. For workers and the precariat to have an adequate income, something like a basic income is simply essential.

Let us take the argument step by step, considering the rationale for moving in this direction, the criticisms and the potential advantages. At the heart of a Precariat Charter must be a struggle for economic security. Social democrats have done nothing to reverse the growth of insecurity, merely offering means-testing, behavioural condition-ality and workfare. Any progressive should want a society in which everyone has basic security, regardless of age, gender, race, marital status, labour status, disability or whatever. This is so fundamental as to challenge the progressive credentials of anyone rejecting it.

Defining a basic income

The proposal is that every individual in society should have the right to a basic income. This should be defined carefully. *First*, the term 'basic' has a double, complementary significance. The amount should be basic – enough to survive on but not enough to provide full security; that induces carelessness, one reason for opposing vast wealth. And the income should be seen as basic in the sense that, without it, other rights cannot be realized. There cannot be a meaningful right to education or a right to work without basic security. A basic income is also a claim or republican right, in that policies should be judged by whether they move towards its realization.

Some argue that the amount paid should be the average income (van Parijs 1995). While this may be a long-term goal, it is not what is proposed here. The amount should be sufficient to cover basic material needs, while facilitating the pursuit of other life-enhancing goals. For that reason, the level should be linked to the median income, so that it does not freeze a minority in poverty.

Second, it must be paid individually, probably with a lower amount for a child. It should not be paid to some notion of a household or family. They are what economists call endogenous units that vary quite properly. It is paternalistic and moralistic, not moral, to set benefits according to household type or some measure of 'marriage' or degree of permanence of a relationship. That has led to Type 1 errors (as was noted in Article 18), as well as arbitrary, unnecessarily intrusive and costly administrative mechanisms.

Third, it must be paid in cash, not in vouchers or subsidized goods. Benefits in kind limit freedom of choice and are paternalistic. It should also be a regular, predictable payment, probably paid monthly. *Fourth*, it should be provided unconditionally, without behavioural rules. In other words, it should be a right of citizenship or legal residence, subject to some pragmatic rule on migration, to be discussed later. *Fifth*, it must be universal, with the transfer clawed back from the better-off through taxes. This is more efficient than means-testing, for reasons given earlier, notably with respect to poverty traps.

Some distinguish between 'partial' and 'full' basic income, usually in considering practical methods of converting existing benefits. We will not go into that debate, and will just say that moving towards a basic income could be achieved by converting existing selective transfers into unconditional grants and then extending them to other groups, or it could be built up from a very modest grant. But it is crucial that its core should rise with economic growth.

The ethical justification

A moral reason for a basic income is that the wealth of anyone in society is far more the result of the endeavours of our forebears than anything we do ourselves. But we do not know whose forebears made greater or smaller contributions. And we do not know whose forebears suffered unfairly and thus could not pass on wealth to their descendants. Thus, behind a 'veil of ignorance' about where we would be in the distribution of outcomes, we should wish to equalize the advantages handed down to us all.

A basic income could be seen as a social dividend derived from our forebears' investments and hard work. Although he did not put it quite like that, Thomas Paine, champion of the rights of man and courageous participant in both the French Revolution and the American War of Independence, had essentially this view in his pamphlet *Agrarian Justice* ([1797] 2005).

In 2013, I was invited to present *The Precariat* in Middlesbrough, a birthplace of the Industrial Revolution in the nineteenth century, which in a few years went from being a nondescript hamlet to a hub of the economy and the British Empire (Heggie 2013). It was the site of the first ironworks, later branching out into steel and chemicals. Statues of the figures who had built the industries stand in the town centre; plaques marking some personality or place remind the visitor of a proud past. Australia's Sydney Harbour Bridge and San Francisco's Golden Gate Bridge were built in or near Middlesbrough, as was much of the Indian railway system. On a gate is emblazoned: 'Born of iron, made of steel.'

Now, Middlesbrough's old town hall stands derelict on a hill, surrounded by wasteland and weeds. In dilapidated estates studied by Tracy Shildrick and colleagues (2012), many of the houses are boarded up, with concrete blocks where there were once windows, and weeds growing in the crevices. Still, 140,000 people continue to live in the town. They suffer the cruelty of history. The wealth today of those living in the south of England and in other affluent parts of the country was generated in part by the people of Middlesbrough. Why should people living in these well-endowed places have lives so much more comfortable and secure than the descendants of those who built the country's wealth and power? Thinking of Middlesbrough, and it is far from alone, should remind us of Paine's argument in 1797. A basic income can be seen as a transfer to people in the likes of Middlesbrough from more affluent folk who are benefiting from the wealth created by those ironworkers and their successors.

There are other ethical reasons for supporting a basic income. It is the only measure that would satisfy the Security Difference Principle, in that it would improve the economic and social security of the most insecure groups in society. No other form of social protection would have that desirable property. It would also satisfy the Paternalism Test Principle, in that it would impose no controls on any specific group, and in that regard would enhance personal freedom, which both libertarians and progressives should wish. And it would satisfy the Rights-not-Charity Principle, by removing bureaucratic discretion to decide who is deserving and who is not, and whose behaviour merits pity and whose merits sanction.

Basic income would also satisfy both the Dignified Work and Ecological Constraint Principles. It would allow people to choose more rationally what work they wished to do, and what labour they would be prepared to accept in pursuit of income. And in altering the trade-off between labour and reproductive work, such as caring for others or growing vegetables, it would help re-orient work from resource-using to resource-reproducing activities.

The economic justification

The economic justification for a basic income stems from globalization itself, in which flexible labour relations have gone with a dismantling of institutions and mechanisms of social solidarity and social protection. However, there is no going back. Social insurance systems could function reasonably if most were able to contribute to an insurance fund and if people had a roughly equal probability of being hit by a bad event. But those conditions have been destroyed by economic and political developments. Individualism and flexibility have made outcomes increasingly unequal, while social mobility has declined, both upwards and downwards. Those in and out of the labour force cannot make regular or sufficient contributions, nor can those in and out of jobs in the precariat.

In a flexible global labour market, more workers will be paid wages that are uncertain and inadequate to provide a dignifying standard of living, however hard they labour. Topping up low wages with tax credits is expensive, distorting, inefficient and inequitable, as well as moralistic in its selective conditionalities. A basic income would not be distortionary, as it would be universal and would allow bargaining and freedom of choice.

From a macro-economic perspective, social insurance once provided an automatic stabilizer role, since spending on benefits increased in recessions, stimulating consumption and thus moving the economy back to growth. By contrast, the austerity regime, by cutting benefits in a recession, is pro-cyclical.

A basic income system could also be counter-cyclical, if designed with three tiers. The first would be a fixed amount, determined by financial need for subsistence and adjusted only for changes in national income per capita. The second could be an economic stabilizer grant, which would rise in recessions and fall in boom times. A third could be based on the additional costs for extra needs of those with a physical or mental disability, compensating them as befits a citizen.

The criticisms

Criticisms of a basic income have come from the conventional left and right. Although these have been refuted numerous times, they persist, testifying to the power of a paradigm. Let us take the main ones in turn. *First*, there is the claim that a basic income is unaffordable. But back-of-the-envelope calculations, multiplying some amount considered a basic income by the population size, are poor economics. The issue here is to *shift* expenditure to a basic income from subsidies, tax breaks and means-tested benefits. A basic income would also produce more tax revenue, since it would induce more labour to enter the tax system from the shadow economy, and would have beneficial cost-saving effects on health and schooling.

In 2012, Sir Mervyn King, then Bank of England Governor, stated his opposition to so-called 'helicopter drops of money' – giving money directly to people (King 2012). Yet the bank under his leadership effectively did the same in the form of 'quantitative easing', except that the benefits went to rich investors. On one calculation, the £375 billion in quantitative easing between 2009 and 2012 could have financed a cash windfall of £6,000 for every man, woman and child in Britain. The $2 trillion equivalent in the USA was worth $6,500 per person (Kaletsky 2012). Money can be released; it is feasible and has been done. However, most of the funds for a basic income would come from switching away from regressive subsidies and diverting part of the proceeds of financial capital, as explained in Article 26.

A *second* objection is that a basic income is utopian; it has never been introduced, so it must be wrong. Albert Hirschman (1991) noted how any new big idea is initially attacked on grounds of futility (it will not work), perversity (it would have unintended negative consequences) and jeopardy (it would endanger other goals). Critics said that about unemployment benefits and then about family benefits. Common sense only prevails when the old paradigm breaks down and cannot supply answers to the challenges of the time. Then we learn to respect the great 'broad church' of proponents through the ages, the likes of Thomas More, William Morris, Bertrand Russell, and Nobel prize-winning economists such as James Meade, Jan Tinbergen and James Tobin. The roll call is a distinguished one.

A *third* claim is that a basic income would be inflationary because it would stimulate aggregate demand, raising prices and creating inflationary expectations. This is incorrect, since the basic income would be phased in to substitute for other spending. In a deflationary era, as in Japan for the past three decades and in Europe since 2008, increased aggregate demand would stimulate the supply of goods and services, limiting pressure on prices. There would also be a positive effect from the twist in aggregate demand in favour of basic goods and services produced within local economies. Pilot basic income schemes in Africa and India suggest that the elasticity of supply of local goods and services tends to be high, so the effect may well be less inflationary pressure.

Fourth, it is claimed that a basic income would reduce pressure to pursue full employment. There are several responses. What pressure? Is putting as many people as possible into low-paying, resource-using labour a worthy objective of a civilized society? Are there not better activities for our time, such as self-chosen work and creative leisure?

The *fifth* objection is probably the most common, that a basic income provided unconditionally and regardless of work status would reduce labour supply and induce idleness. This is a common claim in countries influenced by the Lutheran 'work ethic', such as Finland (Ikkala 2012). It is an insult to the human condition; the vast majority would not be content with just a basic income. There is also evidence, from psychological studies, opinion polls, and cash transfer and pilot basic income schemes in various countries, including Canada and Brazil, which refutes that claim. The real disincentive to labour is means-tested benefits, as poverty and precarity traps make it irrational to move from benefits to low-wage labour.

As a right, a basic income would avoid the poverty trap. Any income earned above the basic income would be taxed at the standard rate or whatever rate is set for low-paid labour income. By reducing the marginal rate of tax compared with means-tested benefits, a basic income would act as an incentive to labour. As Clive Lord (2012) puts it:

> The CI [citizen's income] says to 'Scroungers', 'We are tired of trying to force you into work. Just take the money. But, by the way, there will be one difference. You will now be better off if you get a job instead of being no better off.

A *sixth* claim is that a basic income would induce in-migration. As with any benefit, this justifies pragmatic rules. A sensible one would be to restrict entitlement until people had been legally in the country for two years, unless there was a mutual agreement between the countries of origin and legal residence.

Seventh, critics say basic income would lead to lower wages, because employers would argue that workers already had their subsistence covered. But that is precisely what tax credits do; they also make it easier for workers to accept lower wages, knowing these will be topped up by the state. A basic income would strengthen workers' bargaining position to hold out against worse exploitation, especially if they believed an employer could pay more. It is conditional means-tested benefits that help drive down wages.

Eighth, some claim a basic income would undermine the solidaristic base of the welfare state. This is an old argument of social democrats, most notably in Germany (Liebermann 2012). It was a rather limited solidarity, and the horse has bolted. A universalistic base would set the scene for a new broader form of solidarity.

Ninth, it is argued that a basic income would be politicized, tempting governments to raise the amount before general elections. The way to deal with this is to set up an independent basic-income committee, analogous to central bank committees, with a mandate to set the level and rate of change according to affordability, real economic growth and financial need.

In sum, the objections can be answered. The real criticism is usually unstated: rulers and their followers do not like the idea of people having full freedom. They like to talk about shocking inequality and insecurity more than take effective action to reduce them.

Trade unions and basic income

Traditionally, trade unions were mostly vehemently against a basic income. They advocated radical redistribution of income and yet were stubbornly labourist in thinking that only those doing labour should receive income. The modern young union member may think differently. Addressing an international summer school of trade unionists in 2012, I asked why unions opposed basic income. One Italian ventured that it would give workers more control and they would not then wish to join a union. As he recognized, that does not say much for unions; they should attract members through a struggle for work rights and redistribution.

Contrary to what some commentators seem to believe, however, having basic security makes collective social action more likely rather than less. It is a theme running through this book that social solidarity, sacrificed in the globalization era, must be revived. A basic income would not achieve that by itself, but is vital for its reconstruction.

The advantages

Psychologists have shown that people with basic income security are more inclined to be altruistic and generous towards those less fortunate (Frohlich and Oppenheimer 1993). They have also shown they are more productive in their labour and work, and are more tolerant towards strangers and others who might otherwise be seen as a competitive threat. These are virtues under stress. But they are supplemented by other advantages.

The liquidity effect

Liquidity matters. Precariat life typically involves a combination of low and uncertain income, which feeds into indebtedness, payday loan crises and an inability to plan and construct a life. A regular assured injection of financial liquidity can provide a modicum of control. This was one of the striking findings of a series of pilot basic income schemes conducted by the author and SEWA colleagues in a number of Indian villages in 2011–13 (Standing 2013c). The regular modest payments enabled villagers to cut debts and make savings to protect themselves against common hazards and shocks. Predictability is what matters. Universal schemes provide every individual with more predictability than targeted, conditional schemes.

Community effects

The liquidity effect contributes to beneficial community effects, often ignored in assessments of benefits. Unconditional universal cash transfers enable families and neighbours to pool funds for community improvements and help out those hit by some disaster. If one person in a community receives a benefit, it may be unknown to others or it may lead to envy, criticism or worse. When all members of the community receive the same benefit, this creates not just pooling opportunities for social or economic purposes, but also a positive atmosphere of moral suasion. This was seen in a pilot scheme in Namibia. If a child is not going to school, neighbours feel they can legitimately ask why not.

However, the main community effect is its transformative potential. For different people, different constraints are eroded. This is what happened in those Indian villages (Standing 2013c). A community with basic income security becomes more vibrant, more confident, more inclined to invest and to improve the local environment.

If conditional benefits are tailored to selected groups, there may be a bigger short-term impact on the specific conditional behaviour, such as jobseeking or school enrolment. But evidence from randomized control trials and other pilots show that longer-term positive effects are greater for unconditional universal schemes, because they enable individuals and families to address the constraints they themselves face. For instance, if someone suffering from depression is forced to look for a job every day, this may lead to more jobseeking for a while, and so be cited as successful. But it may worsen the depression. Unconditional basic income would reduce anxiety and allow the person to get better in his or her own time, leading later to more effective (and voluntary) job search. Bureaucrats imposing conditions cannot be presumed to know better than the individual concerned.

Positive community effects were observed in the unconditional guaranteed minimum income pilots conducted in Canada in the late 1970s (Forget, Peden and Strobel 2013). The effects were surprisingly large on schooling and health care. When some teenagers decided to stay on at school, others decided this was a desirable thing to do. That was not a condition; it was a community effect. Similar demonstration effects occurred with health care and economic activity. There was no need to impose conditions.

Making labour markets efficient and equitable

Labour market transactions depend on bargaining power. With high unemployment and labour slack, where income support is uncertain, the bargaining position of labour suppliers is weak. They are exposed to exploitation. This contributes to labour inefficiency. Employers can pay low wages and make a profit easily enough, rather than try to make sure labour is used properly. And workers will be sufficiently desperate that they will take the first job they can just to obtain money, while looking for something else. Allocative efficiency will be poor. Labour turnover or negative reactions in workplaces will be high.

A basic income would facilitate efficient job search, by allowing workers to be more selective and deliberative, and by putting more pressure on employers to use labour efficiently. Dissatisfaction would be more likely to lead to exit. And a basic income would allow incentives to function, since there would be no poverty trap discouraging entry to low-wage jobs.

There would be another advantage in tertiary labour markets. Although minimum wages may hold up wages in flexible labour markets, they do not do so very effectively, beyond setting a moral standard. Minimum-wage advocates should also acknowledge the moral hazards, in that some labour is not undertaken because a potential employer believes its value is not worth the minimum wage. So labour that is desired is not done. Immoral hazards include the surreptitious practice of insisting that the worker does the labour 'in the black' or does more hours of labour than he or she is paid to perform.

A basic income would allow more sensible bargaining. Suppose you wish to build a shed. You cannot afford the minimum wage, but you would like to have the work done if you could pay, say, half. A neighbour's son might like to do the work. In a sensible economy, there could be a bargain. Drawing arbitrary lines between what is legal and what is not makes little sense.

A basic income could also improve dynamic efficiency. The increased bargaining power of workers would put pressure on employers to make jobs more productive and attractive, giving a 'labour-humanizing bias' (Wright 2010). This is surely what we should want.

The precariat's perspective

Basic income would address the insecurities and needs of all three varieties of precariat. Manual workers have lost acquired rights, and would gain. Migrants are denied citizenship rights; a basic income would strengthen their sense of citizenship. And the progressive part of the precariat would gain not just a sense of security but also more liberty to work, labour and 'leisure' constructively and reproductively.

Moving from means-testing and behaviour testing towards a basic income would have two other positive effects for the precariat. It would remove the poverty trap, since nobody would lose their basic income when starting to earn from labour; they would pay just the standard rate of income tax on their earnings. And it would diminish precarity traps, since the person would receive the basic income regardless of any labour market transition. That would encourage more positive labour mobility.

Overcoming moralistic surveillance

A basic income would be a modest advance for liberty at a time of growing use of moralistic conditionality, libertarian paternalism, close monitoring of personal behaviour, surveillance and dataveillance. It would lessen economic uncertainty due to the constant tightening of conditionality. And it would reduce the need for the most intrusive of questions: Why are you poor? Lionel Stoleru noted that a basic income is 'based on the need to help those who are poor, without trying to establish whose fault it is that they are poor; it makes no distinction between the "deserving" and "undeserving" poor' (cited in Rimbert 2013). Michel Foucault made a similar point in a lecture in 1979 (Rimbert 2013): 'After all, we take no interest, and it is quite proper that we should take no interest, in why people have fallen below the level at which they can take part in the social game.' He recognized that a basic income would be less bureaucratic and disciplinarian than a full employment system, and saw the welfare state as a way of stigmatizing and marginalizing groups.

Addressing inequalities

The precariat is at the wrong end of income inequality. It also faces inequality in all the other crucial assets that shape life's chances – security itself, control over time, access to quality space, education in the liberating sense of the term, financial knowledge and financial capital. A basic income would be an effective way to reduce income inequality, since being equal and universal it obviously comprises a higher share of income for someone with a low income. It would also reduce the inequality in security, and enable the precariat to have more resources and freedom to pursue education in a non-commodified sense. A basic income could also help address unequal access to financial knowledge (Article 22), especially if policymakers and recipients see it as enabling people to purchase advice or spend time learning how to handle financial matters. As for financial capital, we will come to that in Article 26.

Liberating time and the right to work

In an industrial economy, workers are exploited mostly in workplaces, so it makes sense to limit exploitation with regulations on hours of labour, overtime and overtime pay rates. In a tertiary society, with 'always-on' connectivity, work and labour are done almost every-where. Placing regulatory limits on hours of labour will have little effect, as France has found.

The primary issue is control over time. The precariat has least control over this key asset. It is expected to labour whenever required, and to do much work-for-labour and other forms of work forced upon it – hence the rise in job-related stress and insecurity (e.g. Gallie et al. 2013). A basic income would give people more control of their time, and enable them to bargain for a more dignifying pace of labour. Stress due to loss of control over time is linked to stress due to loss of public space. A basic income would gently reassert some control of both time and space. It should be part of a new politics of time (Standing 2013b).

Overcoming uncertainty

Uncertainty is the bane of the age. It is the most threatening form of insecurity for the precariat. Uncertainty can be so great that it induces inertia. The risks of any course of action seem prohibitive. People realize their situation is fragile and that if any shock occurs, they could be ruined. In short, they lack resilience.

After assessing the likelihood of rare events, which he dubs 'black swans', Nassim Taleb (2012) has developed the idea of 'anti-fragility'. He believes it is a mistake to try too hard to avoid shocks. An efficient system needs moderate volatility, and that helps prepare people to deal with shocks. The principle can be applied to career choices. If a person has a secure job in a large firm, he or she develops a sense of dependency, so that sudden loss of that job can be a major shock; those in occupations with more variable earnings and demand are less vulnerable to shocks. In other words, moderate insecurity prepares people for shocks and enables them to gain from the unexpected. But the key word is moderate.

A basic income would provide a buffer against uncertainty and shocks. As such, it could give people more courage and confidence to take entrepreneurial risk, in the sense of taking potentially life-enhancing actions. If you know you are not going to be out on the street if you fail, you are more likely to risk learning new skills or leaving a soulless job to try your luck as an independent craft-worker.

Basic income versus capital grants

Among those believing everyone should have equal basic security, there has been a debate on whether it would be better to provide capital grants or modest regular amounts. One could have both. But the arguments for each differ. The most successful relevant example is the Alaska Permanent Dividend, discussed in Article 26. It is a hybrid of a basic income and a capital grant, since it pays an annual dividend to every resident citizen of Alaska derived from the Permanent Fund set up in 1976.

Some have proposed large grants, either annually (Murray 2006) or on reaching age 21 (Ackerman and Alstott 1999). In 2013, a former adviser to the New Labour government recommended that:

> Instead of squandering the public stake in the rescued banks with a share giveaway… the proceeds ought to be used to pay down the country's debt while funding a capital endowment for citizens at the age of 18 – a bolder version of the child trust fund. A universal capital grant would help support an expanded social housing programme based on shared equity (Diamond 2013).

Capital grants offer routes to security, but suffer from one overriding drawback. They pander to weakness of will, the temptation to splurge on large items or to take big risks. Risky options (such as investment in speculative stocks) could make some people rich, but will make many poor. Then what would the state do? The loss could have been due to unlucky timing of the receipt of the capital grant, or to somebody else's bad investment. It would be better to provide everybody with a modest amount regularly.

Rethinking the contribution principle

Basic income should not be discussed without considering the desirable features of an overall social protection system, which should be based on compassion, solidarity and empathy rather than seeking to control and penalize the disadvantaged. A basic income should be seen as the floor of a multi-tiered system geared to twenty-first-century realities.

In 2013, Labour responded to welfare cuts by announcing it would resurrect the contribution principle. Accusing the government of 'divide and rule' policies, Labour's spokesman, Liam Byrne (2013), seemed intent on moving the UK closer to the continental welfare system, as in France where the state rewards insiders, disadvantaging the precariat and underclass, and eroding solidarity between the salariat and precariat. He said that Labour would reward people who paid contributions and encourage local councils to give social housing to those who had.

This is peculiarly divisive. Why should those devastated by reckless economic policies take more cuts in living standards? Labour would introduce its own version of 'divide and rule', rewarding those with incomes from labour, denying social housing to those without. Many in the precariat will not have had an opportunity to contribute, because they are too young or have been unemployed or outside the labour market. Relying on a contributory system would only be 'fair' if everyone was in full-time employment earning 'decent' wages. But they are not and will not be.

Basic income would overcome the 'social democracy trap'. The core of social democracy was labour decommodification, a shift of labour remuneration from wages to security-providing non-wage benefits paid by firms or government. As the wage dwindled as a share of social income, the motivation to labour efficiently fell, since whether one laboured hard or not made little difference to income. And it impeded mobility, since benefits were tied to staying in a job.

As labour flexibility spread, the precariat lost non-wage and contributory benefits. They became regressive, retained mainly by the salariat, and intensified 'security inequality'. The social democracy trap was made worse by the transfer to government of responsibility for labour security, which eroded the need for community benefits. Neighbourhood, institutional and family networks of solidarity faded because they were not seen as needed in a welfare state. When the state turned to labour recommodification, these networks were once again needed but they no longer existed. As a result, the insecurities had more devastating effects.

It would be folly if social democrats tried to restore contributory benefits as the answer to economic insecurity. The benefits would go to the salariat and core working class, to the detriment of the precariat. It would not be a fair system, replacing 'something for nothing' by 'something for something'. The precariat might work just as hard as the salariat, but would be disadvantaged by its low status, insecurity and income volatility. Rather, contribution-based benefits should be part of a multi-tiered social protection system, supplementing a basic income, with principles of mutualism incorporated into insurance funds to ensure the precariat is not penalized.

In short, the state can either leave inequalities and insecurities to fester or it can escape from the labourist trap by providing the missing basic security as a universal right. It should aim to decommodify people ('labour power'), rather than labour. As argued in *The Precariat*, for efficiency and equity reasons, labour should be fully commodified.

Living wage campaigns

Living wage campaigns have become popular since 2008, notably in Canada, the UK, the USA and New Zealand. Such campaigns deserve support, but not too much should be expected. Firms agreeing to pay decent wages could even be at a disadvantage if they are undercut by others who do not. Living wages should be paid by all those tendering for government contracts. But this could result in big firms being favoured over small ones, or established firms over newcomers. Some firms might simply be unable to afford the higher amount. The UK Labour Party announced its support for living wages, only to propose shortly afterwards that the long-term unemployed should be required to take minimum-wage jobs, which could only put downward pressure on wages in general.

A living wage is desirable, but it is not an alternative to a basic income. A basic income would strengthen the bargaining position of the precariat, most of whom are not in sectors or firms paying or likely to pay living wages, or are working too few hours to benefit. And it would encourage a shift from wage labour to reproductive work of many kinds.

* * *

Politicians have been scared by the proposition that everybody should have a right to basic economic security. Even those who believe in it have rationalized staying silent, for fear of being pilloried as 'unrealistic' and 'utopian', or being unpopular with moralists and the 'middle class'. Now, facing the abyss, it is the time for political and ethical courage.

Politicians may find they are moving with the tide of opinion. The precariat is supporting moves for a basic income. Basic income networks now exist in many countries, under the umbrella of an international network, BIEN (Basic Income Earth Network). In April 2013, a petition signed by over 50,000 people was handed in to the Italian parliament. European Green parties have included it in their manifestos. At the time of writing, signatures were being collected for a European Citizens' Initiative (ECI) that would require the European Commission to study the feasibility of basic income and to conduct pilots. ECIs require networks in at least seven countries and the collection of a million signatures within a year of being recognized by the Commission. The barrier of a million is too high, but the institutional network has been strengthened. Precariat groups should persist in demanding that pilots be conducted, by local authorities or by governments in selected areas. Only a precariat movement can change the utilitarian mindset of the political establishment.

Article 26: Share capital via sovereign wealth funds

A new system of distribution must be built so that all those who contribute to society can share in the financial wealth and the social dividends of natural resources and technological innovation. National capital funds can achieve these realistic goals.

Every individual in the world is born therein with legitimate claims on a certain kind of property, or its equivalent.

Agrarian Justice, Thomas Paine (1797)

Paine was referring to natural resources, land in particular. We should go further. There must be a progressive redistribution of the profits and rents gained by tiny elites who have been given control of mineral resources, technological breakthroughs that have a long string of contributions over generations, and windfall gains due to shifting terms of trade and luck. The way ahead is through the creation of democratic sovereign wealth funds (SWFs). These already exist in embryonic form. By 2013, over 60 countries had an SWF of some kind. Most so far have been vehicles for elite enrichment. But several have been used to reduce economic insecurity and inequality.

The greatest source of inequality globally is the shift in the functional distribution of income. The share of national and global income going to capital is rising and the share going to those earning income from labour is falling. The precariat has reason to oppose what is happening and to support measures to reverse the trend. The development of SWFs could be the most promising vehicle, ethically, socially and economically, to help address the real tragedy of the commons and the increasingly rentier character of rich countries in the global market system.

What is behind capital inequality?

There were two major reasons for the shift of income from labour to capital in the globalization era. The first was the automatic shift in the ratio of labour to capital as the global labour supply trebled while capital stock rose only gently. This weakened the bargaining power of those earning income from wages, reinforced by neo-liberal measures to curb collective bargaining and trade unions. The second was the series of technological revolutions in this period, notably in information and communication technologies. It is not necessary to adhere to the 'lump of labour' fallacy – that there is only a certain amount of 'work' to go round and that new technologies are reducing that amount – to appreciate that technological change may tilt income distribution away from those doing labour to those receiving rental income from technological innovation (and the patents they are granted).

Moreover, 'skills' and 'control' over labour and work may be reduced by technological advance. For instance, robots are taking over functions in many forms of production. The Luddites rebelled against machines taking over manual labour. Now labourists want to halt the inroads into spheres of mental labour to head off 'technological unemployment'. This stems from a fetish for jobs.

There is nothing wrong with machines doing tasks that humans have done in the past if they can do them as well or better. Using robots to perform factory tasks and service functions is acceptable if it means humans have more time and income to do what they would like to do with their lives. Robots increase productivity and the income generated by the production. But in a globalizing market economy, technological advance results in more income going to the recipients of capital income, not labour. The political right justifies this as necessary to stimulate innovation and entrepreneurial risk-taking. But while that may make some sense at the micro-level, at the macro-economic or societal level it is worrying.

Instead, we must find ways of sharing capital income. Some propose tax credits; others favour incentives to individuals to purchase stocks (e.g. Smith 2013). However, the second is problematic. Many US firms, for instance, are de-listing and going private. Some favour incentives to induce big firms to list themselves, to increase share purchase possibilities. But that would be yet another subsidy to capital, and would not tackle the issue of investment risk. While the elite and salariat can bear the cost of a drop in share prices, the precariat cannot.

A classic response is to collectivize risk, by pooling money to be spent on shares. There are several variants. One is for the government, or an agency acting on its behalf, to purchase a portfolio of shares for individuals. This would have the advantage of enabling individuals to benefit from the expertise enshrined in the body undertaking the investment. But it would leave them exposed to risk, without the responsibility of taking the decisions. It would be paternalistic, without providing economic security.

The portfolio would be an insurance against the risk of losing income security derived from labour. But it would suffer from the weakness-of-will effect. Someone given a portfolio of financial capital would presumably have the right to sell it for capital gain. They might splurge on riotous living, ending up poorer than at the start. Neo-liberals would not worry, because they are not worried by inequality of outcomes. Others would be concerned, since such outcomes could come about through rational behaviour, and because that loss of income would leave people exposed to income insecurity and poverty.

So, there are inter-related challenges. How can capital income be redistributed so as to reduce inequality, without distorting legitimate market mechanisms that promote investment and efficient allocation of resources? How can capital income be collectivized while overcoming the weakness-of-will problem? The answer is some form of collective or national SWF.

A caveat

Existing capital funds, including occupational pension funds, are powerful forces in global capitalism. SWFs are a specific genre. There is a need to regulate private capital funds or democratize them. That is not what is proposed here. Indeed, funds that exist for legitimate social reasons should be protected from political capture. The UK government aims to channel £20 billion from private pension funds to finance infrastructural investment, so as to lessen pressure to raise taxes. This is inconsistent with the principle of a private insurance fund, which is sold to savers on the expectation that its experts will invest in profitable avenues. Pension funds have a fiduciary duty to invest on behalf of their contributors, not the general public or the government. Just as private capital funds must be protected against political capture and distortion, even more so must SWFs.

How sovereign capital funds operate

The idea of an SWF is that part of the profits from resource-based production is taxed and paid into a fund, which is used for designated types of investment. Such funds have become the biggest sources of capital investment in the globalized model of capitalism; the three largest Chinese state capital funds have become owners of household-name corporations in Europe and elsewhere. Most SWFs are run by the global plutocracy and elite, and most have increased income inequality and monopoly capitalism, bolstering privileges and strengthening their market power. They are virtually risk-free rentier mechanisms. In embryo, however, such funds could be turned into publicly owned resource-based funds that could pay a social dividend to all in society and thus finance a basic income system. The Alaska Permanent Fund has led the way, and another country, Iran, has, surprisingly, set an even stronger precedent (Tabatabai 2012).

It should be noted that any resource can be regarded as the people's inalienable property. The Romans divided property into common property (*res communes*), state property (*res publicae*) and private property (*res privatae*), while the Magna Carta included air, running water, fisheries, forests, the sea and shorelines as common wealth. Then and now, through common law, natural resources are held in trust for the benefit of all citizens. There is evident justification in saying that citizens should benefit from all three forms of property.

Publicly owned resources can include not only natural resources such as energy and minerals, but something as non-natural as finance (Flomenhoft 2012). Any rental income arising from a privilege granted by the state should be considered as potential revenue for the fund, since it is the people, through their governments, who permit private interests to earn what are really 'windfall profits', or rents. Thus exploiters of natural resources earn rents, returns greater than the minimum income required to attract labour, capital and expertise to extract them. And with rising commodity prices, rents have risen. A tax on rents, such as a mining levy, is a way of raising revenue without lowering the motivation to produce.

Another source of revenue for a national capital fund is a windfall profits tax. If a country has commodities that rise in price in real terms in export markets because of terms-of-trade effects, then part of the extra revenue should go into the sovereign capital fund. Risk-free profits should also be regarded as monopoly rents. For example, banks protected as 'too big to fail' have received huge subsidies and the promise of more if needed. The public deserves part of their profits, since it is the public that is providing the banks and bankers with income security. Part of bankers' bonuses should flow into the SWF, along with a share of banks' net profits. Any commercial entity where the state underwrites the risks should have to pay into the fund, as a matter of equity and progressive politics.

Hedge funds are another potential revenue source. They have grown prodigiously – managing over \$2.2 trillion in assets in 2012, up fourfold since 2000 – even though they have delivered a rate of return below inflation and enriched their investors less than themselves. Then there is the 'Tobin tax' on financial transactions. Eleven European Union member states are planning to introduce a tax on securities trading, raising an estimated €30–35 billion annually. In the USA, a financial transaction tax charged at only 3 cents for every \$100 trade would raise \$352 billion over ten years, according to the Congress Joint Committee on Taxation. The costed plan would exempt the first sale of stocks and all bond deals, so that the cost of raising capital would be unaffected. Critics claim that such a tax would be hard to collect, but so are most taxes, which does not make them illegitimate. Most financial trading has no social or productive purpose. The tax could help check bubbles and frenzied trading, and reduce short-term investment shifts.

In sum, an integrated system can be devised for channelling resource-based revenues to a fund for the benefit of the whole community. The people's resources should be preserved for the people and rented out only to those prepared to pay a sustainable rent.

The Alaska Permanent Fund

Started in a modest way, the Alaska Permanent Fund has become a beacon of common sense. It was set up in 1976 by the late Jay Hammond, a liberal Republican governor, who introduced it after a referendum. It has three elements – a resource-based revenue (25 per cent of the state government's oil royalties), a savings fund for making investments, which also acts as a stabilization fund, and a Permanent Fund Dividend, an annual social dividend determined by the returns from the fund's investments. This is paid at the end of each year to every legal resident of Alaska (Widerquist and Howard 2012a, 2012b).

The dividend is calculated as 52.5 per cent of the fund's nominal investment income averaged over the previous five years divided by the number of eligible recipients – all who have lived in the state for at least five years. It is a savings fund in that the principal builds up, with only a share of investment income being given out as a citizenship right. It is known as a bird-in-the-hand fund, intended for future as well as current generations to benefit.

The Alaska model has worked well for four decades. It is popular with the citizenry; it has distributed about $1,400 every year to every Alaskan; and Alaska has gone from being a poor and unequal state to being the state with the lowest poverty and inequality. In 2013, the governor of Oregon proposed a similar model in his state, where timber is the main natural resource. There is no reason to think it would not work anywhere where there are natural resources. The main obstacle is elite capture aided by craven politicians serving corporations.

The Alaskan model throws up challenges, the main one being governance. The fund must be independent of government, so that investments and levels of payout are not dictated by electoral cycles. Ideally, these should be decided by a parallel democracy system, with all interests represented in the fund's governance and decisions on investments oriented to the reproduction and preservation of the resources and environment. Another challenge is to maintain the fund's long-term viability while distributing dividends in an equitable and sustainable way. This poses a democratic quandary, as the current generation, particularly older members of society, would wish to maximize short-term returns, whereas youth would wish to ensure dividends are continuing and higher in the future. So, the governance should give Voice to several generations.

Today, it would be political suicide for a politician to propose to end the Alaska Permanent Fund Dividend (Goldsmith 2012). Even Sarah Palin, in her last year as governor of Alaska, used the state budget to add $1,200 to the dividend of $2,069 paid that year to all eligible inhabitants. The Alaska fund is truly transformational.

North Sea oil, the Norwegian fund and Britain's historical error

Norway has been ranked as the happiest country according to an index of prosperity calculated by the Legatum Institute. It grew rich through North Sea oil in the 1970s, but to overcome the risk of 'Dutch disease' (a rise in the exchange rate due to oil revenues), it set up a sovereign wealth fund now worth over £460 billion. When the global crash came, Norway was immunized by its fund. Nationally, salaries rose by nearly two-thirds between 2000 and 2012, while the average length of work-weeks has fallen to just over 27 hours, compared with 39 in Greece, for example. According to the OECD, Norwegians rate their life satisfaction more highly than almost anywhere else. The wealth fund has been used to improve social security and other social entitlements.

The contrast with the UK is stark. The Thatcher government made the unforgivable error of selling the UK's North Sea oilfields to the prospecting companies at a time when the oil reserves were still unknown. There were alternative progressive proposals, but these were brushed aside. Profits flowed to an elite and then to foreign capital, while the windfall gains from privatization were used to cover the social costs of deindustrialization and mass unemployment. Later, a Chinese capital wealth fund bought up a large profitable stake in Scottish oil. Privatization led to foreign state ownership!

Gordon Brown when Prime Minister made a similar mistake after 2008. The government should have taken a permanent public stake in the rescued banks, which would have provided the basis for a financial capital wealth fund and enabled the British public to receive dividends from the banking industry once profits were restored.

The neo-liberal model erodes political rights as it constructs a global market system. Privatization of utilities and natural resources creates space for foreign state capital to take over. Just as privatizing North Sea oil led eventually to Chinese state capital taking over British natural resources, so privatizing the Greek port of Piraeus, under pressure from the international financial agencies and 'the troika' from the European Union, has turned the port into an operational base for China's state-owned shipping company, a modern Trojan horse. The state is thereby leveraging a global brand of capitalism, weakening national democratic control over the economy and resources. This erodes political rights and reduces democratic governance.

A shale-gas fracking fund?

Fracking ('hydraulic fracturing') has become a Wild West gold rush. The technique, which involves releasing oil or gas from shale rock by pumping high-pressure water and chemicals underground, is depicted as rescuing countries from dependence on coal and imported oil. Virtually unregulated fracking is booming in the USA, resulting in land despoliation, depletion and pollution of water sources, and other environmental costs as drillers move from site to site. While paying lip service to the need for regulation, the UK has moved in a similar direction.

Fracking poses an ecological threat to communities that have up to now considered themselves immune to such threats. This presents an opportunity to mobilize opposition from a broad alliance of social groups. The elite and financial capital may dangle the incentive of cheap energy and faster economic growth, but this may cut little ice if your village, commons and forest land are sites for drilling and destruction. An opinion poll in 2013 found that 44 per cent of the British favoured fracking, but the proportion dropped significantly when asked if they would support drilling in their community. The 'veil of ignorance' principle was at work.

Shale gas belongs to the people. It is part of the commons. Giving it away to private interests amounts to expropriation. The Chancellor of the Exchequer has promised generous tax breaks to fracking companies, as well as financial bribes for local councils to agree to fracking on their land. A more equitable policy would be to establish a Shale-Gas Capital Fund along the lines of the Alaska Permanent Fund. It could be used to pay social dividends or contribute to a national pot for a basic income for all.

* * *

Large capital funds are part of the landscape of global capitalism. Most have been dominated by the plutonomy, reflecting the power of the elite and greatly enriching it. They must become the locus of a struggle by and for the precariat. When neo-liberals declare that inequality is necessary, and hold out the prospect of 'trickle-down' benefits of growth, the answer must be that democratically governed sovereign wealth funds coupled with basic income grants are the way to advance economic security and reduce income inequality. There is an alternative.

Article 27: Revive the commons

> The physical, social and information commons must be protected
> and revived. It matters more for the precariat than for any other
> group or interest.

Historically, what goes under the generic name of 'the commons' has
been important for the working classes of the time. The Charter of
the Forest of 1217, which was derived from the Magna Carta, was
mainly about asserting the right to land, water and other essential
resources for reproducing the welfare of peasants, small-holders and
others in a predominantly rural society. In protecting the commons
from external power, it put a limit on privatization.

Modern debates have been influenced by a perspective known as
'the tragedy of the commons' (Hardin 1968), the view that land open
to all to use would become depleted and exhausted. It is a convenient
view for neo-liberals, since it was used to claim that resources not
owned by private firms or individuals would be squandered. Some
have contested this perspective, saying it only applies to spaces that
all can individually exploit. Others, notably Elinor Ostrom (1990),
have noted that, left to themselves, people in small communities
adapt and preserve the commons, reproducing their environment
through cooperation, trust relationships and 'user managers'.

Today, the neo-liberal model is resulting in systematic erosion of
the commons and of quality public space, to the detriment of the
precariat. That must be reversed. Quality space is one of the key assets

over which the redistributive struggle must be waged. It is becoming more unequally distributed. This was absurdly illustrated when, in March 2013, the Emir of Qatar bought six Greek islands, taking advantage of a great society suffering under an austerity regime. While the plutocracy gains more quality space, the precariat is being crowded into less, and its quality is declining. As the crowding continues, so the anger grows.

The commons in social income

The commons, or public quality space in general, comprise part of social income. They have always provided a source of economic security, for collecting firewood or water, and a source of meat and fish, fruit and vegetables. They have also had social and political roles, providing the *agora* or 'gathering place' in Greek city states and meeting places for citizens up to modern times.

The tragedy of the commons is not primarily that they were over-used but that they became prone to commercialization; the enclosure movement was only the most conspicuous instance of that process. The state has been instrumental in the destruction of the commons, taking away that vital informal source of social income. Recalling that social income consists of all types of income anybody can receive, the further down the class spectrum one goes, the greater the relative contribution of the commons. Shrinking the commons thus increases social income inequality and reduces the income of the precariat and those beneath it.

The Lauderdale paradox

The threat to the commons and public space can be interpreted in terms of the 'Lauderdale paradox', stated by the Earl of Lauderdale in 1804. It figured in classical economics, but has fallen out of fashion. Lauderdale argued that in a capitalist system, public wealth declines as private riches increase. 'Public wealth may be accurately defined to consist of all that man desires, as useful or delightful to him' (cited in Foster and McChesney 2011). But private riches require 'a degree of scarcity', so private riches can increase if scarcity is contrived. That is what capitalism tends to do, whether by monopolistic practices, by patents, by depletion of scarce resources, or by strategies to limit the reproduction of those resources. Economies can 'grow' faster if resources are being used up so that their prices rise. But this is at the cost of diminished public wealth. That is why less emphasis should be put on growth and more on preserving the commons.

The Lauderdale paradox may be illustrated by the conversion of parkland into shopping malls. It was this prospect that sparked the inspiring demonstrations in Istanbul in 2013. The mall is a symbol of financial capitalism, signalling a zone planned to induce more consumption than people can afford, or even contemplate or want. Initially, shopping malls seemed to provide a quasi-public space in which people socialized as well as consumed. But insatiable commercialism soon revealed their true function, a glossy means of private enrichment. As those Turkish protestors understood (Göle 2013), a shopping mall in Gezi Park meant private capital's confiscation of the commons. Lauderdale's paradox was clear.

The allotment as metaphor

The time-honoured institution of the allotment – or community garden, as it is known in the USA, or 'victory garden' as it was called in the UK during the Second World War – should be a metaphor for the commons. Allotments have existed in many countries and cultures, including Germany (where they are known as *Schrebergärten*), Italy (where they boomed in the Second World War, hence their name *orti di guerra*), the Netherlands, Denmark, Norway (where people can wait up to 20 years for one) and Sweden.

Allotments have always been part of the social income of their holders, providing a source of informal social protection. This was graphically shown in the aftermath of the break-up of the Soviet Union. Russia and Ukraine suffered a terrifying period of plunging national income and hyper-inflation. In Russia, life expectancy also plunged, with male life expectancy falling from 64 to 58. But in Ukraine, the poorer country, life expectancy fell only a little, from a similar starting point. What distinguished Ukraine was that, before the break-up of the Soviet Union, the authorities had arranged for all urban residents to have small plots on which to grow vegetables, principally potatoes. These plots saved many lives, even if the work done on them was not recognized as productive activity.

Allotments combine several socio-economic roles and images, meshing production with a civilizing role of leisurely work, or working leisure. In many countries, they were once like an outside equivalent of the bistro – Balzac's 'parliament of the people' – where conviviality flourished. In the twentieth century, allotments were colonized by bourgeois or petit-bourgeois families, intent on weekend escapes from the urban bustle. Nowhere was this more so than in Germany and, as dachas, in Russia and Ukraine. In recent years, allotments have come to be dominated by pensioners. But their progressive role should not be neglected. Nor should we overlook their economic and cultural roles, helping to reproduce a sense of community and standing against commercialization. They have also had a political role, enabling families and friends to discuss politics, facilitating reflective talk, undisturbed by commercial pressures or bosses' demands.

For the precariat, allotments may prove a harbinger of a struggle for revival of the commons. They offer a symbolic vision of desirable elements of a good life, including not just nutritional benefits but an assertion of the value of reproductive work over the dictates of labour. The precariat must find ways of combating two threatening trends – the shrinkage of the land allocated for allotments and the marginalization of the work done on them. The latter is a crucial part of the campaign to legitimize all forms of work that are not labour. Work on allotments, whatever the reason, is real work, creating a little space as valuable and productive an activity as putting cans and boxes on shelves in a supermarket.

While allotments originated in rural areas and thrived around small towns in the eighteenth century, the allotment movement began with industrialization and the emergence of metropolitan areas. In the UK, demand for allotments surged at the beginning of the twentieth century, leading to the Small Holdings and Allotments Act of 1908, parts of which are still in force. Demand for plots has always outstripped the supply of land, only partly explained by the fact that the public ownership principle was preserved to keep down the price, to respect the idea that allotments were part of the commons.

In the UK and elsewhere, responsibility for providing and allocating allotments was delegated to local councils. Since 1908, the amount of land made available has fluctuated dramatically. By 1913, there were 600,000 allotments in England and Wales. In the First World War, more land was requisitioned for allotments to increase food supply, so that by 1918 there were around 1,500,000. Much of the land was returned to its old owners after 1918. But the wartime spurt had shown that land for common use could be mobilized quickly, could be put to productive use by working people and was thus an appropriate response to national crises.

The number of allotments shrank in the 1920s, before troubled economic times led to a new revival. In 1926, the Quakers (Society of Friends) launched a scheme in South Wales called Allotment Gardens for the Unemployed to provide food and work (Acton 2011). This was successful and spread throughout Britain, initially supported by a government keen to deflect social unrest. Allotments boomed again during the Second World War, before gradually shrinking in number afterwards, mainly due to a diminishing supply of land.

The allotment involves work for reproduction. It induces respect for the soil, for nature, for a balanced life. But in today's neo-liberal paradigm, if you work on your allotment rather than in the labour market, you risk being called a 'skiver' and a 'scrounger', because you are not jobseeking or in a job. Allotments offer a place for retreat, a place to dissipate stress. They exude a sense of security and a link with generations of folk. They convey a sense of citizenship, a welcome combination of cultural, social and economic rights, because of the connection to the land and the economic right to produce for family, friends and the community. There may be a ban on the commercial selling of produce, as in the UK, but informal exchange and barter have never gone amiss. There is a pride and status in the reproductive work that gardening conveys.

Modes of attack on the commons

Four main methods have been used by the neo-liberal state to whittle away at the commons. The primary way has been through privatization, rationalized on grounds of efficiency, growth and austerity. Selling off communal land and turning it over to housing or other development is only the most visible form of privatization.

A *second* means of attack on the commons is the closure of public amenities, including parks, swimming pools and libraries. The city of Manchester was so underfunded that it closed all but one of its public toilets. When central government hit local councils with swingeing budget cuts, many were left with little option than to cut non-structural spending.

One example was the 2012 decision by the London Borough of Tower Hamlets to sell a great sculpture by Henry Moore, which he sold to the former London County Council well below the market price on the understanding that it would be placed in east London, a run-down part of the city. Entitled Draped Seated Woman and nicknamed Old Flo, it was initially placed in the midst of a Tower

Hamlets council estate, much to Moore's delight. Selling it betrays his legacy. As one critic of the sale put it:

> Placed amid tower blocks, it was a rare moment of quality, a sign that someone cared... as long as it was there it created the possibility that some might be inspired, intrigued, or provoked into seeing the world in a different way (Moore 2012).

Old Flo was later moved to a sculpture park for safekeeping but remains in Tower Hamlets' ownership. The mayor said the sale was necessary as the council could not afford to insure it. A public outcry and a question of ownership held up the sale. But the state vandalism was clear. The decision by Tower Hamlets followed the sale of 35 paintings by Bolton Council. Austerity was used to reduce public wealth and increase private riches.

A *third* attack on the commons is the destruction or limitation of the reproductive capabilities of public spaces – less cleaning, less monitoring for public safety, less repair of public services, less investment in equipment and amenities. It blends into the micro-politics of privatization (see Chapter 4), eroding the public's appreciation of these spaces and facilities until few people have the spirit to contest their sale or closure.

A *fourth* form of attack is loss of public, accountable control over the externalities generated by commercial production. This includes erosion of the public capacity to limit pollution and the destruction of species and ecosystems. If a piece of the commons – a public good – is privatized, the duty to care is weakened, for a user no longer part-owns the space and knows that the owner can change the use at whim. Privatization weakens the public sense of social responsibility.

The relationship of trust and common wealth is replaced by opportunism and individualism. Throwing litter on a property developer's urban wonderland is less likely to induce a citizen's protest than it would on the commons.

Austerity, labourism and the shrinkage of the commons

The combination of austerity and the primacy given to job creation has created a utilitarian logic for shrinking the commons. However, from the outset, the neo-liberal project has included strategic dismantling of the commons. Margaret Thatcher's decision in the 1980s to sell off land used by state schools for play and sport was symbolic, an act of state vandalism.

Deindustrialization and the Great Convergence have had their impact. In 2009, a former member of the Welsh National Assembly recalled how the transfer of the Burberry factory to China, after 60 years in the Rhondda Valley, had led to a spiral of decay:

> We've also lost our hospital, we've lost our ambulance station, we had an infants' school, an excellent infants' school, that's gone. We've lost our recycling centre and now we're going to lose our swimming pool. Our local theatre is under threat. Above all, there are fewer young people about, especially children (Engel 2009).

Numerous other areas have suffered a similar fate. But it is the wanton destruction of the commons in the austerity era that marks out a qualitative shift in state policy. A poignant example occurred in Spain, in a context where it was well known that construction companies had been pouring money into the governing People's Party. In 2012, near the coastal town of Tarifa, plans were drawn up to build a huge tourist complex in one of the last unspoilt beach areas of southern Spain, a habitat of rare protected species. The local council said the scheme was needed to generate jobs. Environmentalists and conservation groups protested that a glorious piece of Spain was to be destroyed. A movement called *Salvemos Valdevaqueros* (Saving Valdevaqueros) sprang into Twitter action within hours of the council decision, leading to a campaign supported by *los indignados*, as well as Greenpeace, *Ecologistas en Acción* and other conservation bodies. Characteristically, the opposition Socialist Party voted with the governing People's Party in favour of the project. Critics pointed out that the country had a million empty homes. But another bit of Spain was to be destroyed, in order to generate short-term jobs and profits for construction companies. This was symbolic of a last spasm of labourism. Soon, enough people will come to realize that short-term jobs are the wrong answer to the wrong question.

In the UK, allotments are under threat as local councils consider selling the land for commercial development, using well-worn rationalizations about growth and job creation. The neo-liberal agenda is advanced by stealth. Government looks kindly on property developers who offer donations to their party coffers and possible future board memberships. And they look opportunistically at allotment areas that could be made 'productive' and bring jobs.

Take the Farm Terrace allotment area in Watford, near London, set up in 1896 on land known for its fertile soil, and in 2013 consisting of 60 working sites overlooked by Watford General Hospital (Harris

2013). The council, in partnership with a corporate developer, drew up plans to sell the land to the developer to build a 'health campus' and a 'business incubator and retail units', including a hotel, restaurant and cafes. In quick time, this was approved by the government's 'communities' minister. Allotment holders were told they would be offered alternative plots two miles away, on what all agreed was less fertile soil. A time-honoured economic right was shredded. One allotment holder who had worked on her plot for five years put it well:

> Emotionally, it's been very hard. The thing is, how could you recreate somewhere like this? And I'm worried about the detrimental effect that getting rid of these plots will have on people's health. For a lot of us, this is physical work – but there is also the emotional release you get.

Similar encroachments occurred elsewhere. The National Society of Allotment and Leisure Gardeners reported in early 2013 that it was hearing of new threats to allotments every day, and that three-quarters of allotment holders were worried their plots might be sold.

The government believes nothing should impede growth. It is even allowing development in London near world heritage sites, to the consternation of UNESCO and conservationists. The skyline is part of the commons. It belongs to all of us.

The 2013 UK budget, ostensibly to boost growth and jobs, launched a £3.5 billion scheme for interest-free loans for buyers of new homes built on greenfield sites (i.e. part of the commons), while relaxing planning rules for construction on them. It was a regressive subsidy, giving to people not among the most insecure, and followed intensive lobbying by commercial developers, who stood to gain most. In stimulating house-building, freeing up mortgages and making it easier to build on 'green' land, the debate was cast in terms of increasing the supply of homes, with jobs and growth having priority over other considerations. But the commons were a victim of the measures, which enriched construction companies and property investors.

Private profit, growth and jobs always triumph in the neo-liberal utilitarianism. The commons have no 'value' in the growth scenario. A representative of a conservation group in Scotland wrote a poignant letter to *The Guardian* (2013):

> You may wonder what Cairngorms National Park is thinking when it allows housing development on such a large scale that one small town, Kingussie, is approved to double in size; another small town, Aviemore, is to be extended by an adjacent new town of 1,500 houses within sight of the most precious landscape on our island, home of the osprey, the wildcat, the red squirrel and many other protected species of fauna and flora; and two further small villages are also approved for new developments. Affordable housing, but for whom? Employment in the area is mostly restricted to low-paid, temporary, seasonal and part-time work in hotels. The housing is 'affordable' only as second homes – now for more people with the 'spare home subsidy'.

Austerity has been used to justify erosion of the social as well as the physical commons. The UK's Arts Council, which channels funds to arts venues, theatre groups and galleries, had its budget cut by nearly a third. Opponents of the cuts emphasized the commercial importance of its work, notably in generating tourist revenues. But the loss of cultural rights continued. The closure of regional theatres and art galleries deprived the precariat of access to culture and ways of participating in its reproduction. Meanwhile, hundreds of libraries have been closed, set for closure or reduced to shells. But libraries are not just places for borrowing books. They are also a vital piece of the social commons, where the precariat can find some respect and solace.

The commons and justice principles

The existence of public spaces, parks, libraries, allotments and other areas of common sharing has positive effects on the economy, society and people's values. Their erosion, therefore, can be expected to have corresponding negative effects.

Erosion offends the Security Difference Principle, because it is the precariat and other low-income groups who make most use of the commons. The commons are a safety valve and form a greater part of their social income. They are also a block on controls over people, so that losing them offends the Paternalism Test Principle. And erosion of the commons offends the Rights-not-Charity Principle, since the use of public property is a communal right not dependent on bureaucratic discretion. The commons are ours, collectively.

As for the Dignified Work Principle, the commons are a reminder of the importance of use value rather than exchange value, of work rather than labour. To say that labour for wages on a farm owned by an agribusiness is productive work, whereas producing vegetables on an allotment is not, is nonsensical, concealing an ideology.

Above all, erosion of the commons offends the Ecological Constraint Principle; it reduces the reproduction of an environment that can be shared, not just between classes but also between humanity and nature, and the species that have shared the commons throughout history.

* * *

The precariat is not passive in the face of the shrinking commons. Indeed, the struggle for quality public space is proving to be a formidable means by which the precariat is turning from a class-in-the-making into a class-for-itself. It is the only group in the global market system with an urgent need to fight for the revival of the commons. This is what it is doing, often showing courage, usually exhibiting the 'primitive rebel' stage of its evolution.

The elite and plutocracy have their sun-blessed islands, mountain retreats and numerous homes. The salariat has its gardens, leafy neighbourhoods and second homes. The old working class clings on, watching council estates crumble in dereliction until the better bits are gentrified and lost to private ownership. By contrast, the precariat lives for and in the commons, and feels the pain of shrinking public spaces. It has nowhere else to go. That is why it is leading the fightback, be it in São Paulo, New York, Istanbul, Jakarta or Madrid.

In Istanbul in May 2013, plans to convert the iconic Gezi Park into a shopping mall, by selling it to property developers, prompted a mass occupation and protests demanding it be kept a public space. The brutal police response emphasized the conflict between society and the state. The occupiers of the park and nearby Taksim Square came together spontaneously. They were primitive rebels, knowing what they were against, but were not yet a political force. Prime Minister Recep Tayyip Erdogan branded them as *çapulcu* (riff-raff), which protesters appropriated as a badge of pride, posting the word on tents (*çapulcu* homes), on banners and even on biscuits. One woman told a newspaper, 'I came because the park should be kept for children. I came to stand up for the weak' (Beaumont 2013).

Shortly afterwards, Brazilians surged onto the streets to protest at 'eventism' – use of public resources by the state for profit-making activities in preparation for the 2014 football World Cup and the 2016 Olympic Games. Although sparked by a rise in public transport fares, which is why the protests were dubbed 'the 20-cent revolution', shrinkage of the commons was high on the list of concerns, as wasteful stadiums and amenities depleted public spaces.

More mundanely, the precariat must join the struggle to preserve allotments. No allotment area should be sold without the agreement of the holders, and no bribery in the form of compensatory payments should be allowed, since this is a public good handed down by past generations and held for the next. The struggle line must be drawn. And those principles must be taken into other forms of the commons.

There is a final political point for reflection. In the UK, the Green Party appears to attract disproportionately large support from the progressive part of the precariat – well-educated but low-income (Mortimer 2013). Struggling for the commons resonates politically. It must.

Article 28: Revive
deliberative democracy

> Deliberative democracy is the only way to overcome the
> commodification of politics and thinning of democracy, and to
> ensure that the aspirations and insecurities of the precariat are
> given priority over utilitarian trends.

It is vital to promote deliberative democracy, the form of democracy that involves public debate on policies, to combat the combined threat of thinning democracy, the commodification of politics, 'post-truth' politics, politics as a stepping-stone occupation, and the utilitarian consensus.

Neo-liberalism has achieved the commodification of politics, just as it commodifies every aspect of life. Politicians rely on financial backing, mainly from the plutocracy, the elite and financial institutions. They use buzzwords and simplistic images to manipulate enough of the people for enough of the time to win elections. To this is added the dark art of 'wedge politics' (appealing to the prejudices of part of the supporters of another party), practised by public relations consultants who hire themselves out to politicians and political parties, who in turn package themselves to appeal to the plutocracy and elite.

Post-truth politics played out in the media adds to the deadly mix. It feeds on political illiteracy, reinforced by the commodification of education where the pursuit of 'human capital' crowds out ethics, moral education and philosophy. Lack of respect for the political process leads to thinning democracy: fewer people are attracted to party politics, fewer join political parties, fewer campaign for them and fewer vote. So-called 'think tanks' are the breeding and grooming ground for aspiring politicians, who too often see a period in politics as a stepping stone for lucrative positions in commerce.

This trek to phoney democracy must be reversed. The alternative is not to opt out by cutting involvement in electoral politics. It is to demand the construction of countervailing mechanisms to revive political rights. Deliberative democracy means revival of the ancient Greeks' idea of *schole*, public participation in the political debate. Experiments show that deliberative democracy increases commitment to altruism and to the 'social floor' principle enshrined in basic income (e.g. Frohlich and Oppenheimer 1993). It could also combat the trend towards post-truth politics, in which politicians and their backers can present misleading assertions and factoids without challenge, by exposing people to all points of view (and truthful factual information). It is the deliberative process that is vital.

Thinning democracy

To be healthy and legitimate, democracy requires widespread participation by the electorate. There has been an unhealthy decline in the range of institutions subject to democratic accountability and in the participation of adults in political parties, elections and debate. In the US presidential election of 2012, just over half the electorate voted, and just over half of those who voted did so for Obama. With over 3 million 'felons' and others denied a vote altogether, less than 30 per cent voted for Obama. In Germany too, only a third of the electorate voted for Chancellor Angela Merkel in the September 2013 general election; another third stayed at home, In the UK, a 2012 report by Democratic Audit concluded that democracy was in 'terminal decline'. The thinning of democracy is a global crisis.

There are many reasons, which need not be discussed here. But some points are worth mentioning. If the costs of voting exceed the expected return, it is rational not to vote and to take a free ride on others doing so. This rationale grows stronger if the perceived differences between the parties are small. Parties have become almost indistinguishable. The progressive flame has been dimmed in recent years. But that may not last. We are not in a 'post-democratic' or 'post-political' age. We are in a period of transition.

A reason the precariat should re-engage with electoral politics is that the thicker the democracy, the more likely distributional and ecological concerns will predominate. Effective democracy may slow economic growth, since social objectives become more important. This was found in research on Chinese local government reform (Martinez-Bravo et al. 2011). Thinning democracy leads to growth becoming over-emphasized, because elites gain. What do they care about the disappearing commons? Reviving deliberative democracy could restore a balance in favour of social and environmental objectives.

Commodification and corruption of politics

It is scarcely news that the plutocracy and multinational financial capital have bought politics. Successful politicians rely on them, at every level. At the 2010 British general election, the City of London provided more than half of Conservative Party funding. In his US presidential re-election campaign, Obama was partially funded by contributions from Goldman Sachs, which also financed some of his opponents. Many corporations do the same, hedging their bets to ensure the eventual winner is in their debt. In the commodification of politics, above all in the USA, corporations have been given more citizenship rights than people. The precariat is most threatened, although anybody claiming to be a democrat should oppose what is taking place. Too many proclaiming democratic credentials stay silent. The essence of rights is universalism, based on the principle that everybody has equal rights.

Political rights require that each citizen should have an equal voice in the public space, in influencing opinion and in making political decisions. Democracy is rule by the people for the people. Yet corporations – archetypal representatives of the elite – are allowed and encouraged, by tax deductions for donations and by assured access to policymakers, to devote substantial funds to their preferred political causes, politicians and ideology. They have vastly more weight in the democratic process than any but the very richest individuals.

As capital has become more concentrated, the number of corporate citizens with the capacity to shape political decisions has shrunk to a fraction of the proverbial 1 per cent. Winner-takes-all markets lead to a plutocratic form of commodified democracy; witness the B20 corporate lobby group set up to persuade governments to be even more business-friendly than they have been.

The only way this will be reversed is through civil action and demands that corporations should not be allowed to contribute to political parties or individual politicians. The moral case is not hard to make. A Precariat Charter must call for an end to such practices. It is most unlikely to come from existing political parties, since they are enmeshed in the culture of corporate funding.

Lobbying must be curbed. The lobbying industry in the USA spent $3.5 billion in 2009 alone to influence the federal government, and half of retiring senators now join lobby firms. David Cameron when in opposition warned of the 'far too cosy relationship between politics, government, business and money' and said that a scandal over 'secret corporate lobbying' was waiting to happen.

> We all know how it works. The lunches, the hospitality, the quiet word in your ear, the ex-ministers and ex-advisers for hire, helping big business to find the right way to get its way (Sparrow 2010).

Yet he did nothing to stop it. During his premiership, the Conservative Party's co-treasurer was forced to resign after he was secretly filmed offering access to Cameron in return for large donations to the party. In the last days of the previous Labour government, three ex-Cabinet ministers were also filmed offering services for money.

Many go into politics as a stepping stone into the elite. On leaving office, various New Labour ex-ministers rushed to become company directors. In 2012, Mervyn Davies, former business minister, became chairman of Chime Communications, a public relations firm; Lord

Myners became director of MegaFon, a Russian telecoms firm; and former business secretary, Lord Mandelson, was appointed chairman of Lazard Ltd, an investment bank.

The precariat could not trust a party whose leaders so flagrantly serve the interests of financial capital. A way to check this is through building mechanisms that give everyone the chance to put pressure on politicians to respect the public Voice.

Combat 'pollitis'

Opinion polls have become dangerously influential tools in politics. They displace deliberative democracy, since they steer political rhetoric and legitimize prejudice. And the questions, and hence results, are often biased, deliberately so or due to prejudiced views by those who devise them or who pay for them to be conducted.

Take a sensitive subject for the precariat. An ICM/Guardian poll in 2013 reported that nearly half 18–24 year-olds disagreed with the statement that most unemployed people receiving benefits were 'unlucky rather than lazy'. Overall, a third of voters thought most unemployed were lazy. Yet there is no evidence whatever to support this view. Opinion has been manipulated by the post-truth assertions of politicians and the media keen to justify conditional social policies.

According to other polls, by 2013 over half of British people believed unemployment benefits were too high, compared with a third who said that in the 1980s. Yet the real value of unemployment benefits fell sharply over that period. People should have been asked how much they thought the average unemployed person was receiving. Only after being told the correct amount, should they have been asked if the amount was too low, too high or about right.

One improvement would be to insist that both the questions and responses should be presented in mainstream media. However, that would not be enough. Public views are manipulated as much by what is not asked as by what is asked. Registered opinion polls should be based on a form of mutualism. There should be a regulatory board, on which a cross-section of political and social groups, including the precariat, is represented, to monitor the adherence of polls to ethical codes and professional standards for sampling and question design. While there should not be a ban on any poll, those who wish to demonstrate legitimacy and be taken seriously by the media should accredit their organization to that board.

Opinion polls are used to reinforce politicians' positions, to court popularity. First, corporations and the plutocracy ensure, through donations and lobbying, that politicians and political parties promote their interests. Then they ensure that these views are projected in the media they control, moulding public opinion. That opinion is subsequently reflected in polls that appear to validate the policies politicians are advocating. The polls complete the circle in favour of manipulative power. That circle must be broken.

Deliberation grants

The Precariat proposed linking basic income to a moral, not legally binding, commitment to vote in national elections and to participate at least once a year in town-hall or village-hall meetings convened to enable the people to interrogate representatives of mainstream political parties.

As a condition for receiving the basic income (Article 25), or social dividend from capital funds (Article 26), there should be a commitment to register to vote, done online when registering to receive the basic income. That would help reverse the trend towards thin democracy whereby under two-thirds of the potential electorate vote in general elections, often because they are not registered to do so. This is important for progressives, since those in the precariat – 'the poor', migrants, youth and people with disabilities – are the least likely to register (and thus vote).

The proposal stems from a very old model. In ancient Greece, Pericles arranged for all citizens to receive a grant, a sort of basic income, in return for their participation in political life, for going to the *agora*, the public centre, to listen to and speak at meetings called to decide on policies. Participation was not a condition for receipt of the grant since, with moral education ingrained in that society, there was no need for conditionality. It was a payment for presumed participation. The moral suasion was sufficient to induce social responsibility. That is how it should be in the twenty-first century.

In addition, as proposed by Ackerman and Ayres (2002) and Johnson (2012), every legal resident should be given a card, credited with a modest amount, which can be spent only on national election campaigns. Each person could choose which party should receive the money, which would encourage more political involvement. It would help offset the power of the plutocracy to buy politicians and parties, and give a moral prod to participate in the political process.

Deliberation days

The deliberation idea is based on rich historical experience and recent experimental evidence that the process of deliberation leads to more mature, more altruistic and more progressive outcomes. It draws on the ancient Greek *ekklesia*, the assembly of all free citizens. The modern 'assemblies' of the Occupy movement have their roots there. Ackerman and Fishkin (2005) have proposed a national holiday in the USA two weeks before a presidential election to enable all potential electors to participate in public events to review the issues at stake. A 'Deliberation Day' should be institutionalized in every vibrant democracy.

It cannot be divorced from growing online political activity, which has been so important in the movement of the squares around the world. Online activities have limits, and seem best for reacting to events rather than for launching progressive initiatives. There is a need for more off-screen involvement, to draw on energies that can be dissipated in petitioneering. Signing online petitions in a good cause is too easy and, while petitions may be good weathervanes, they may soon be absorbed by the political system and manipulated by the corporate elite. Deliberation in the public arena would be more robust.

* * *

The precariat has most to gain from more deliberative democracy. It is a route back to class-based rather than commodified politics, and is a way to combat the utilitarian consensus. Thinning democracy means the modal voter becomes older and more conservative, as progressives and sceptics become disillusioned and detached. While there are good reasons for disaffection, it plays into neo-liberal hands. Minority views become majority votes. Strengthening democracy is a progressive imperative. In sum, deliberative democracy must be reinvented for the twenty-first century. The precariat's Voice must be strengthened, if a progressive politics is to be revived.

Article 29: Re-marginalize charities

> The role of charity should be reduced to a residual, providing supplementary comfort, empathy and environmental revival. It should not be a substitute for rights-based state policy.

Charity is no substitute for justice withheld.

Saint Augustine

The neo-liberal state has reduced public provision of services, so as to facilitate tax cuts and subsidies for selected interests, and has been helped by drawing on people's goodwill to fill the gap with charity. It is vital to re-marginalize the role of charity in society. It is being used to cover up regressive policies, imposing unfair pressures on donors and on supplicants. The contrived centrality of charity is linked to the religification of social policy. From an ecumenical and progressive perspective, that must be reversed. Charity should be marginal and appreciated all the more for that.

Charity displaces rights, gives discretionary power to potential 'donors' and is moralistic. It does not help that in English the word is ambiguous. When the Bible speaks of charity being the greatest of sentiments, the meaning is clearly 'love'. But charity has come to mean benevolent giving and forgiving. Charity is associated with pity, and pity is akin to contempt. And to be a recipient of charity is to be a supplicant, a beggar, a failure in society. To receive or ask for charity is a demeaning experience.

With the construction of welfare states, charity seemed to be relegated to the margins. That was appropriate with the extension of rights. But the neo-liberal deconstruction of rights has allowed a growing space for charity and its plutocratic variant, philanthropy. Charities are promoted as the means of replacing functions performed by the public sector, enabling governments to push ahead with cuts in public provision by providing a palliative against intolerable deprivation. Without the charity sector, the neo-liberal state would not be able to get away with it.

'Do-gooding' has become a global business, with global ambassadors, salariats and spokespeople. The plutocrats choose their priorities, directing policy behind the scenes, with support from industry, governments and international organizations. The United Nations, set up to promote human rights, seeks to participate in and legitimize global charity.

Charities are also reproducing the global class structure. There are the plutocrats and elites in the charity business, there are the well-paid salariat executives managing charity empires, there are proficians skipping between charities on consultancies, there is a poorly-paid core of staffers, and there are numerous charity workers who are in the precariat themselves, one day providing charity services, the next expecting to be a recipient.

It is ironic that while the neo-liberal state is putting more onus on charities to deal with the growing insecurities and inequalities flowing from its policies, many charities are floundering. In 2013, the UK's Charities Aid Foundation estimated that one in six were close to collapse due to falling donations or surging demand for help.

UK jobcentres, supposedly an arm for social rights, are sending jobseeker 'clients' to food banks and other charities to cover delays in processing welfare claims, rather than providing advances. Partly this reflects cuts to staffing, partly it reflects increased use of complex assessment tests, partly it is deliberate. One experienced Citizens Advice worker wrote to the author:

> For voluntary agencies, is it better to be part of it and try to do what we can, or turn down council funding and be closed? I loathe food parcels and utility vouchers. It is outrageous that they're needed, and of all the responses to poverty, they must be among the most inadequate and humiliating. They ease hunger for a few days. That's all.

Growth of charity is related to the growing conditionality and paternalism of social policy. And it goes with the moralistic tone of conventional thinking. For example, in January 2013, Demos, a think tank formerly linked to New Labour, issued a report favouring a shift from cash benefits to pre-paid cards that would 'open up the potential to exercise some control over how benefits are spent'.

The report, sponsored by MasterCard, concluded: 'Whatever the future of prepaid cards, it's clear that they enable more creative and innovative thinking regarding how people relate to local and national government and public services.' This is paternalism, close to social engineering.

Shortly afterwards, the government abolished the centrally run social fund, which gave out small loans and grants to desperate people for crises such as broken boilers or lack of food, and handed responsibility for emergency help to local councils at the same time as cutting the total available. Most of England's 150 councils planned to replace cash grants and loans with one-off vouchers that could only be used for certain items such as food or nappies (diapers), in the form of prepaid supermarket cards. Some planned to give charity food parcels or support food banks. Birmingham City Council, which issued cards to be used only in Asda supermarkets, said it had decided not to pay cash in order to 'build in an element of control by utilising payment cards'. Another council, Bristol, said the cards 'should not be used for cigarettes, alcohol or entertainment' and that if 'misuse occurs it will seek repayment'. Soon, bureaucrats will check supermarket receipts to make sure spending is only on permitted items. Even if they do not, vouchers and prepaid cards are a restriction of freedom. They are condescending, infantilizing and stigmatizing, branding citizens (or denizens) as incapable of making rational decisions. And administrative costs are large – typically 20 per cent of the total allocated to them.

Besides chipping away at freedom, vouchers weaken social solidarity. It is part of the meaning of society (Big or Small) that those hit by misfortune should receive assistance from the state. This also underpins the social insurance contributory principle – cross-subsidizing those who have a higher risk of deprivation and ill luck. If that principle is killed, one cannot fairly demand altruistic 'socially responsible' behaviour from those victimized by the volatility and uncertainty of an open market system.

Because vouchers are stigmatizing, many who should qualify for help will not apply on those grounds (Type 1 error), which suits a government with moralistic objectives intent on cutting public social spending. Indeed, some libertarian paternalists argue that stigmatization is a necessary step towards weaning people off state dependency. In the USA, only three-quarters of those qualifying for food stamps apply for them.

Shifting to vouchers erodes the capacity to function in a money economy. They actually increase dependency, impair the ability to make rational decisions and chip away at personal responsibility. Some US states prohibit people from using food stamps to buy fizzy drinks (sodas), on the grounds that they could cause obesity. Vouchers are not a way of asserting equality before the law. As Zoe Williams (2013) put it, 'When you relegate people to a world outside money, you create a true underclass: a group whose privacy and autonomy are worth less than everyone else's, who are stateless in a world made of shops.'

The state is converting the social system into an arm of philanthropic paternalism, with coercion and denial thinly concealed. Local authorities have introduced entitlement rules, and some have added conditionalities, including requiring recipients to sign up to 'expected behaviours and actions'. The paternalism is part of the utilitarian trend, defying the Rights-not-Charity and Paternalism

Test Principles. Like so many elements in the libertarian paternalistic model, the policy increases immoral hazards. Desperate people denied cash to meet their needs in moments of crisis may try to obtain cash in risky or criminal ways. Others may turn to loan sharks.

The paternalists should be consistent. Those recommending such policies should convert pocket money they give to their children into extra portions of greens which, as most parents know, are 'good for you'. Why do they not do that? It is because pocket money gives freedom, helping youngsters learn how to handle money responsibly. The precariat are to be infantilized instead. They are not like our children!

In response, the precariat must campaign against those who perpetuate such paternalism, naming, shaming and voting against them. And those providing charity should object too, since their goodness is being exploited, their 'work' no more than unpaid labour. Charities must play their part. They should organize not just to make their activities more integrated, efficient and transparent, but also to do what is the hardest for them, demand to be re-marginalized. The growth of the charity state is one reason for advocating a basic income as a right. It offers a route for reversing the trend towards a begging society. Knowing that your fellow citizen has the same rights as you do humanizes us all.

6

There is a future

Rise like lions after slumber,
In unvanquishable number
Shake your chains to earth like dew,
Which in sleep had fallen on you.
Ye are many – they are few.

'The Masque of Anarchy', Shelley, 1819

The precariat is beyond the stage of being a despondent mass of defeated people experiencing insecurity and deprivation, with occasional acts by primitive rebels to lift the spirits. It is beyond the period of recognition. The numbers are multiplying, so that however hard they try, establishments cannot deny the existence of the precariat or what it stands for. A new progressive politics will come as new entrants swell the precariat into something close to a majority, at least among active members of society.

When mainstream political parties cut the numbers working in public social services, the libertarian-paternalist road to conditionality will collapse in inefficiency, inequity and contradictions. Costs will escalate, Type 1 errors will proliferate, as numerous citizens lose rights without justification. The morale of civil servants will collapse. Whistleblowers will proliferate, and become bolder as they find themselves compromised ethically, required to deliver an illiberal system that could turn on them, their relatives or friends. Resistance from within could be as powerful as the resistance provided by the precariat and its allies. The sooner the better.

The scourge of uncertainty

To adequately understand the precariat's dilemma, or the times we live in, we must understand the scourge of uncertainty. The neo-liberal model generates chronic uncertainty. For the precariat, uncertainty is pervasive: Where will the next shock come from? Will I need assistance or a loan? What will happen if I lose my job or fall sick? Will I be able to obtain benefits to survive? Will I lose my home? The precariat must also reckon with constant tightening of the benefit regime, without opposition from those paid to oppose.

The multiple character of uncertainty is what unites supplicants. They may put their heads down and grind their teeth in their structured humiliation. But from time to time, a little extra pressure makes them snap, individually or collectively. Silent grimacing gives way to groans, and groans give way to the realization that the situation is unendurable. This is a global condition. Indian farmers facing price uncertainty commit suicide in horrifyingly large numbers. In the industrialized world, suicides have soared since the onset of austerity (Stuckler and Basu 2013). It is not homes and family that drive people to these extremes; it is the lack of society, which the neo-liberal dystopia denies. When Margaret Thatcher – described by David Cameron as the country's 'greatest peace-time prime minister' – said that 'there is no such thing as society', she meant that in the neo-liberal vision 'there should be no such thing as society'. It is the deconstruction of supportive communities, and the disregard for the ethics, rituals and reciprocities that make up occupational, social and cultural communities, that is so rotten about the neo-liberal model. Chronic uncertainty is the outcome, without a strategy to overcome it.

The importance of alliances

In forging a political programme for the precariat, it will be essential to build cross-class alliances in favour of particular aims. In some cases, alliances should be relatively easy. Thus, proficians and much of the salariat should want to see education decommodified (Article 23). All classes should be drawn to fight for a revival of due process, fearing they could be next to be denied this ancient civil right. Proficians will see how today's official concepts and statistics on labour and work distort their reality as much as the precariat's. And the salariat will see how idiotic and expensive today's recruitment mechanisms have become.

The core of the old working class may have difficulty in supporting a right to a basic income, seeing their short-term interest in defending the old social security system. But that system is crumbling rapidly, while wages will continue to tumble. Indeed, it is perhaps around income poverty that a cross-class alliance will emerge. Here the block on progress is the labourist bias of social democracy. Characteristically, celebrating in 2013 the fiftieth anniversary of the civil rights march on Washington and Martin Luther King's 'I have a dream' speech, American labourists used it to argue for a rise in the minimum wage. In fact, King (1967: Chapter 5) argued cogently for a basic income for all.

> I am now convinced that the simplest approach will prove to be the most effective – the solution to poverty is to abolish it directly by a now widely discussed measure: the guaranteed income... New forms of work that enhance the social good will have to be devised for those for whom traditional jobs are not available... a host of positive psychological changes inevitably will result from widespread economic security. The dignity of the individual will flourish when the decisions concerning his life are in his own hands, when he has the assurance that his income is stable and certain, and when he knows that he has the means to seek self-improvement.

One could not say it much better.

From supplicant denizens to rights-bearing citizens

There must be an onslaught on moralistic social policy. On this there should be an alliance between libertarians, including classic liberals, and progressives. Neither should favour paternalism or its inevitable drift into coercion. Moralistic social policy must be displaced by rights-based policy. With the latter, there is a presumption of innocence, unless another conclusion is reached by due process. With moralistic policy, there is a tendency to presume guilt until a person demonstrates innocence, a tendency to believe that if someone is in difficulties it is their own fault, or due to laziness or personal deficiencies. People are required to prove they are deserving before being granted anything.

If a man in a boat ran into rocks and fell overboard, we would not ask if it was his fault before rescuing him, or throw him back if he had been careless. Nor would we ask him to prove anything before we gave him food and clothes. We would draw on moral sentiments and recognition that everybody has a right to live and to be treated with dignity. Social policy no longer proceeds on that basis. It demands proof of behavioural propriety before help is provided.

Politics has experienced a retreat of virtue as it has become more moralistic towards society's disadvantaged. Greed is legitimized by neo-liberalism, and those who promote its ideology behave accordingly, cheating on expenses, taking bribes, squirreling money into overseas bank accounts... the list goes on. A minister in charge of welfare reform benefits from huge farm subsidies that his government refuses to cap. Meanwhile, he preaches against 'benefit dependency' and imposes ever tougher conditionalities on desperate supplicants.

Moralistic policy goes with paternalism, which becomes harder as its advocates become more messianic. Ever increasing numbers are affected by loss of due process and the growth of snooping, intrusive questions and compulsion, in the benefit system and elsewhere. Sooner or later, enough of the salariat and proficians will feel the infringements on liberty dangerously close to themselves and their relatives and friends. They will reject the ideologues and moralists. They must.

Recapture the language of progress

In the post-1945 era, the language of public discourse favoured rights and egalitarianism. Then the neo-liberals captured the language, devising images suited to their ideology. Thus, for example, welfare changed from being a positive word for well-being to being a badge of failure and 'state dependency'. Disability benefits have been turned into 'allowances', converting a term suggesting rights into one suggesting a discretionary conditional payment. The unemployed are called 'clients' and those dealing with them 'advisers', when what is happening is that the unemployed are being told what they must do, on pain of being sanctioned. The language is abused with intent. And social democrats were all too eager to adapt, adding to the lexicon of anti-progressive terms.

Still, a feature of the austerity era and the spread of the precariat has been a wry invention of subversive words and phrases, with crisis slang satirizing politicians and bankers. It has helped clear the air. Now is the time to go further, to create a language of positive images.

Reviving the future

Some sombre voices have said that the future died in the 1970s, with the world now condemned to endless consumption predicated on continued growth. To those Jeremiahs we might say that an ecological vision of a Good Society could only emerge fully once the neo-liberal dystopia of permanent growth was exposed as unsustainable and socially divisive. The 'end of the future' seems to recur in the dying phase of epochs, before the next transformation begins. It occurred in the late Middle Ages, before the Renaissance; it recurred in the late eighteenth century, before the upsurge of romanticism; and it occurred in the late nineteenth century before the upsurge of socialism. Now a future is emerging from the failings of the neo-liberal project.

The future must have a base of certainty. Here the precariat will find unity. For the first variety, falling out of old working-class communities, chronic insecurity has fuelled loss of citizenship, loss of acquired rights. The welfare state was built for them. Now they look back and listen to the sirens of populism. A basic income as a right would restore a sense of security and a feeling that they are citizens, showing that the state does care for them, which at present they doubt.

For the second variety, most migrants and minorities know they are denizens, and do not feel they belong fully to any community. Even if large in number, many feel they have neither a present nor a future. For them, even if they had to wait, a basic income would amount to an assertion that they are members of society, with an economic right that would be the basis of citizenship, promoting involvement in the *agora* and in the life of the *polis*.

For the third variety, the vanguard of the precariat, the Promethean spirit of educated youth encourages a desire to combine work with the leisure of *schole*, meaning constant learning and participation in public life. Currently, they too are denizens, without rights in the state. They understand the threat posed by commodification, and are the victims of educational commodification in particular, provided with a costly lottery ticket worth little, promised a 'career' but unable to build one.

What makes this part of the precariat progressive is that it is detached from labourism. Its members can see the value of work and *schole*. For them, a basic income would not just be a source of security but would also be liberating, in enabling them to obtain the other key assets of a tertiary society – more control of time, more quality space, non-commodified education and a share in financial capital.

The essence of a Precariat Charter is the assertion that many elements must come together; no single measure is a panacea or magic bullet. It is an ethos that must be reconstructed, built on the great values of compassion and empathy. You should not risk waking up years from now, thinking you have no moral right to complain because you did nothing when you had the energy and did not like the future-less realities around you. Change can only come if we act, not if we simply complain.

Triumph will come only when the precariat has abolished itself. Then society could be based on the general pursuit of a life of occupation, work and leisure. It is too early to tell if there will be a future after that. The job at hand is to accelerate the arrival of the next one.

BIBLIOGRAPHY

Ackerman, B. and Alstott, A. (1999), *The Stakeholder Society*. New Haven and London: Yale University Press.

Ackerman, B. and Ayres, I. (2002), *Voting With Dollars: A New Paradigm for Campaign Finance*. New Haven and London: Yale University Press.

Ackerman, B. and Fishkin, J. S. (2004), *Deliberation Day*. New Haven and London: Yale University Press.

Acton, L. (2011), 'Allotment gardens: A reflection of history, heritage, community and self'. *Papers from the Institute of Archaeology (PIA)*, 21: 46–58.

Arendt, H. ([1951] 1986), *The Origins of Totalitarianism*. London: André Deutsch.

—(1958), *The Human Condition*. Chicago: University of Chicago Press.

Balls, E. (2013), 'Ed Balls: Britain needs real welfare reform that is tough, fair and that works'. *PoliticsHome*, 4 January. http://www.politicshome.com/uk/article/69052/ed_balls_britain_needs_real_welfare_reform_that_is_tough_fair_and_that_works.html [accessed 24 September 2013].

Barcelona Social Forum (2004), *Charter of Emerging Human Rights*. Barcelona: Institut de Drets Humans de Catalunya.

Beaumont, P. (2013), 'Recep Tayyip Erdogan struggles to make sense of Turkey's trauma'. *The Observer*, 15 June. http://www.the guardian.com/world/2013/jun/15/erdogan-misses-point-turkish-unite-defend-rights [accessed 9 December 2013].

Berg, A. G. and Ostry, J. D. (2011a), 'Equality and efficiency'. *Finance and Development*, 48, (3): 12–15. http://www.imf.org/external/pubs/ft/fandd/2011/09/Berg.htm [accessed 9 September 2013].

—(2011b), 'Warning: Inequality may be hazardous to your growth'. *iMF Direct*, 8 April. http://blog-imfdirect.imf.org/2011/04/page/2/ [accessed 11 September 2013].

Birrell, I. (2012), 'Don't mock "hug a hoodie". It was and still is the right message'. *The Guardian*, 1 June, p. 44.

Blanchflower, D. G. and Bell, D. N. F. (2013), 'Underemployment in the UK revisited'. *National Institute Economic Review*, 224, (1): F8–F22.

Blanden, J., Gregg, P. and Machin, S. (2005), *Intergenerational Mobility in Europe and North America*. London: Centre for Economic Performance, London School of Economics.

Bobbio, N. (1990), *L'età dei diritti* [*The Age of Rights*]. Rome: Einaudi.

Boffey, D. (2012), 'Iain Duncan Smith's advisers warn of consequences of benefit crackdown'. *The Guardian*, 22 December. http://www.theguardian.com/society/2012/dec/22/iain-duncan-smith-jobseekers-allowance [accessed 22 September 2013].

Boffey, D. and Urquhart, C. (2013), 'Soldiers, teachers, cashiers and nurses: Faces of the benefit cuts'. *The Observer*, 6 January, p. 28.

Boubtane, E., Coulibaly, D. and Rault, C. (2013), 'Immigration, growth and unemployment: Panel VAR evidence from OECD countries'. CESifo Working Paper No. 4329. Munich: Center for Economic Studies and Ifo Institute.

Bowcott, O. (2013), 'Grayling climbdown over legal aid change'. *The Guardian*, 2 July, p. 4.

Braga, R. (2012), *A política do precariado* [*The Politics of Precariat*]. São Paulo: Boitempo Editorial.

Brinks, D. and Gauri, V. (2012), *The Law's Majestic Equality*. Washington, DC: World Bank.

Brooklyn Rail (2012), 'The debt resistors' operations manual'. *Brooklyn Rail*, 4 October. http://www.brooklynrail.org/2012/10/local/the-debt-resistors-operations-manual [accessed 25 September 2013].

Brubaker, W. R. (1989), 'Membership without citizenship: The economic and social rights of non-citizens', in W. R. Brubaker (ed.), *Immigration and the Politics of Citizenship in Europe and North America*. Lanham, MD: German Marshall Fund of the United States, pp. 145–62.

Brynjolfsson, E. and McAfee, A. (2012), 'The great decoupling'. *International Herald Tribune*, 12 December, p. 8.

Buddelmeyer, H. and Wooden, M. (2011), 'Transitions out of casual employment: The Australian experience'. *Industrial Relations*, 50, (1): 109–30.

Burgess, J. and Campbell, I. (1998), 'Casual employment in Australia: Growth, characteristics, a bridge or a trap?' *Economic and Labour Relations Review*, 9, (1): 31–54.

Burke, M. (2013), 'Economics and the debate on immigration'. *Socialist Economic Bulletin*, 29 March. http://socialisteconomicbulletin.blogspot.co.uk/2013_03_01_archive.html [accessed 23 September 2013].

Byrne, L. (2013), 'Why Conservative benefit cuts won't get Britain working'. *The Observer*, 6 April, p. 6.

Cappelli, P. (2012), *Why Good People Can't Get Jobs: The Skills Gap and What Companies Can Do About It*. Philadelphia: Wharton Digital Press.

Colley, H. (2013), 'What (a) to do about "impact": A Bourdieusian critique'. *British Educational Research Journal*, online 8 July. DOI: 10.1002/berj.3112

Collini, S. (2012), *What are Universities for?* London: Penguin Books.

Collins, J. L. (2008), 'The specter of slavery: Workfare and the economic citizenship of poor women', in J. L. Collins, M. di Leonardo and B. Williams (eds), *New Landscapes of Inequality: Neoliberalism and the Erosion of Democracy in America.* Santa Fe, NM: SAR Press, pp. 131–52.

Collinson, P. (2013), 'Private equity firms behind expansion of Wonga.com'. *The Guardian*, 26 July. http://www.theguardian.com/business/2013/jul/26/wonga-private-equity-firms-backers [accessed 9 December 2013].

Crisp, R. and Fletcher, D. R. (2008), 'A comparative review of workfare programmes in the United States, Canada and Australia'. Department for Work and Pensions Research Report No. 533, Sheffield: Centre for Regional Economic and Social Research, Sheffield Hallam University.

DePaulo, B. (2007), *Singled Out: How Singles are Stereotyped, Stigmatized, and Ignored, and Still Live Happily Ever After.* New York: St. Martin's Griffin.

Diamond, P. (2013), 'One nation? Not yet'. *The Guardian*, 1 March, p. 38.

Doogan, K. (2009), *New Capitalism? The Transformation of Work.* Cambridge: Polity.

Duncan, R. (2012), *The New Depression: The Breakdown of the Paper Money Economy.* Hoboken, NJ: John Wiley & Sons.

Economist (2011), 'Exporting jobs: Gurgaon grief'. *The Economist*, 24 September, p. 25.

—(2012a), 'Free exchange: Decline and small'. *The Economist*, 3 March, p. 69.

—(2012b), 'Mobile moans'. *The Economist*, 28 April, p. 66.

—(2012c), 'The nationalisation of markets: The rise of the financial-political complex'. *The Economist*, 26 May, p. 64.

—(2012d), 'The hollow men: The hollowing out of Japan'. *The Economist*, 9 June, p. 56.

—(2012e), 'Free exchange: Savers' lament'. *The Economist*, 1 December, p. 40.

—(2012f), 'A season of dolour and dole'. *The Economist*, 15 December. http://www.economist.com/news/britain/21568421-squeezing-welfare-budget-popular-tories-may-still-suffer-it-season [accessed 27 September 2013].

—(2013a), 'The Irish economy: Fitter yet fragile'. *The Economist*, 5 January, p. 57.

—(2013b), 'Filing taxes: It shouldn't be so hard'. *Economist.com*, 2 April. http://www.economist.com/blogs/democracyinamerica/2013/04/filing-taxes [accessed 25 September 2013].

—(2013c), 'Unions, Inc.'. *The Economist*, 6 April, pp. 58–9.

—(2013d), 'Welfare reform: Chipping away'. *The Economist*, 6 April. http://www.economist.com/news/britain/21575778-sweeping-changes-welfare-system-many-them-loudly-opposed-are-less-radical-they [accessed 27 September 2013].

Ehrenreich, B. (2001), *Nickel and Dimed: On (Not) Getting By in America.* New York: Metropolitan.

Ellsberg, M. (2012), *The Education of Millionaires: Everything You Won't Learn in College About How to be Successful*. New York: Penguin Books.

Engel, M. (2009), 'Dispatch from the Rhondda'. *FT Weekend*, 28–9 March, pp. 16–17.

Fernández-Aráoz, C., Groysberg, B. and Nohria, N. (2009), 'The definitive guide to recruiting in good times and bad'. *Harvard Business Review*, May. http://www.berlin-civil-society-center.org/wp-content/uploads/ The-Definitive-Guide-to-Recruiting-in-Good-Times-and-Bad.pdf [accessed 21 September 2013].

Flomenhoft, G. (2012), 'Applying the Alaska model in a resource-poor state: The example of Vermont', in K. Widerquist and M. Howard (eds), *Exporting the Alaska Model: Adopting the Permanent Fund Dividend for Reform around the World*. New York: Palgrave Macmillan, pp. 85–108.

Fogg, A. (2013), 'The homeless aren't "negative impacts" – they are living victims of policy'. *The Guardian*, 30 May. http://www.theguardian.com/ commentisfree/2013/may/30/homeless-negative-impacts-victims-policy [accessed 28 September 2013].

Forget, E. L., Peden, A. D. and Strobel, S. B. (2013), 'Cash transfers, basic income and community building'. *Social Inclusion*, 1, (2): 84–91.

Foster, J. B. and McChesney, R. W. (2011), 'The internet's unholy marriage to capitalism'. *Monthly Review*, 62, (10). http://monthlyreview.org/2011/03/01/ the-internets-unholy-marriage-to-capitalism [accessed 27 September 2013].

Friedman, T. (2013), 'The professors' big stage'. *New York Times*, 5 March. http://www.nytimes.com/2013/03/06/opinion/friedman-the-professors-big-stage.html?_r=0&gwh=99CEA939643ADDAD6136F5819A3DF0C9 [accessed 25 September 2013].

Frohlich, N. and Oppenheimer, J. A. (1993), *Choosing Justice: An Experimental Approach to Ethical Theory*. Berkeley and Los Angeles, CA: University of California Press.

Fumagalli, A. (2013), 'Cognitive biocapitalism, the precarity trap, and basic income: Post-crisis perspectives'. Paper for the Espanet Conference, 'Italia, Europa: Integrazione sociale e integrazione politica', University of Calabria, Rende, 19–21 September.

Fumagalli, A. and Morini, C. (2012), 'The poverty trap and basic income: The labour market in cognitive bio-capitalism. The Italian case'. Presentation to BIEN Congress 2012, Munich, 14–16 September.

Gallie, D., Felstead, A., Green, F. and Inanc, H. (2013), *Fear at Work in Britain: First Findings from the Skills and Employment Survey 2012*. London: Centre for Learning and Life Chances in Knowledge Economies and Societies, Institute of Education.

Gautie, J. and Schmitt, J. (eds) (2010), *Low-Wage Work in the Wealthy World*. New York: Russell Sage.

Gentleman, A. (2012), 'Disability charities welcome increase in award of unconditional benefits'. *The Guardian*, 23 October. http://www.theguardian. com/society/2012/oct/23/disability-charities-welcome-award-benefits [accessed 24 September 2013].

Goldsmith, S. (2012), 'The economic and social impacts of the Permanent Fund Dividend on Alaska', in K. Widerquist and M. Howard (eds), *Exporting the Alaska Model: Adopting the Permanent Fund Dividend for Reform around the World*. New York: Palgrave Macmillan, pp. 49–64.

Göle, N. (2013), 'Public space democracy'. *Eurozine*, 29 July. www.eurozine. com/articles/2013-07-29-gole-en.html [accessed 27 September 2013].

Goodhart, D. (2013), *The British Dream: Successes and Failures of Post-War Immigration*. London: Atlantic Books.

Goodley, S. (2013), 'Budget wishlists: "We should be talking about tax cuts for the public as well as for business"'. *The Observer*, 17 March. http://www. theguardian.com/uk/2013/mar/17/budget-wishlists-tax-cuts-public-business [accessed 25 September 2013].

Gordon, D., Mack, J., Lansley, S., Main, G., Nandy, S., Patsios, D. and Pomati, M. (2013), *The Impoverishment of the UK: PSE UK First Results: Living Standards*. http://www.poverty.ac.uk/sites/default/files/attachments/ The_Impoverishment_of_the_UK_PSE_UK_first_results_summary_report_ March_28.pdf [accessed 11 September 2013].

Grant, A. (2013), 'Welfare reform, increased conditionality and discretion: Jobcentre Plus advisers' experiences of targets and sanctions'. *Journal of Poverty and Social Justice*, 21, (2): 165–76.

Green, T. H. ([1879] 1986), *Lectures on the Principles of Political Obligation and Other Writings*. Cambridge: Cambridge University Press.

Gregg, P. A. (2009), *Job Guarantee: Evidence and Design*. Bristol: Centre for Market and Public Organisation, University of Bristol.

Guardian (2013), 'Letters: Battle lines over house-building'. *The Guardian*, 25 March, p. 29.

Gunn, B. (2012), 'We need to rethink the way we treat ex-prisoners'. *The Guardian*, 10 October, p. 35.

Hammar, T. (1994), 'Legal time of residence and the status of immigrants', in R. Baubock (ed.), *From Aliens to Citizens: Redefining the Status of Immigrants in Europe*. Vienna: European Centre, pp. 187–98.

Hardin, G. (1968), 'The tragedy of the commons'. *Science*, 162, (3859): 1243–8. DOI: 10.1126/science.162.3859.1243

Harding, J. (2013), 'Forty years of community service'. *The Guardian*, 9 January, p. 35.

Harris, J. (2013), 'Turf wars escalate in the battle for Britain's allotments'. *The Guardian*, 31 May. http://www.theguardian.com/lifeandstyle/2013/may/31/turf-war-escalates-britains-allotments [accessed 27 September 2013].

Heery, E. (2009), 'The representation gap and the future of worker representation'. *Industrial Relations Journal*, 40, (4): 324–36.

Heggie, J. K. F. (2013), *Middlesbrough's Iron and Steel Industry*. Stroud, UK: Amberley Publishing.

Herndon, T., Ash, M. and Pollin, R. (2013), *Does High Public Debt Consistently Stifle Economic Growth? A Critique of Reinhart and Rogoff*. Amherst, MA: Political Economy Research Institute, University of Massachusetts.

Hessel, S. (2010), *Indignez-Vous [Time for Outrage]*. Montpellier, France: Indigène Éditions.

Hirschman, A. (1971), *Exit, Voice and Loyalty: Responses to Decline in Firms, Organizations, and States*. Cambridge, MA: Harvard University Press.

—(1991), *The Rhetoric of Reaction: Perversity, Futility, Jeopardy*. Cambridge, MA: Harvard University Press.

Hobsbawm, E. ([1962] 1977), *The Age of Revolution*. London: Abacus.

Hodson, H. (2013), 'Crowdsourcing grows up as online workers unite'. *New Scientist*, 7 February. http://www.newscientist.com/article/mg21729036.200-crowdsourcing-grows-up-as-online-workers-unite.html#.UkcOxtJmiSo [accessed 28 September 2013].

Hollinger, P. (2011), 'Opposition grows to multiculturalism'. *Financial Times*, 17 February, p. 2.

Horowitz, S. (2012), *The Freelancer's Bible: Everything You Need to Know to Have the Career of Your Dreams – on Your Terms*. New York: Workman Publishing Company.

Houlder, V. (2013), 'Nations on defensive as anger grows over tax avoidance'. *Financial Times*, 28 April. http://www.ft.com/intl/cms/s/0/e99c202e-a0fb-11e2-990c-00144feabdc0.html [accessed 26 September 2013].

Hussein, S. (2011), 'Estimating probabilities and numbers of direct care workers paid under the national minimum wage in the UK: A Bayesian approach'. *Social Care Workforce Periodical*, 16. http://www.kcl.ac.uk/sspp/kpi/scwru/pubs/periodical/issues/scwp16.pdf [accessed 21 September 2013].

Hutton, W. (2013), 'We must not allow scholarship to become the preserve of the wealthy'. *The Observer*, 6 January, p. 33.

Ikkala, M. (2012), 'Finland: Institutional resistance of the welfare state against a basic income', in R. K. Caputo (ed.), *Basic Income Guarantee and Politics*. New York: Palgrave Macmillan, pp. 63–82.

International Network of Civil Liberties Organizations (2013), *'Take Back the Streets': Repression and Criminalization of Protest Around the World*. New York: INCLO.

Inui, A., Higuchi, A. and Hiratsuka, M. (2013), 'Precarious transition in Japan'. Presentation to Youth Studies Conference 2013, 9 April, Glasgow.

Johannsen, C. (2013), 'Student debt crisis: "It's like carrying a backpack filled with bricks"'. *The Guardian*, 28 May. http://www.theguardian.com/ commentisfree/2013/may/28/student-debt-lasts-lifetime [accessed 25 September 2013].

Johnson, S. (2012), *Future Perfect: The Case for Progress in a Networked Age*. London: Allen Lane.

Junius (1812), 'Letter XXXVII to the printer of the public advertiser, March 19, 1770', reproduced in *Junius: Stat nominis umbra*. London: Dowall, p. 183.

Kaletsky, A. (2012), 'How about quantitative easing for the people?' *Reuters*, 1 August. http://blogs.reuters.com/anatole-kaletsky/2012/08/01/how-about-quantitative-easing-for-the-people/ [accessed 26 September 2013].

Kaplan, G. and Schulhofer-Wohl, S. (2012), 'Understanding the long-run decline in interstate migration'. NBER Working Paper No. 18507. Cambridge, MA: National Bureau of Economic Research.

Kearney, M., Harris, B., Jácome, E. and Parker, L. (2013), *A Dozen Facts about America's Struggling Lower-Middle Class*. Washington, DC: The Hamilton Project, Brookings.

Kendzior, S. (2013), 'Managed expectations in the post-employment economy'. *Aljazeera*, 12 March. http://www.aljazeera.com/indepth/opinion/2013/03/20 1331116423560886.html [accessed 21 September 2013].

King, M. (2012), *Speech Given by Mervyn King, Governor of the Bank of England, to the South Wales Chamber of Commerce*. London: Bank of England.

King, M. L. (1967), *Where Do We Go From Here: Chaos or Community?* New York: Harper & Row.

Kington, T. (2013), 'Is Beppe Grillo the bogeyman a disaster waiting to happen, or can his activist army heal Italy?' *The Guardian*, 23 February. http://www. theguardian.com/world/2013/feb/23/beppe-grillo-italian-elections [accessed 27 September 2013].

Kozek, B. (2012), 'Precariat's world'. *Green European Journal*, 4, 13 December. www.greeneuropeanjournal.eu/precariats-world/ [accessed 12 September 2013].

Kraus, M. W., Côté, S. and Keltner, D. (2010), 'Social class, contextualism, and empathic accuracy'. *Psychological Science*, 21: 1716–23.

Kuchler, H. (2013), 'Employers increase zero hours contracts'. *Financial Times*, 7 April. http://www.ft.com/intl/cms/s/0/04a86a6c–9f8a–11e2-b4b6– 00144feabdc0.html?siteedition=intl [accessed 12 September 2013].

Kuper, S. (2012), 'Why citizenship tests are full of holes'. *Financial Times*,

13 July. http://www.ft.com/intl/cms/s/2/d7489dc2-caea–11e1–8872–
00144feabdc0.html [accessed 23 September 2013].

Kvam, B. (2010), 'Italy's young hope to work before they're old'. *Nordic Labour
Journal*, 1 July. http://www.nordiclabourjournal.org/i-fokus/in-focus–2010/
theme-youth-outsiders../italys-young-hope-to-work-before-theyre-old
[accessed 22 September 2013].

Liebermann, S. (2012), 'Germany: Far, though close – problems and prospects
for BI in Germany', in R. K. Caputo (ed.), *Basic Income Guarantee and
Politics*. New York: Palgrave Macmillan, pp. 83–106.

Lord, C. (2012), 'The poverty trap: Scroungers of the world unite'. *CliveLord*,
2 November. http://clivelord.wordpress.com/2012/11/02/the-poverty-trap-
scroungers-of-the-world-unite/ [accessed 25 September 2013].

Lundahl, L., Erixon Arreman, I., Lundström, U. and Rönnberg, L. (2010),
'Setting things right? Swedish upper secondary school reform in a 40-year
perspective'. *European Journal of Education*, 45, (1): 46–59.

Makowski, J. (2012), 'Erasmus generation, you're Europe's last hope'. *PressEurop*,
24 October. http://www.presseurop.eu/en/content/article/2933441-erasmus-
generation-you-re-europe-s-last-hope [accessed 27 September 2013].

Malik, S. (2012), 'Sick and disabled braced for enforced work-for-benefits
programme'. *The Guardian*, 1 December, p. 23.

—(2013), 'Iain Duncan Smith: Shelf-stacking as important as a degree'. *The
Guardian*, 17 February. http://www.theguardian.com/society/2013/feb/17/
iain-duncan-smith-shelf-stacking [accessed 25 September 2013].

Marsh, P. (2012), *The New Industrial Revolution: Consumers, Globalization and
the End of Mass Production*. New Haven, CT: Yale University Press.

Marshall, T. H. (1950), 'Citizenship and social class', in T. H. Marshall,
Citizenship and Social Class, and Other Essays. Cambridge: Cambridge
University Press.

Martinez-Bravo, M., Padró i Miquel, G., Qian, N. and Yao, Y. (2011), 'Do local
elections in non-democracies increase accountability? Evidence from rural
China'. NBER Working Paper No. 16948. Cambridge, MA: National Bureau
of Economic Research.

Mason, R. (2013), 'Coalition's £1bn youth deal failing to create permanent jobs
– labour'. *The Guardian*, 14 August, p. 7.

Mattei, U. (2013), 'Protecting the commons: Water, culture, and nature: The
commons movement in the Italian struggle against neoliberal governance'.
South Atlantic Quarterly, 112, (2): 366–76.

McGettigan, A. (2013), *The Great University Gamble: Money, Markets and the
Future of Higher Education*. London: Pluto Press.

McNally, D. (1993), *Against the Market: Political Economy, Market Socialism,
and the Marxist Critique*. London: Verso.

ME Association (2009), 'New figures on work capability assessments – government press release'. *ME Association*, 13 October. http://www. meassociation.org.uk/2009/10/new-figures-on-work-capability-assessments- government-press-release/ [accessed 24 September 2013].

Mead, L. (1986), *Beyond Entitlement: The Social Obligations of Citizenship*. New York: Free Press.

Mettler, S. (2011), *The Submerged State: How Invisible Government Policies Undermine American Democracy*. Chicago: University of Chicago Press.

Miliband, E. (2013), 'A one nation plan for social security reform'. *Labour Party*, 6 June. http://www.labour.org.uk/one-nation-social-security-reform- miliband-speech [accessed 26 September 2013].

Milkman, R., Luce, S. and Lewis, P. (2013), *Changing the Subject: A Bottom-Up Account of Occupy Wall Street in New York City*. New York: Murphy Institute, City University of New York.

Millar, M. (2012), 'Need a job? Learn to impress the robots'. *BBC Business News*, 3 September. http://www.bbc.co.uk/news/business–19440255 [accessed 21 September 2013].

Mishel, L., Bivens, J., Gould, E. and Shierholz, H. (2012), *The State of Working America*. New York: Cornell University Press.

Mishel, L. and Sabadish, N. (2012), *CEO Pay and the Top 1%*. Washington, DC: Economic Policy Institute.

Mitchell, W. and Welters, R. (2008), '*Does casual employment provide a 'stepping stone' to better work prospects?*' Proceedings of the 10th Path to Full Employment Conference and the 15th National Unemployment Conference, 4–5 December 2008, Newcastle, NSW, Australia, pp. 132–46.

Moore, R. (2012), 'Should Tower Hamlets council sell off its £20m Henry Moore?' *The Observer*, 4 October. http://www.theguardian.com/ artanddesign/2012/nov/03/henry-moore-tower-hamlets-sculpture-sale [accessed 27 September 2013].

Morsy, H. (2012), 'Scarred generation'. *Finance & Development*, 49, (1): 15–17.

Mortimer, J. (2013), 'Greens: A middle-class party? Think again'. *Bright Green*, 3 June. http://brightgreenscotland.org/index.php/2013/06/think-greens-are-a- middle-class-party-think-again/ [accessed 27 September 2013].

Murray, C. (2006), *In Our Hands: A Plan to Replace the Welfare State*. Washington, DC: AEI Press.

Newman, J. H. ([1852] 1907), *The Idea of a University Defined and Illustrated*. London: Longman.

New Zealand Council of Trade Unions (2013), *Under Pressure: A Detailed Report into Insecure Work in New Zealand*. Wellington: NZCTU.

O'Connell, J. (2012), 'Soaring childcare costs see parents working for nothing'. *The Observer*, 2 September, p. 39.

OECD (2010), 'A family affair: Intergenerational social mobility across OECD countries', in *Going for Growth*. Paris: Organisation for Economic Co-operation and Development.

—(2012), 'Labour losing to capital: What explains the declining labour share?', in *OECD Employment Outlook 2012*. Paris: Organisation for Economic Co-operation and Development.

Office of Fair Trading (2013), *Payday Lending Compliance Review: Final Report*. London: OFT.

Office of the UN High Commissioner for Human Rights (2013), '"Legal aid, a right in itself" – UN special rapporteur'. *News Release*, 30 May.

Oger, H. (2003), '"Residence" as the new additional inclusive criterion for citizenship'. *Web Journal of Current Legal Issues*, 5 [no pagination].

Ortiz, I. and Cummins, M. (2013), *The Age of Austerity: A Review of Public Expenditures and Adjustment Measures in 181 Countries*. New York: Columbia University and Geneva: South Centre.

Ortiz, I., Daniels, L. M. and Engilbertsdóttir, S. (eds) (2012), *Child Poverty and Inequality: New Perspectives*. New York: Division of Policy and Practice, United Nations Children's Fund (UNICEF).

Ostrom, E. (1990), *Governing the Commons: The Evolution of Institutions for Collective Action*. Cambridge: Cambridge University Press.

Paine, T. ([1797] 2005), 'Agrarian justice', in *Common Sense and Other Writings*. New York: Barnes & Noble, pp. 321–45.

Peev, G. (2012), 'Striking low paid workers to lose benefit payments topping up their wages'. *Mail Online*, 17 June. http://www.dailymail.co.uk/news/article-2160624/Striking-low-paid-workers-lose-benefit-payments-topping-wages.html [accessed 27 September 2013].

Pennycook, M., Cory, G. and Alakeson, V. (2013), *A Matter of Time: The Rise of Zero-Hours Contracts*. London: Resolution Foundation.

Perlin, R. (2011), *Intern Nation: How to Earn Nothing and Learn Little in the Brave New Economy*. London and New York: Verso.

Pierce, J. and Schott, P. (2012), *The Surprisingly Swift Decline of U.S. Manufacturing Employment*. http://faculty.som.yale.edu/peterschott/files/research/papers/manuf_229.pdf [accessed 8 September 2013].

Polanyi, K. ([1944] 2001), *The Great Transformation: The Political and Economic Origins of Our Time*. Boston, MA: Beacon Press.

Pollin, R. and Ash, M. (2013), 'Austerity after Reinhart and Rogoff'. *Financial Times*, 17 April. http://www.ft.com/cms/s/0/9e5107f8-a75c-11e2-9fbe-00144feabdc0.html#axzz2eK6O264S [accessed 8 September 2013].

Przeworkski, A. (1985), *Capitalism and Social Democracy: Studies in Marxism and Social Theory*. Cambridge: Cambridge University Press.

Pun, N. and Chan, J. (2013), 'The spatial politics of labor in China: Life, labor, and a new generation of migrant workers'. *South Atlantic Quarterly*, 112, (1): 179–90.

Ramesh, R. (2012), 'Atos wins £400m deals to carry out disability benefit tests'. *The Guardian*, 2 August. http://www.theguardian.com/society/2012/aug/02/atos-disability-benefit-tests [accessed 24 September 2012].

—(2013), 'How private care firms have got away with breaking the law on pay'. *The Guardian*, 13 June. http://www.theguardian.com/society/2013/jun/13/care-firms-law-on-pay [accessed 21 September 2013].

Rawls, J. (1971), *A Theory of Justice*. Cambridge: Cambridge University Press.

Reinhart, C. and Rogoff, K. (2010), 'Growth in a time of debt'. NBER Working Paper No. 15639. Cambridge, MA: National Bureau of Economic Research.

Rifkin, J. (2009), *The Empathic Civilization: The Race to Global Consciousness in a World in Crisis*. New York: Tarcher.

Rimbert, P. (2013), 'Deserving and undeserving poor'. *Le Monde Diplomatique*, May. http://mondediplo.com/2013/05/03income [accessed 26 September 2013].

Robinson-Tillett, S. and Menon, C. (2013), 'Work doesn't pay for multi-part-time employees'. *The Guardian*, 13 April, p. 3.

Rothkopf, D. (2009), *Superclass: The Global Power Elite and the World They Are Making*. New York: Farrar, Straus and Giroux.

—(2012), *Power, Inc.: The Epic Rivalry Between Big Business and Government – and the Reckoning That Lies Ahead*. New York: Farrar, Straus and Giroux.

Ruskin, J. ([1860] 1986), 'Unto this last', in *Unto This Last and Other Writings*. London: Penguin Books.

Saez, E. (2012), *Striking It Richer: The Evolution of Top Incomes in the United States (Updated with 2009 and 2010 Estimates)*. Berkeley, CA: Econometrics Laboratory Software Archive (ELSA), University of California.

Savage, M., Devine, F., Cunningham, N., Taylor, M., Li, Y., Hjellbrekke, J., Le Roux, B., Friedman, S. and Miles, A. (2013), 'A new model of social class? Findings from the BBC's Great British Class Survey experiment'. *Sociology*, 47, (2): 219–50.

Sawhill, I. (2008), *Trends in Intergenerational Mobility*. Washington, DC: The Pew Charitable Trusts.

Schwartz, M. (2013), 'Opportunity costs: The true price of internships'. *Dissent*, Winter. http://www.dissentmagazine.org/article/opportunity-costs-the-true-price-of-internships [accessed 21 September 2013].

Seils, E. (2013), 'Is job creation useful to fight poverty and social exclusion?' *Social Europe Journal*, 25 July. http://www.social-europe.eu/2013/07/is-job-creation-useful-to-fight-poverty-and-social-exclusion/ [accessed 13 September 2013].

Seldon, A. (2013), 'British universities should be educating Gita'. *The Times*, 18 February, p. 18.

Shierholz, H., Sabadish, N. and Finio, N. (2013), *The Class of 2013*. Washington, DC: Economic Policy Institute.

Shildrick, T., MacDonald, R., Webster, C. and Garthwaite, K. (2012), *Poverty and Insecurity: Life in Low-Pay, No-Pay Britain*. Bristol: Policy Press.

Smith, N. (2013), 'The end of labor: How to protect workers from the rise of robots'. *The Atlantic*, 14 January. http://www.theatlantic.com/business/archive/2013/01/the-end-of-labor-how-to-protect-workers-from-the-rise-of-robots/267135/ [accessed 26 September 2013].

Social Security Advisory Committee (2012), *Report on the Draft Universal Credit Regulations 2013, the Benefit Cap (Housing Benefit) Regulations 2012 and the Draft Universal Credit, Personal Independence Payment, Jobseeker's Allowance and Employment and Support Allowance (Claims and Payments) Regulations 2013*. London: Her Majesty's Stationery Office.

Sparrow, A. (2010), 'David Cameron vows to tackle "secret corporate lobbying"'. *The Guardian*, 8 February. http://www.theguardian.com/politics/2010/feb/08/david-cameron-secret-corporate-lobbying?guni=Article:in%20body%20link [accessed 27 September 2013].

Squires, N. (2013), 'Pope accused of encouraging illegal immigration'. *The Telegraph*, 10 July. http://www.telegraph.co.uk/news/religion/the-pope/10171289/Pope-accused-of-encouraging-illegal-immigration.html [accessed 23 September 2013].

Standing, G. (1990), 'The road to workfare: Alternative to welfare or threat to occupation?' *International Labour Review*, 129, (6): 677–91.

—(1996), *Russian Unemployment and Enterprise Restructuring: Reviving Dead Souls*. Basingstoke: Macmillan.

—(1999), *Global Labour Flexibility: Seeking Distributive Justice*. Basingstoke: Macmillan.

—(2002), *Beyond the New Paternalism: Basic Security as Equality*. London and New York: Verso.

—(2009), *Work after Globalization: Building Occupational Citizenship*. Cheltenham and Northampton, MA: Edward Elgar.

—(2011), *The Precariat: The New Dangerous Class*. London and New York: Bloomsbury Academic.

—(2013a), 'Why a basic income is necessary for a right to work'. *Basic Income Studies*, 7, (2): 19–40.

—(2013b), 'Tertiary time: The precariat's dilemma'. *Public Culture*, 15, (1): 5–23.

—(2013c), 'The poor are responsible too'. *Financial Express* (India), 6 June. http://epaper.financialexpress.com/c/1170252 [accessed 26 September 2013].

Stuckler, D. and Basu, S. (2013), *The Body Economic: Why Austerity Kills*. New York: Basic Books.

Subramanian, A. (2011), *Eclipse: Living in the Shadow of China's Economic Dominance*. Washington, DC: Peterson Institute for International Economics.

Summers, A. B. (2007), *Occupational Licensing: Ranking the States and Exploring Alternatives*. Los Angeles: Reason Foundation.

Tabatabai, H. (2012), 'From price subsidies to basic income: The Iran model and its lessons', in K. Widerquist and M. Howard (eds), *Exporting the Alaska Model: Adapting the Permanent Fund Dividend for Reform Around the World*. New York: Palgrave Macmillan, pp. 17–32.

Taleb, N. N. (2012), *Antifragile: Things that Gain from Disorder*. New York: Random House.

Thaler, R. and Sunstein, C. (2008), *Nudge: Improving Decisions About Health, Wealth, and Happiness*. New Haven and London: Yale University Press.

Thompson, D. (1984), *The Chartists: Popular Politics in the Industrial Revolution*. New York: Pantheon.

Torgovnick, K. (2013) 'Who controls the world? Resources for understanding this visualization of the global economy'. *TED Blog*, 13 February. http://blog.ted.com/2013/02/13/who-controls-the-world-resources-for-understanding-this-visualization-of-the-global-economy/ [accessed 30 August 2013].

UNCTAD (2011), *World Investment Report 2011*. Geneva: United Nations Conference on Trade and Development.

—(2012), *Trade and Development Report 2012: Policies for Inclusive and Balanced Growth*. Geneva and New York: United Nations for United Nations Conference on Trade and Development.

—(2013), *World Investment Report 2013*. Geneva: United Nations Conference on Trade and Development.

UNICEF Office of Research (2013), 'Child well-being in rich countries: A comparative overview'. Innocenti Report Card 11. Florence, Italy: UNICEF Office of Research.

Vanham, P. (2012), 'Virtual working takes off in EMs'. *Financial Times*, 23 May. http://blogs.ft.com/beyond-brics/2012/05/23/virtual-working-takes-off-in-ems/#axzz2pX96TiN1 [accessed 9 December 2013].

Van Parijs, P. (1995), *Real Freedom for All: What (if Anything) can Justify Capitalism?* Oxford: Clarendon Press.

Walker, N. (2008), 'Denizenship and the deterritorialization in the EU'. Working Paper LAW 2008/08. Florence, Italy: Department of Law, European University Institute.

Watt, N., Mulholland, H. and Malik, S. (2012), 'Unpaid jubilee jobseekers: Downing Street dismisses criticisms', 6 June. http://www.theguardian.com/

society/2012/jun/06/unpaid-jubilee-jobseekers-downing-street [accessed 9 December 2013].

Wearden, G. (2013), 'Sir Mervyn King: Don't demonize bankers'. *The Guardian*, 20 May, p. 20.

Weil, D. (2013), 'Student loans: The financialized economy of indentured servitude'. *Daily Censored*, 1 June. http://www.dailycensored.com/student-loans-the-financialized-economy-of-indentured-servitude/ [accessed 25 September 2013].

Wells, M. and Schwarz, P. (2013), 'The political significance of Beppe Grillo's Five Star Movement'. *World Socialist Web Site*, 9 March. http://www.wsws.org/en/articles/2013/03/09/gril-m09.html [accessed 27 September 2013].

Wessel, D. (2012), 'Software raises bar for hiring'. *Wall Street Journal*, 31 May. http://online.wsj.com/article/SB10001424052702304821304577436172660988042.html [accessed 21 September 2013].

Whyte, M. (2010), *Myth of the Social Volcano: Perceptions of Inequality and Distributive Injustice in Contemporary China*. Redwood City, CA: Stanford University Press.

Widerquist, K. and Howard, M. (eds) (2012a), *Alaska's Permanent Fund Dividend: Examining its Suitability as a Model*. New York: Palgrave Macmillan.

—(2012b), *Exporting the Alaska Model: Adopting the Permanent Fund Dividend for Reform around the World*. New York: Palgrave Macmillan.

Williams, Z. (2013), 'Nobody wants to have their groceries served with pity'. *The Guardian*, 28 March, p. 50.

Wilson, A. N. (2013), 'Michael Philpott is a perfect parable for our age: His story shows the pervasiveness of evil born out of welfare dependency'. *Mail Online*, 2 April. http://www.dailymail.co.uk/debate/article-2303071/Mick-Philpotts-story-shows-pervasiveness-evil-born-welfare-dependency.html [accessed 27 September 2013].

Wintour, P. (2010), 'Douglas Alexander outlines Labour's stance on welfare'. *The Guardian*, 5 November. http://www.theguardian.com/politics/2010/nov/05/douglas-alexander-labour-welfare [accessed 25 September 2013].

Wolf, G. (2013), 'We can't spend our way out of crisis. But we can cut taxes'. *The Observer*, 17 March, p. 40.

Wolf, M. (2010), 'Three years on, fault lines threaten the world economy'. *Financial Times*, 14 July, p. 11.

World Bank (2013), *Capital for the Future: Saving and Investment in an Interdependent World*. Washington, DC: World Bank.

Wright, E. O. (2010), *Envisioning Real Utopias*. London and Brooklyn, NY: Verso.

Zolberg, A. R. (2000), 'The dawn of cosmopolitan denizenship'. *Indiana Journal of Global Legal Studies*, 7, (2): 511–18.

INDEX

Page references in bold denote figures/boxes